THE AMERICAN HOME FRONT

REVOLUTIONARY WAR
CIVIL WAR
WORLD WAR I
WORLD WAR II

by

James L. Abrahamson

1983

National Defense University Military History

Patrick Henry University Press
Colorado Springs, Colorado

The American Home Front:
Revolutionary War, Civil War,
World War I and World War II

by
James L. Abrahamson

ISBN 1-58963-061-0

Copyright © 2001 by
Patrick Henry University Press

Reprinted from the 1983 edition

Patrick Henry University Press
An imprint of
Fredonia Books
Colorado Springs, Colorado

http://www.PatrickHenryUniversityPress.com

All rights reserved, including the right to reproduce
this book, or portions thereof, in any form.

THE AMERICAN HOME FRONT

To Marigold

CONTENTS

Foreword xi
Preface xiii
The Author xv
Acknowledgments xvii

WAR AND SOCIETY IN AMERICA: SOME QUESTIONS 1

1. **THE AMERICAN REVOLUTION** 5
   The Price of War 6
   A Revolutionary Society at War 8
   The Revolutionary Economy 22
   The Politics of Mobilization 26
   The Political Consequences of War 31

2. **THE CIVIL WAR** 43
   The Northern Economy at War 44
   The Collapse of the Southern Economy 52
   Southern Mobilization 56
   Southern Politics 60
   Northern Politics 61
   Mobilizing the Union for War 67
   Civil War and American Society 71
   Organizing the Nation 83

3. **WORLD WAR I** 87
   Neutrality: Prelude to Mobilization 88
   Workingmen, Workingwomen, and the European War 94
   Mobilizing the American Economy 101
   A Divided Public 112
   Mobilizing Public Opinion 116
   Roots of Social Tension 123
   An Uncertain Economic Future 126
   Political Upheaval 127

4. WORLD WAR II ... 131
Controlling the Wartime Economy ... 133
The Economic Consequences of Total War ... 148
Liberal Reform and Total War ... 155
The Politics of Total War ... 165

WAR AND SOCIETY IN AMERICA: A FEW ANSWERS ... 171

Notes ... 177
Glossary of Acronyms ... 219
Index ... 221

FIGURES AND TABLES

Figures

1.1	Index of Wholesale Prices, 1774–1785	7
1.2	Depreciation of Continental Currency, 1777–1781	30
2.1	Production of Pig Iron and Rails, 1860–1870	50
2.2	Southern Agricultural Capital, 1850–1880	54
3.1	Tractors on American Farms, 1914–1920	94
3.2	Price and Wage Trends, 1914–1921	100
3.3	General Wholesale Prices and Prices of Selected Basic Commodities, 1914–1918	109
4.1	Price and Wage Trends, 1939–1949	154

Tables

1.1	Southern Exports to England and Scotland, 1769–1778	23
1.2	Emissions of Continental Currency, 1775–1779	29
2.1	Annual Export of Pork, Beef, Corn, and Wheat Products, 1860–1865	45
2.2	US Imports and Exports, 1860–1865	47
2.3	Sales of Reapers and Mowers, 1862–1865	49
2.4	US Output and Decennial Rates of Change, 1849–1889	51
2.5	Southern Agricultural Production, 1860–1866	52
2.6	Indicators of Southern Manufacturing, 1850–1880	56
2.7	Average Annual Prices, 1861–1865	68
2.8	United States Immigration, 1820–1860	74
3.1	American Foreign Commerce, 1913–1921	89
3.2	Gross National Product, 1914–1918	90
3.3	Indices of Industrial Production, 1914–1918	92
3.4	Farm Profits and Production Index, 1914–1921	93
3.5	Production and Average Annual Prices of Selected Farm Products, 1914–1918	95

3.6	Number of Women per One Thousand Employees in 474 Firms Doing War Work, 1916–1919	96
3.7	Industrial Wages and Living Costs, 1913–1921	98
3.8	Strikes and Lockouts, 1914–1919	99
3.9	Index of Annual Earnings in Selected Occupations, 1913–1921	110
3.10	Ethnic Americans in 1910	114
4.1	Federal Civilian Employment, September 1939–July 1945	133
4.2	Output of Selected Farm Products, 1939–1945	138
4.3	Gross National Product and Federal Finances, 1939–1946	139
4.4	Wartime Work Stoppages, 1940–1946	144
4.5	Volume of Intercity Freight Traffic, 1939–1945	146
4.6	Output of Selected Industries, 1939–1945	149
4.7	Index of Selected Farm Prices, 1939–1945	153
4.8	Net Black Interregional Migration, 1920–1950	162

FOREWORD

This latest National Defense University military history seeks to broaden the perspective of those who are interested in understanding the effects of the wartime mobilization of American society. Through a comparative analysis of the economic, political, and social results of America's four principal wars, this study reveals the major issues faced by each wartime administration and sketches the consequences of the mobilization policies adopted.

As the author, Colonel James L. Abrahamson, US Army, explains, each conflict occurred in unique circumstances, required varied policies, and produced different effects on American institutions. He therefore avoids offering a simplistic list of the expected domestic consequences of any future conflict. Nevertheless, certain common factors, which may inform modern mobilization planners, surface in his analysis of these four wars. The author suggests that if planners are aware of the implications of their mobilization choices, they can better devise effective policies for drawing forth the material and human essentials of victory.

The National Defense University is pleased to have hosted Colonel Abrahamson as a Visiting Senior Research Fellow from the US Military Academy history faculty, so that he might research and write this instructive historical study. Studies such as this may help us all better understand the potential societal effects on the American home front should any future crisis again require America to go to war.

John S. Pustay
Lieutenant General, US Air Force
President, National Defense
University

PREFACE

This study seeks to inform two quite different audiences.

The first consists of those individuals, both civilian and military, who have a responsibility to plan against the possibility of our involvement in another major war. My observations of their background, reinforced by the historical experience recounted in the pages that follow, lead me to the conclusion that most of those war planners have little knowledge of wartime life on the home front. They remain unfamiliar, for instance, with the means by which the government has traditionally sought (and sometimes failed) to mobilize human, industrial, agricultural, and financial resources; or the past military consequences of the social, economic, and political disruptions that inevitably accompany war; or the extent to which our wars have left this nation in quite a different condition than anyone imagined (or even desired) at their outbreak. Also lacking such knowledge, previous generations of wartime leaders have tended to repeat the errors made in earlier conflicts or to be caught off guard by developments they might well have anticipated. Hoping to prevent history from repeating itself, I have written this book.

The second audience is a younger one, those college students enrolled in survey courses in American history or perhaps preparing for a career in the military services. American history texts typically ignore the impact of war, perhaps because their authors share the traditional American antimilitarism and wish to avoid anything remotely related to the armed services or because they prefer to focus on either a war's origins or its principal diplomatic and international consequences. To that audience, I offer this book as a supplement that will add another dimension to their study of American history and reinforce their understanding of the social, economic, and political evolution that continues even when the nation takes up arms against a foreign or domestic foe.

Because one slim volume cannot supply to both audiences a fully detailed account of American life on the home front, I have made several compromises in scope and depth of coverage. The study, for one, describes the impact of but four American wars—one from the eighteenth century (the Revolutionary War), one from the nineteenth (the Civil War), and two from the twentieth (World Wars I and II). Although a complete description of each war's impact would both assess how the war affected those who fought it and explain the wartime evolution of literature and the arts as well as popular culture, I have set those subjects aside and instead focused on war's principal political, economic, and social effects. In regard to the latter category, this study takes particular cognizance of war's consequences for those Americans disadvantaged by their race, sex, ethnic background, or religious beliefs.

Rather than a fully detailed study of each war, I thus offer an introductory account based exclusively on published sources. To compensate somewhat for that brevity of scope and detail, I have made liberal use of endnotes. Newcomers to the subject will wish to ignore them, at least until they want to gain more information about a particular aspect of the topic. When they do, the notes will guide them to the principal published sources.

THE AUTHOR

James L. Abrahamson researched and wrote this study while a Visiting Senior Research Fellow at the National Defense University. He is currently a professor at the United States Military Academy, where he has taught American history since 1975.

A 1959 graduate of the Military Academy, he holds advanced degrees from the Graduate Institute of International Studies, Geneva, Switzerland, and Stanford University, where he completed his Ph.D. in 1977. In 1981 Macmillan published his dissertation, *America Arms for a New Century: The Making of a Great Military Power*, which examined the relation between military reform and American society between 1880 and the end of World War I.

His military assignments include duty with the 11th and 15th Armored Cavalry Regiments in Vietnam and Germany, respectively, and the Combat Developments Command. He is also a graduate of the Command and General Staff College.

ACKNOWLEDGMENTS

My principal intellectual debts are owed to the authors of several hundred monographs and articles that treat some aspect of war's social, economic, or political influence. Standing upon the foundation laid by those specialized studies, I have gained the perspective needed to attempt this synthesis that summarizes the domestic impact of four American wars.

Several other people helped in more mundane ways. To insure that I found the latest periodical literature, Michael Ridgeway of the US Military Academy Library introduced me to the mysteries of the Lockheed Dialog system, and Rosie L. Nabritt of the National Defense University Library helped me obtain on Inter-Library Loan the items not readily available at the Library of Congress, whose Main Reading Room staff kept in shape toting the many volumes consulted in the preparation of this study.

Four former members of the Military Academy's Department of History—Martin W. Andresen, David W. Hazen, Montgomery C. Meigs, and Terry R. Moss—gave me the benefit of their expertise by reading a portion of the manuscript. Then, five members of a review panel—Dr. Dean Allard of the Office of Naval History, Mr. Samuel Tucker, formerly of the Office of the Secretary of Defense, and three fellow researchers at the National Defense University, Nick Andrews, Richard Darilek, and John Reinertson—and the staff of the Center of Military History gave the revised manuscript their careful examination and shared their views on its strengths and weaknesses. I mention them here out of gratitude for their assistance and not to lessen my own responsibility for any surviving errors of fact or interpretation.

Colonel Franklin D. Margiotta and the staff of his Research Directorate rendered invaluable administrative and logistical support at every step of this project, and I owe a special debt to Colonel Frederick T. Kiley and Ms. Evelyn Lakes for their editorial assistance. Fred's sharp mind improved my style, and his ready wit kept everything in perspective and mellowed even the severest criticism.

Brigadier General Thomas E. Griess and Colonel Roy K. Flint, in their turn heads of the Military Academy's Department of History, enabled me to spend a year in Washington doing the necessary research. And once again,

Marigold permitted me to uproot our household and did her best to insure that this researcher worked in a happy and supportive home.

J. L. A.

West Point, New York
November 1982

WAR AND SOCIETY IN AMERICA: SOME QUESTIONS

> *It is a very improbable supposition, that any people can long remain free, with a strong military power in the very heart of their country. . . . History, both ancient and modern, affords many instances of the overthrow of states and kingdoms by the power of soldiers, who were rais'd and maintain'd at first, under the plausible pretense of defending those very liberties which they afterwards destroyed. Even where there is a necessity of the military power, . . . a wise and prudent people will always have a watchful & jealous eye over it; for the maxims and rules of the army, are essentially different from the genius of a free people, and the laws of a free government.*
>
> Samuel Adams[1]

That 1768 excerpt from the *Boston Gazette* suggests that Samuel Adams, then that city's leading revolutionary, had, like many other Americans, already begun to incorporate into his political philosophy a set of antimilitary beliefs borrowed from English radicals who maintained that a standing army threatened to subvert their nation's unwritten constitution and rob its citizens of their liberties. The impending struggle with Great Britain reinforced that nascent antimilitarism, and subsequent events made it a central theme of the continuing debate over war's impact on American society.

Decades of debate also stretched the antimilitarists' argument well beyond the basic proposition that a powerful standing army might overthrow republican government and sustain a tyrant. Soon they saw danger in both war and an assertive foreign policy because each justified the maintenance of large regular forces. In addition, the antimilitarists discovered more subtle threats than a simple military coup d'état. A large standing army, they argued, would create patronage and prestige for an ambitious elite, provide wealth to its suppliers while it impoverished the citizenry, and strengthen the central government, which would use the army to justify new taxes and to coerce its domestic opponents. Worse yet, military service would corrupt a soldier's morals and instill an unrepublican submissiveness and respect for authority that he would carry back into civil life. War, and the regular forces it required, thus became something that American antimilitarists strongly believed the nation must avoid—or risk the loss of its republican institutions.[2]

Although sharing the antimilitarists' commitment to republican government, other Americans rejected their belief in its vulnerability to an internal military foe. Rather, they reversed the argument and described war as sometimes both a useful instrument of national policy and the palladium of liberty in its battle against tyranny.

In so doing, they became neither the first nor the last Americans to make that connection. When still calling themselves Englishmen, colonial Americans had relied upon warfare to secure and extend their settlements in the New World and sustain their efforts to build model societies. Later, even as they denounced Great Britain's alleged attempt (using a standing army) to crush local self-government, Americans had resorted to war—and raised their own standing army—in order to achieve national independence. Then, in 1812, they raised another army and made war on Britain in defense of their newly won independence—or out of a desire for North American empire, which the war's stalemated results initially left unfulfilled. More successfully in the remainder of the nineteenth century, the United States militarily expanded its national domain—the so-called realm of free government—at the expense of Indians, Mexicans, and Spaniards. Midway in that century, Americans also engaged in a civil conflict, in defense of two differing concepts of individual liberty and self-government. On a global scale, America's twentieth-century wars manifested the same paradox: the use of war, in the opinion of some a threat to representative government, to create an international environment conducive to the growth of democracy both at home and abroad.

Despite that legacy of armed conflict in behalf of representative government, many Americans have continued to regard war as a grave danger to the nation's democratic institutions and way of life. Beyond the obvious death and destruction, those Americans have claimed that war also diverts capital and labor to unproductive uses and creates a crushing burden of new taxes. In addition, they have alleged that war leads to social regimentation, inattention to the correction of injustices, criticism of dissenting opinion, and a hatred of foreigners ultimately extending even to domestic aliens and strange customs. War, they have also asserted, draws two related political dangers in its train. An ambitious President (or one of his successful generals) might use the regular military forces to establish one-man rule—continuing in peacetime the sometimes arbitrary use of executive power justified by wartime emergencies. Because war also expands the general scope and authority of government at the expense of individual choice, they have observed, it might produce a militarized population that too willingly surrenders its civil liberties to governmental authorities who merely reenact the rituals of representative government before an intellectually enslaved public. Such, anyway, have been the recent views of many American liberals, most radicals, and even a few conservatives.

A more complete assessment of war's effects, however, suggests a need to modify such dire predictions, which to some seem exaggerated in light of the American military experience. While acknowledging wartime death and destruction, historians have also recorded war's occasionally beneficial social, economic, and political consequences. Economically, wars appear sometimes to have created prosperity or caused an industrial reconstruction that both compensated for wartime losses and led to dramatic postwar advances. Socially, wars may have permitted lasting social gains by underprivileged groups, a liberalizing effect that somewhat compensates for any illiberal consequences of wartime regimentation. Politically, war has occasionally insured the survival of liberal, democratic regimes, and in the case of the United States, the expanded authority of wartime government has become a useful model for guiding the nation's response to grave domestic crises. Nor has war been the only, or even the most important, factor in the growth of the size, scope, and power of central governments or the rise of absolutism.[3]

Despite such findings, which seem to challenge aspects of the liberal presumption about war's special dangers to representative government, American historians have for the most part confined their investigations of war's impact to a single conflict or a specific group, institution, or issue. They have, in other words, done little in a systematic, comprehensive way to assess the broad impact of war across their society and have left unanswered general questions about war's influence upon the economy, political institutions, and society's constituent groups.

This book takes a preliminary step toward answers to those questions. Limited to the nation's four major wars—the American Revolution, the Civil War, World War I, and World War II—and relying essentially on secondary works, its conclusions have a necessarily tentative character. They should nevertheless expose those aspects of the subject requiring further primary research and provide a frame of reference for comparable attention to the nation's minor wars and the conflicts of the Cold War era.

1
THE AMERICAN REVOLUTION

There is nothing more common, than to confound the terms of American revolution with those of the late American War. The American War is over: but this is far from being the case with American revolution. On the contrary, nothing but the first act of the great drama is closed.

Benjamin Rush[1]

Previous studies of the influence of the American Revolution have generally focused on the consequences of independence—the developments that accompanied either the severing of formal ties to Great Britain or what Benjamin Rush—physician, patriot, and the Continental Army's Surgeon General—characterized as the effort of the American people "to establish and perfect [their] new forms of government" and to bring their "principles, morals, and manners" to republican perfection.[2] The distinction that Rush, also a signer of the Declaration of Independence and member of the Continental Congress, has drawn between war and independence (the freedom to complete the American revolution) therefore has particular relevance to this survey. Unlike previous studies, this chapter seeks to reveal the developments that stemmed not from independence alone, but from the fact that eight years of war accompanied the emergence of nationhood. That task requires attention both to the direct social, economic, and political effects of the military struggle and to the indirect influence that the military experience would have on the ways that Americans subsequently used their new national freedom.

That indirect effect of war possesses a perhaps paramount importance. For had Great Britain yielded to colonial demands in 1776, or ended the war even after Burgoyne's defeat at Saratoga the next year, Americans would surely have drawn quite different conclusions about what Rush called the "weakness and other defects" of American society and its institutions.[3] A long and difficult war tested values, assumptions, and institutions, and more quickly than decades of peace made Americans aware of the need to reexamine many of their social, economic, and political views.

The Price of War

Assessing the direct influence of the War for Independence can begin with an accounting of its costs. Estimates of the number who fought in the Revolutionary armies—the Continental Line and the states' militia—vary from 100,000 to almost four times that number, a result of poor record keeping and an inability to identify all those who enlisted more than once.[4] Accepting a figure just below 200,000 as the best guess, John Shy has calculated that 25,000 of those Revolutionary soldiers died—in about equal parts from battle, disease, or the hardships of primitive military prisons. Although that number might at first glance seem small, it represents well over 10 percent of the men who served and would be, on a per-capita basis, equivalent to more than two million deaths in the nation's present population. Nor does that number include another 25,000 men left permanently crippled by wounds or disease.[5] All 200,000, of course, suffered the disruption of their lives for periods that varied from a few months to more than three years, during which they experienced often incredible privation, occasional stark terror, and frequent stupefying boredom.

Figure 1.1 indicates that both soldiers and civilians suffered in another way—from a wartime inflation unparalleled in American history except by the Confederacy's economic collapse in the final stages of the Civil War. Although that inflation hurt all Americans on fixed incomes, it treated soldiers with special cruelty. It destroyed the value of their monetary enlistment bonuses, and a soldier's wage, sometimes more than a year behind in payment, became increasingly inadequate.[6]

The Continental soldier's family suffered most of all. Not only was its breadwinner generally underpaid, often unpaid, and usually absent, but local governments failed to provide wives and children the assistance the laws required. In 1778, for example, the wife of a Continental private wrote that she was "without bread, & cannot get any, the Committee will not supply me, my Children will Starve, or if they do not, they must freeze, we have no wood, neither Can we get any—*Pray Come Home.*" Another, whose soldier husband had gone four years without pay, complained that creditors had seized "her Household Goods, even her Bed . . . and . . . brought her & Children to great Distress, having neither Wood nor Bread."[7]

Although the cost to the United States of waging the war came to only between $158 and $168 million, some Americans paid a far heavier price. The loss of the former colonists' primary overseas market dislocated the economic lives of those who offered products for export or handled that trade.

**Figure 1.1
Index of Wholesale Prices, 1774-1785
(1850-59=100)**

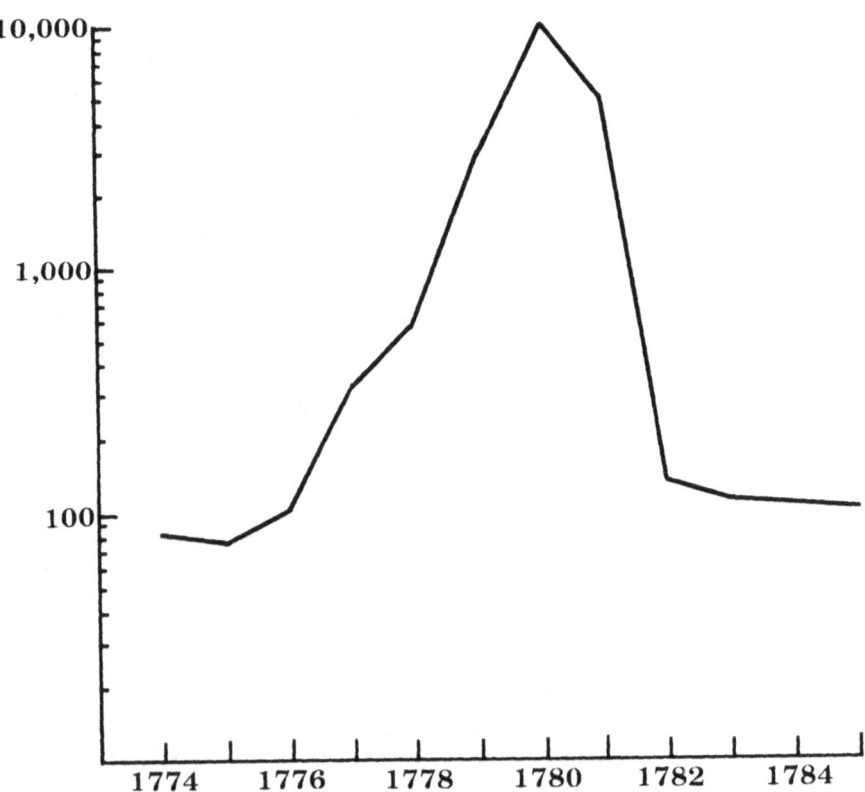

Source: US Department of Commerce, Bureau of the Census, *Historical Statistics of the United States, Colonial Times to 1970*, Bicentennial ed., 2 vols. (Washington, DC: US Government Printing Office, 1975), 2:1196.

Commerce was further disrupted by Britain's naval blockade, which also virtually destroyed New England's fisheries. Those who lived near the scene of active military operations risked damage to their homes, farms, and businesses and suffered again when hungry or rapacious soldiers seized their goods and livestock. The 100,000 Loyalists, slaves, and Indians who by war's end had fled to British-controlled areas in Canada or the Caribbean lost almost everything. Although that number may now seem small, it represented 4 percent of the prewar population and at least five times the number of emigres that left France to escape the terrors of its revolution.[8]

The war also injured the nation's intellectual life. Schools closed as the war and government service enlisted teachers and intellectuals. At various times the contending armies used the facilities of seven of the country's nine colleges* as hospitals, barracks, or stables.[9]

Such general descriptions of the more dire consequences of the War for Independence, although important to maintaining a proper perspective of the conflict, nevertheless conceal the often positive ways that Americans reacted to calamity. Those reactions, along with the significance of achieving political independence, offer valuable insights into the war's meaning and its contribution to national development. To gain that insight, we can best begin by first studying the impact of the war on the principal racial, ethnic, religious, and other subgroups that constituted American colonial society.

A Revolutionary Society at War

Even before the Continental Congress declared America's independence, free blacks and a few blacks still held in slavery had taken their places in the Revolutionary forces seeking to coerce Great Britain into recognizing American rights. As members of the states' militia, they had fought at Concord and later joined the army besieging the British troops in Boston. Nor was such service unusual. Despite laws formally barring blacks from military service—on the racist assumption that they were innately cowardly or the more practical fear that once trained to arms they might attempt to free fellow Afro-Americans held in bondage—black Americans had habitually served in both the militia and the expeditionary forces raised for the major international wars and Indian campaigns of the colonial period.[10]

---

*Harvard (1636); William and Mary (1693); Yale (1701); College of New Jersey, later Princeton (1746); Franklin's Academy, later University of Pennsylvania (1751); King's College, later Columbia College (1754); Rhode Island College, later Brown University (1764); Queen's College, later Rutgers (1766); and Dartmouth College (1769).

Although George Washington and the Continental Congress at first sought to reject that tradition and exclude blacks, slave or free, from the Continental forces, Virginia's last royal governor, John Murray, Earl of Dunmore, took an action that unintentionally reinforced the tradition of black military service and highlighted the question facing all Afro-Americans: how might they best use the war to their own advantage?[11]

Lord Dunmore's decree of 7 November 1775, suggested one way: Any slave willing to bear arms for Britain might gain his freedom by escaping to the British lines. Anxious to counter that offer and, later, to overcome the shortage of white volunteers, the Continental Army began enlisting those free blacks who had prior military experience, and most of the states' militia recommenced general recruitment of Afro-Americans. By 1778, Rhode Island had raised two regiments containing black soldiers, one of which combined free blacks, slaves, and Indians under white leadership. Elsewhere the practice of enlisting blacks, both slave and free, quickly spread throughout New England and the Middle Atlantic States. Because the inequitable conscription laws of most states permitted one who had been drafted to hire a substitute, they also encouraged black enlistments whenever wealthier Americans who could not purchase the services of a poor or landless white citizen instead sent their servants or slaves. Even Virginia, which refused to enlist slaves, accepted the services of such "free" blacks, and only Georgia and South Carolina steadfastly refused Congressional urgings to enlist Afro-Americans—although both states widely used their labor in support of military operations. In the end, perhaps 5,000 blacks fought in the Patriot armies, and black seamen served extensively in the Revolutionary naval forces without raising any of the troubling questions posed by service on land.[12]

Many American blacks also accepted offers like that of Lord Dunmore, who was but the first British commander to offer freedom in return for service with His Majesty's forces. More than 500 won their freedom through service in the British ranks, and between 1775 and 1783 another 65,000 escaped their masters through flight to British-occupied areas. One third of that number eventually left the country, but the remainder swelled the ranks of the new nation's emerging community of free blacks. Because of the leadership they would offer to both Afro-Americans and later antislavery forces, historian Willie Lee Rose characterized their escape as the "most immediate and significant consequence of the Revolution for blacks."[13]

If freedom gained through American military service gave blacks an implicit claim on the rights of a citizen, the Revolution's very meaning reinforced that claim for all who were held in bondage. As Abigail Adams, wife of the second President and mother of the sixth, explained: "It always appeared a most iniquitous scheme . . . to fight ourselves for what we are daily robbing and plundering from those [slaves] who have as good a right to freedom as we."[14] The wave of ideologically inspired emancipations that soon arose in the Northern States also received help from another source. Nonslaveowning whites, politically dominant in New England and the Middle Atlantic States, responded to the opposition of white workers who both feared the competition of slave labor and regarded the few skilled black laborers in their midst as fully capable of earning their livelihood. By 1783, Vermont and Massachusetts had freed their small slave populations, and Pennsylvania had passed a law providing for gradual abolition. In the next quarter century the rest of New England as well as New York and New Jersey followed suit, approving laws that brought freedom to newborn blacks after an "apprenticeship" usually lasting from twenty-one to twenty-eight years. Most of the states and later the Federal Government also outlawed the importation of slaves, and even some of the Southern States eased their laws permitting private manumission.[15]

Those changes, which did little to diminish racism in the United States and left most black Americans still entrapped by slavery, forced Afro-Americans to rely on individual action to achieve or advance their freedom. During the war, they had gained liberty through military service or by a flight from bondage that Gary Nash called "the first large-scale rebellion of American slaves." Such individual escapes remained the most common route to freedom in the postwar South. Generally confined to society's lowest socioeconomic positions and denied civil and political liberties, even free blacks could not unite politically to demand the further extension of racial justice, as whites had done to abolish slavery in the North. In that region, however, they might speak out, hoping to guide and uplift members of their own race and to convince whites of the injustice of slavery and racism.[16]

White American women similarly benefited from their participation in the Revolution. Even before the outbreak of hostilities, a Continental Congress intent on coercing British merchants had called upon women to boycott British imports and to increase home manufacture of textiles and clothing. Uniting to enforce that boycott, urban women joined the Daughters of Liberty, pledged themselves to use no tea or other imports, and kept an eye on local merchants—even resorting to mass violence against those who hoarded scarce goods in hopes of higher profits. As the war progressed, the Daughters and other ad hoc committees also sewed uniforms for American soldiers.[17]

When husbands left for government or military service, wives also undertook to manage farms and businesses and to cope with Indian raids on the frontier, British assaults on coastal cities, and sporadic fighting wherever it might occur. What is less well known is that about 20,000 American women joined the Continental Army, in which they served as nurses in military hospitals and carriers of water and ammunition for the artillery. Though not uniformed, neither were they camp followers but rather the wives, mothers, and daughters of soldiers and recipients of pay and rations and objects of army discipline. In addition, a handful of women, including the famed Margaret Corbin and Deborah Sampson, donned men's clothing and fought as private soldiers, even though regulations formally barred such duty. A large but indeterminate number of women also fought with the colonial militia, especially in frontier districts. Without the army's women, as George Washington acknowledged, many more soldiers would have deserted.[18]

Such direct and indirect participation in the war did not, unfortunately, bring a significant improvement in women's rights. Throughout the new nation, husbands continued to control their wives' property and earnings, although a few Northern States made divorce somewhat easier. Society continued to regard the home as a woman's proper sphere, unless economic necessity forced her to seek work. Only in New Jersey, and for but a brief period ending in 1807, did women gain the right to vote.[19]

Participation in the war effort had nevertheless shown women that they were neither inherently inferior to men nor incapable of doing a man's work. As daughters saw their mothers successfully cope with new roles, the next generation too may have learned that femininity did not necessarily mean weakness and incompetent delicacy. The Revolution not only sanctioned abandonment of gender roles to engage in men's work that supported the war, but also gave women's work an entirely new political significance. The wartime boycotts and home manufacture of clothing placed women in the midst of the economic struggle to defeat England, and they consequently began to discuss political affairs.[20]

The war thus gave women a new sense of their abilities and linked domesticity to politics. Although a woman's political role remained indirect and deferential, that union of the female sphere with what had formerly been an exclusively male domain became, as Linda Kerber has written, a step in women's "political socialization." It also served as a basis for both the nineteenth-century "cult of true womanhood" and female involvement in social and political reforms that would protect or improve American families.[21]

The emphasis on a republic's need for an educated citizenry extended the modest political involvement of American women into the postwar period. Because the Founding Fathers believed that the success of America's new governments depended upon an educated and public-spirited citizenry, they concluded that its "Republican Mothers" needed sufficient education and general knowledge of affairs to prepare their sons for citizenship and to reinforce their husbands' commitment to the public good.[22] Motherhood in the new nation therefore demanded that American girls receive an adequate education, one that stressed history, composition, and geography rather than such ornamental accomplishments as needlework, music, and dancing.[23]

That movement to improve the education of women went hand in hand with the revival of a prewar educational trend: supplementing classical education based upon Greek and Latin with a new curriculum of such practical subjects as composition, English, history, geography, and mathematics. In a shift that affected higher education as well, schools gave less emphasis to preparing an elite for the clergy and more to training citizens in the mechanical arts and the requirements of citizenship. America's many new colleges, including new state universities in North and South Carolina, Georgia, and Vermont and fifteen other new schools between 1792 and 1802, began offering law, politics, medicine, chemistry, modern languages, natural history, and similar practical subjects even where the tradition of liberal education prevailed.[24]

Revolutionary ideals and wartime experiences also emphasized the practical in their contribution to American medicine and engineering—professions with few skilled American practitioners prior to 1776. The Revolution, described by one medical historian as "the making of medicine in this country," brought many of the 4,000 doctors who served the armed forces into their first contact with hospitals and the few American doctors who were masters of their craft. The war also prompted the publication of America's first book of medicine—appropriately on the treatment of wounds and fractures—and its first pharmacopoeia. According to Dixon Fox, American engineering, which was in an even more primitive state than prewar medical practice, dates from the arrival of the French military engineers who served with the American forces, men like Duportail, Gouvion, L'Enfant, Laumoy, and La Radiere. America's practical men of science—clockmakers, surveyors, and a few mathematicians—had already, however, contributed to the war effort by making telescopes, artillery instruments, and maps and assisting with the production of cannon.[25]

Although the war failed to erase entirely the differences separating America's three principal white ethnic groups, it did serve to break down many of the social and political barriers of the colonial period and produce a new sense of unity. Revolutionaries within the dominant English community—which constituted about three-fifths of the white population—found that they must share political power and social status with theretofore relatively excluded groups of Scotch-Irish (15 percent) or German (13 percent) ancestry. Military success necessitated the cooperation of those three groups, and participation in the war created an awareness of their combined power, a consciousness that James Olson characterized as "the beginnings of American nationalism."[26]

In 1776 the American population contained relatively insignificant numbers of French, Dutch, Belgians, Welsh, Jews, and Scots—which altogether constituted but one-tenth of the white population. Excluding the Scots, those small groups had their share of both Loyalists and Patriots, and their small numbers and dispersion make it difficult to ascertain precisely the war's influence on their place in American society.[27]

The fate of the Scots is clear, however. Those who had arrived in America from the Scottish Lowlands often held appointive political posts in the royal administration or served as American agents of British trading firms. The Scottish Highlanders, in contrast, were rural folk who had emigrated to America in the quarter century before the Revolution, settled in the backcountry of the South, and retained their loyalty to clan leaders and through them to the Crown. Despite the exploits of a few Patriot heroes of Scots ancestry, like John Paul Jones, Arthur St. Clair, and James Wilson, both groups remained overwhelmingly loyal to Great Britain during the war, and their participation on the losing side eliminated most of the great influence that at least the Lowlanders had in prewar America.[28]

Three different groups of Germans figure in an analysis of the war's impact on that much larger ethnic group. The German pietists—Dunkards, Moravians, Mennonites, Amish, and Schwenkfelders—had begun arriving in Pennsylvania and New Jersey in the late seventeenth century seeking religious freedom and escape from the low social position they held in the war-ravaged Germanic states. Because they were clannish and committed by religion to pacifism and nonresistance, the war subjected them to much the same abuse and exclusion as the Quakers, who will be discussed later.[29]

Some 12,000 "Hessians" suffered from no such beliefs. About 20 percent of the mercenary force sent to North America by Great Britain, they elected to remain in either the United States or Canada. Having few prospects in their native German principalities, the Hessians succumbed to American propaganda, the eventual success of American arms, a desire to escape prisoner-of-war camps, or the appeal of the Congressional offer of land, oxen, cows, and pigs—what John Miller has called "a complete farm except for the *Frau*."[30]

A more numerically significant group were the Lutheran and Reformed Germans who began arriving in large numbers in 1708. Some settled in New York's Mohawk Valley as well as Pennsylvania and New Jersey, but overcrowding forced many into the backcountry of Maryland and Virginia. Unfamiliar with English, not automatically regarded as citizens, without any tradition of participation in politics, clannish by nature, and isolated on the frontiers, German-Americans had taken little part in colonial politics or the prewar agitation against Britain. Although those factors might have encouraged Loyalism or indifference to the Revolution, other considerations prompted the latter group of German-Americans to join the Patriot cause. No national sentiment bound them to England. Nor had life in Europe made them sympathetic to monarchy. To the Anglican church and the taxes and civil liabilities it imposed on dissenters, they felt positive hostility. Because the outbreak of war made them valued citizens, however, the Revolutionary leadership translated laws into German, increased the political representation of German-dominated areas, and gave military commissions, eventually generalcies, to such community leaders as Peter Muhlenberg and Nicolaus Herkimer. The aid given the American army by the "barons" von Steuben and de Kalb similarly enhanced the postwar prestige of German-Americans. By the end of the war, Americans of German ancestry had become politically active and more fully integrated into American society.[31]

Participation in the war also helped the Scotch-Irish become, wrote James Leyburn, "integral parts of the American nation." After 1717 they began arriving in America in considerable numbers from the Scottish Lowlands via Ulster (Northern Ireland), where the British government had settled them in the previous century. Unwanted in New England, whose Congregationalists opposed the Ulstermen's Presbyterian form of Calvinism, most of the Scotch-Irish migrated to Pennsylvania and then into the backcountry. Naturally hostile to the English, opposed to Quaker neutralism in Pennsylvania, and attracted by the tolerant government of the future Revolutionary elite in Virginia, most of the Ulstermen became ardent Patriots. Further to the south, improved representation in the new state governments and the missionary work of Presbyterian clergy made most of the Scotch-Irish at least reluctant Revolutionaries. In the end, the Ulstermen's participation in the Revolution enhanced their social and political position, and they fully melted into the white Protestant English-speaking group that dominated postwar American life.[32]

Except for their Roman Catholic religion, Irish-Americans might similarly have blended easily into the mainstream of American life. Some had apparently tried to do so prior to the Revolution, escaping the civil and social restrictions imposed upon Catholics by abandoning that faith for one of the more acceptable forms of colonial Christianity. The Revolution helped assimilate the rest, who in 1790 accounted for no more than 4 percent of the American population. During the war, George Washington had not only been eager to win the loyalty of Irish Catholic recruits but also to draw to the Patriot side the Catholic French of Canada. Consequently, he took pains to insure that the Continental Army honored St. Patrick's Day and to discourage criticism of the Pope. As a further mark of respect, he made "St. Patrick" the password for the Continentals' occupation of Boston on 17 March 1776. The alliance with France and Washington's later command of its Catholic troops similarly moderated prewar American hostility to Catholicism.[33]

Whether the established colonial church was Anglican or Congregational made little difference to the existence of such hostility. Every colony except Pennsylvania—even Maryland, which had been founded as a refuge for

English Catholics—denied Roman Catholics the vote and placed them under other legal restraints.[34] Surprisingly then, in 1776 American Catholics overwhelmingly followed the lead of Charles Carroll of Carrollton, signer of the Declaration of Independence and the new nation's most prominent Catholic political figure. As Carroll later told George Washington's adopted son, he had become a Revolutionary in the expectation that independence would insure "the toleration of all sects professing the Christian religion." Carroll was not disappointed. The relation of Catholics and Catholicism to the war and the move toward religious freedom inspired by the ideals of the Revolution brought dramatic improvements in the legal and political position of Catholics.[35]

Groups of Protestant dissenters who had supported the War for Independence drew similar advantages from the spread of the Enlightenment ideals that had justified the Revolution. Presbyterians and Baptists, who found the ideology of the Revolution compatible with their religious principles, gave the war their strong support. They benefited, in turn, from the disestablishment of the Anglican Church, which spread during wartime like a wave through the Middle Atlantic and Southern States. As those states wrote their new constitutions or prepared bills of rights, they either entirely disallowed taxes for the support of a church or at least permitted the citizen to select the institution that would receive his money. In every new state, members of all the Protestant faiths gained the right to vote and hold public office. Eight states extended that privilege to Catholics, and half their number gave political rights to Jews as well.[36]

Congregationalism, the established faith in New England, escaped the Revolutionary fate of Anglicanism. No English bishop or largely Tory clergy tied the Congregationalists to the Crown. They believed, moreover, that Revolutionary ideology reinforced their religious principles, and they eagerly fought in the Patriot armies and provided political leadership to Revolutionary governments. As a result, New Englanders initially made no move to disestablish Congregationalism, and Baptists and other local religious minorities— despite their support for the war—had to continue their struggle for severance of church and state in New England.[37]

Other forces associated with the war and independence, however, weakened the influence of churches everywhere, even in New England. The years of warfare having generally disrupted all institutions of social control, public and military service or flight to avoid invasion sometimes even denied Americans access to their community and church. The resulting absence of such peacetime restraints on behavior may have facilitated immorality, just as wartime inflation and new economic conditions encouraged greed and speculation—or at least so Americans thought. President Timothy Dwight of Yale claimed that a decade of political agitation and war had unhinged "the principles, the morality, and the religion of the country more than could have been done by a peace of forty years." And wartime experience prompted Benjamin Trumbull, a Connecticut clergyman and early American historian, to theorize that the "state of war is peculiarly unfriendly to religion. It dissipates the mind, diminishes the degree of instruction, removes great numbers almost wholly from it, connects them with the most dangerous company, and presents them with the worst examples." As a result, war produced "profaneness, intemperance, disregard to propriety, violence, and licentious living." It apparently, he observed, "emboldens men in sin."[38]

As a competitor to the traditional churches, the Revolution also created a civil religion that linked, and often confused, Christian faith with American political ideology. Prior to 1776, Americans had drawn inspiration from the past. They derived their values from the ancient Hebrews, democratic Greece, republican Rome, Anglo-Saxon England, and Christian history as interpreted by the Reformation and Puritan Revolution. They found their heroes in the past and passively relied upon God to make history. In that environment, the church had offered both intellectual leadership and political counsel.[39]

Although never entirely abandoning that heritage, after 1783 Americans increasingly drew inspiration from new sources and sought to shape their own future. They made Liberty their goddess and their Country an object of worship. They gave their struggle for independence heroic proportions and expected to become models for subsequent generations. They believed that God had given them a divine mission to bring political freedom to mankind, and they used the war to test and purify American society in preparation for that millennial task. As a consequence, political theorists and statesmen replaced clergymen as the leaders of American thought, and politics supplanted religion as the field that drew the new nation's best minds. By the close of the Revolution, the churches had begun to respond to rather than shape American culture and institutions.

If the wartime development of a civil religion weakened all churches generally, their individual relation to the war hurt two of them very specifically. Although Anglicans in the Middle Atlantic and Southern States, where they were most numerous, tended to support the Revolution, those in New England had remained overwhelmingly loyal. The church's largely Tory clergy also discredited it in the eyes of many Americans, as did the fact that it was the Church of England and dependent upon that country for its ministers and leadership. Even its religious emphasis on order and the Biblical admonition to submit to established rulers placed Anglicanism at odds with the spirit of the Revolution. The Anglicans thus became, claimed Winthrop Hudson, the war's "greatest casualty."[40]

If so, their injuries only slightly exceeded those of the Quakers and German pietists, who opposed as a matter of religious principle both fighting and the violent overthrow of established authority. The refusal of the Quakers and German sectarians to support the war raised for the new United States important questions about a citizen's duty to the state. Most Americans, however, sidestepped such philosophical questions and chose to regard religious pacifism as evidence of unprincipled neutrality or even Loyalism. The new state governments therefore eliminated the Quakers' exemption from militia service (for the Quakers, hiring a substitute was equivalent to immoral support of the war), demanded oaths of loyalty to the new state constitutions (even though swearing an oath similarly violated Quaker religious principle), and insisted that Quakers pay all special taxes for support of the war.[41]

Those Quakers who refused the demands of the Revolutionary governments risked fines, loss of civil rights, confiscation of their property, imprisonment, and even exile—all for adherence to religious beliefs. Those who submitted, either from a lack of moral courage or, like Philadelphia's Free Quakers, out of a higher loyalty to Revolutionary ideals, incurred the wrath of their coreligionists. The yearly meetings that constituted the Quaker governing body determined to disown any church member who took part in Revolutionary government, hired a substitute, paid any tax likely to be used for a military purpose, or conducted business that would promote the war. (Even accepting Continental paper money became suspect.)[42]

The strains of war thus left Quakers reduced in numbers but purified in spirit. Reinforcing prewar trends, the Revolution also affirmed the Quaker decision to withdraw from government and worldly affairs, yet, while turning inward and cultivating a special way of life, to continue war-initiated efforts at humanitarian relief and the moral improvement of society.[43]

If Quaker pacifism raised questions about a religious dissenter's duty to the state, widespread Loyalism also forced Americans to determine policies defining the status of the Revolution's political opponents. Once again, modern ideas about civil liberties suffered. Following the lead of the Continental Congress, which resolved in December 1775 that "those who refused to protect their country should be excluded from its protection," American Revolutionaries enthusiastically ferreted out those suspected of neutrality or Loyalism and forced them to declare their allegiance to the new government—or, as "enemies of American liberty," to pay a heavy price for their opposition.[44]

Following the First Continental Congress, provincial committees of safety and similar local bodies quickly seized effective control in most of the colonies. Those bodies disfranchised all who refused an oath of allegiance to the Congress, forced possible Loyalists publicly to justify their conduct, inspected mail seized from the post office, and confined the movement and censured the speech of any the committees felt might endanger the Patriot cause. Loyalists were also ordered to billet Revolutionary troops, to accept Continental paper money for supplies, and to perform other services that might compromise their position in the eyes of the British. To increase the disabilities of the Loyalists, every state but Georgia and South Carolina had by 1777 declared any act of direct support to Great Britain to be treasonous, and Congress had recommended the confiscation of Loyalist property.[45]

At the hands of the local committees, the opponents of the Revolution also lost many civil and economic rights. They could neither vote nor hold office. They could neither collect debts nor buy and sell land. They were barred from the practice of law and such other professions as teaching. For any act of opposition, they felt the pain of fines, imprisonment, exile, loss of property, and even execution. Those were the officially imposed punishments.[46]

Many zealous Patriots and a few Americans eager to settle old scores also refused to conduct business with Tories, organized mob attacks on their houses and property, tarred and feathered them, rode them through the streets on rails, locked them in stocks for hours, and on occasion branded them with "GR" for George Rex. Against such private vengeance, local governments offered little protection.[47]

In those efforts to suppress dissent, the militia played a vital role. Except in the presence of the British Army, militia units enforced the 1774 Congressional boycott of British goods and sustained the Revolutionary committees that replaced royal governments. Because the obligation to serve in the militia was nearly universal, a militia muster also helped either to expose those with Loyalist sympathies—who might refuse to appear—or to force them to fight on the Patriot side, which would make them vulnerable to later retribution by the British. Neutrality became difficult if not impossible as the militia forced people to take sides.[48]

By methods that would horrify modern civil libertarians, Revolutionary committees and Patriot militia had almost everywhere by 1775 defeated, intimidated, and disarmed America's Tories. That considerable achievement required the domination of as much as one quarter of the nation's white population and testified to both the energy of the Revolutionaries and the early effectiveness of their political organization.[49]

With the possible exception of upstate New York's "neutral ground," warfare between Tory and Patriot nowhere became more intense and prolonged than in the backcountry of the Carolinas and Georgia. In that region, which mixed Scotch-Irish, Germans, and Scottish Highlanders, each colony's Eastern elite had systematically denied representation and influence to backcountry leaders. When Easterners turned Revolutionary, declared independence, and seized control of provincial governments, the resulting wartime dislocations permitted the eruption of old discontent. They roused both ethnic animosities and an opposition that was less pro-British than traditional Western distrust of an Eastern elite. As a result, a vicious partisan war broke out following the British invasion of the South in late 1778. As elsewhere, the Revolutionary militia responded with propaganda, economic and political coercion, confiscation, banishment, and sheer terror to silence the Revolution's opponents, to win reluctant support from many who preferred neutrality, and, with less justification, to settle old personal scores. On the positive side, the new state constitutions accompanied oppression with the attraction of modest improvements in the representation of the backcountry and the civil rights of its many religious dissenters.[50]

Farther to the West, beyond the Appalachians, a more portentous struggle took place. English settlement of that region had only just begun at the conclusion of the French and Indian War, when France had ceded the area east of the Mississippi to Great Britain. To insure that colonization was orderly, revenue producing, and limited—in order not to unduly provoke the Indians—King George III in 1763 reserved, "for the use of the Indians, all land and territories" west of the Appalachians "without our [the King's] special leave and license for that purpose first obtained." Any settlers already there must, moreover, "forthwith . . . remove themselves."[51]

Disappointing to prospective colonists as well as colonies with claims to the region, the Proclamation of 1763 may have helped prompt the Revolution. The royal announcement did not, however, completely halt settlement. The British lacked the troops to exclude individual settlers willing to risk the wrath of both the King and his Indian subjects. The royal government's Indian agents, moreover, continued to negotiate with the Indians for the opening of new tracts to development. Nevertheless, settlement of the future states of Kentucky and Tennessee proceeded slowly before 1775, and the Proclamation made clear that colonization would occur on British, not colonial, terms.[52]

The course of the war, not simply the establishment of independence, changed that. Seeking to ease Anglo-Indian pressure on the frontier and, perhaps, reaffirm its colonial land claims, Virginia in 1778 dispatched George Rogers Clark and a small military force with the object of seizing Kaskaskia, Vincennes, and ultimately the British base at Detroit. Though Clark never captured Detroit, his five-year battle to hold the Old Northwest may have reinforced the American claim to the region.[53]

His assaults also made the Indians vulnerable to the rush of postwar American settlement, often fueled by land bounties awarded to Revolutionary soldiers. In 1783, for instance, only 12,000 people lived in "Kentucky." Seven years later it contained a population in excess of 73,000, which by 1810 had swelled to over 400,000. Tennessee's growth was similarly dramatic. After some delay, Congress aided Western settlement by distributing some ten million acres—almost fifty acres per soldier—to holders of Federal land warrants. Wartime conquest of the trans-Appalachian West and governmental land bounties thus helped insure that America's population would not be confined to the coast and that, for a time, the United States would become a nation of small farmers.[54]

For Indians the war proved a disaster. Most of the tribes had elected to support Great Britain, whose defeat left them entirely exposed to American anger and land hunger. The few tribes that sided with the United States split confederacies like that of the Iroquois and caused internecine warfare that left the Indians as a group less able to resist subsequent white expansion. Although military operations in the transmontane West remained on the fringes of the war, they seriously disrupted the Indians' ability to preserve their political independence and maintain their territorial claims.[55]

That survey of the Revolutionary frontier does not complete discussion of the war's impact on various social groups. Later sections on politics and economics will describe its consequences for merchants, farmers, and workingmen. At this point, however, a few general observations about the Revolution's overall social effects will facilitate understanding of later material on political developments.

As the eighteenth century progressed, good land became increasingly scarce—a shortage exacerbated by the 1763 closing of the West—and economic opportunity grew ever more restricted. The share of total wealth controlled by the richest 10 percent of Americans increased dramatically, in the case of Bostonians from 42 to 58 percent. Politically, hardly more than 15 percent of the population had even a potential influence on colonial governments that denied the vote to blacks (free as well as slave), minors, women, indentured servants, and propertyless white males—a class that grew in size as the American economy developed. Even the voting minority generally deferred to an elite that dominated government at all levels. Because such differences in the distribution of wealth and power were greatest in colonial cities and regions devoted to commercial (plantation) agriculture, a society characterized by more distinct and rigid class stratification spread as those areas grew in population and extent at the expense of the more egalitarian communities of small farmers. In sum, colonial America inclined toward a rigidly stratified society that set individuals apart from one another by differences in wealth, prestige, and power. Although by European standards still relatively free and fluid, American society had begun to grow more like that of the Old World.[56]

Americans had not for the most part gone to war in order to restructure their society, but the eight years of violent struggle required to win independence nevertheless produced notable social change and reversed that colonial trend toward a society of rigid class distinctions. "When a cataclysmic event like the American Revolution occurs," observed Richard Morris, "great social changes are inevitable. New events bring up new men. New ideas have a forum. . . . In many respects the most remarkable fact about the American Revolution was not that there was social change, but that it was relatively modest."[57]

The politicization of large numbers of white males may have been one of the war's most important consequences. Although the Continental Army never exceeded 50,000 men, four times that number (10 percent of the white population) saw some military service and took political stands as members of either the national forces or the states' militia. Using the militia to force Americans to take sides caused even the "dubious, afraid, uncertain, indecisive" majority of the population, wrote John Shy, "to associate themselves openly and actively with the cause." Involvement in the war thus extended to rural areas the politicization of the urban masses begun by the prewar agitation against British revenue measures. The use of the militia and local Patriot mobs to crush upper-class Loyalists had a similar political significance. Men of the middling and lower classes began "hounding, humiliating, perhaps killing men known . . . as social superiors." Deference could not survive such a blow, as common citizens lost their "unthinking respect for wealth and status."[58]

The creation of a national government, the elimination of appointive royal offices, and the expansion of state legislatures offered those politicized voters new opportunities to exert their influence—even to hold office. Effectively disqualified from office were both the 55 percent of the top colonial office holders who remained loyal to Britain and another 22 percent whose patriotism was suspect. The departure of Loyalists created vacancies at lower levels as well. Those positions, as well as the new ones created by independence, often fell to men of lesser wealth and social status. To the same end, new state constitutions offered more equitable representation and an expanded franchise to Catholics, dissenting Protestants, non-English immigrants, and Westerners who became more politically active and helped give the middle and lower classes a greater role in American government.[59]

Election to a government office or receipt of a military commission also enhanced the social standing of many middling sorts of men. In the same way, monetary and land bounties given to Revolutionary soldiers, quite often men who lacked both property and mechanical skills, resulted in the improvement of their social and economic standing.[60]

Economic changes, too, contributed to a reversal of the prewar trend toward a more rigidly stratified society. The war-inspired confiscation of

Loyalist property probably produced little economic levelling—because only the Revolutionary elite had the funds to buy the seized property—but a lot of property did change hands. More important, the opening of the West made land more available to all. While wartime economic conditions weakened the position of some prewar debt holders and ruined not a few merchants and planters, the war also created opportunities for others in manufacturing and privateering. In addition, many well-established but not extremely wealthy merchants built their fortunes in wartime trade. Those economic changes merit, however, more detailed and systematic examination.[61]

The Revolutionary Economy

That examination is made difficult by the way that the results of independence and postwar developments obscure, at some points overwhelm, the economic consequences of the war itself. Independence, whether or not won in a long and difficult war, implied, on the one hand, America's economic exclusion from the British imperial system. The terms of American access to the ports and carrying trade of that empire would thereafter depend upon diplomacy and calculations of imperial interest. On the other hand, exclusion from the British sphere meant no automatic access to the equally exclusive systems of the other European empires—though American commerce in such formerly "enumerated" articles as tobacco could now go directly to its ultimate markets and Americans could trade more easily with the nations of western and northern Europe. At the same time, the destructive postwar surge in imports, the creation of a strong new central government in 1789, its adoption of new trading policies, and the self-sufficiency imposed upon the United States by two decades of European war beginning in 1793 also had a profound influence upon American economic development—an influence more far-reaching than any direct effect of the Revolutionary War.[62] The war nevertheless produced significant and lasting economic results.

Because 90 percent of all Americans engaged in farming, the war's impact on agriculture produced the most widespread results. Nowhere was that more dramatically true than in the Southern colonies. As shown in Table 1.1, the prewar boycotts and the outbreak of hostilities caused a precipitous drop in Southern exports to England and Scotland by 1778. As military operations shifted to the Southern States after 1778, agriculture there suffered further from capital destruction and the loss of slaves. The profitability of indigo production collapsed with the termination of the British bounty, and rice growers, who had much of their capital sunk in paddy systems, found it difficult to convert to raising sheep, hemp, or flax—for which there was a great wartime demand. In the upper South, however, the war stimulated the prewar trend toward converting from tobacco to grain and livestock (for which

Table 1.1
Southern Exports to England and Scotland, 1769–1778
(In Pounds Sterling)

	Virginia/Maryland	Carolina	Georgia
1769–1774 average	548,636	402,792	67,693
1775	758,357	579,550	103,477
1776	73,225	13,668	12,570
1777	58	2,234	—
1778	—	1,074	—

Source: Lewis C. Gray, *Agriculture in the Southern United States to 1860*, 2 vols. (Washington, DC: Carnegie Institution of Washington, 1933), 2:577. Reprinted by permission of the publisher.

the war increased the domestic demand), and the remaining tobacco crop soon found ways around the British blockade to profitable overseas markets. While the lower South therefore suffered modestly, the Chesapeake area adjusted to new wartime demands and reestablished good overseas markets.[63]

The grain and livestock producers of the Middle Atlantic and New England States suffered some temporary dislocation in their overseas markets but profited greatly from the wartime demand for foodstuffs created by the American, British, and French armies. Wartime inflation also meant higher prices for farm products—a benefit to farmers everywhere. As the wages of farm labor lagged behind inflation and farmers could avoid higher prices for imported goods by engaging in home manufacture, net farm income probably increased while inflation eased the payment of debts and taxes.[64]

By the last years of the war, then, most American farmers carried on normally, except when disturbed by military operations. Though growing for export was risky, the profits were high. Inflation and the armies' demand for foodstuffs boosted prices and made debts less burdensome.[65] Wayne Rasmussen seems correct in his conclusion that the war "stimulated rather than injured" agriculture. It may even have been responsible for the American farmers' subsequent preference for inflation, seeing in easy money, according to John Schlebecker, the "route to agrarian prosperity."[66]

For the most part, American industries profited from the self-sufficiency imposed upon the United States by the prewar boycotts and later outbreak of hostilities. There were difficulties, of course. Labor, always scarce, could demand even higher wages when the armed forces, privateers, and new manufacturers joined the competition for workers, and dislocations in overseas markets temporarily hurt the processors of such primary products as naval stores and bar iron. Military operations also occasionally damaged facilities, and Britain's control of the seas from Canadian bases almost completely disrupted American fisheries.[67]

The war also brought compensations. Patriotism demanded, and for a time zealous local committees insured, that Americans buy only domestic goods. With a similar effect, both warring governments declared their ports closed to the ships and goods of the other, which sheltered American manufacturers much as a protective tariff. Supplying a home market enlarged by the loss of imports and meeting the new demands of the armed forces also encouraged manufacturers to increase output and enabled them to raise prices. The ready availability of paper currency at first facilitated both domestic trade and investment in manufacturers, and local and provincial governments even assisted the establishment of new facilities.[68] Except for cannon, the American economy already produced most of the items demanded by the armed forces. To supply both civil and military needs, manufacturers had simply to expand facilities and output. As a result the American production of gunpowder, paper, glass, pottery, leather goods, firearms, hardware, and other iron products—industries already partially established before the Revolution—jumped dramatically, as did the home manufacture of textiles and clothing.[69]

When peace eliminated military orders and reopened American markets to foreign manufacturers, however, much of that war-induced prosperity temporarily evaporated. Eight years of conflict had nevertheless demonstrated the advantages of greater national self-sufficiency and laid the foundations for later growth. "Indeed, it is likely that had the Revolutionary War not broken out," Robert Heilbroner concluded, "manufactures might have been long delayed."[70]

Unlike agriculture and manufactures, which the war stimulated, American commerce initially had to struggle for survival. The 1774 Continental boycott and Britain's 1775 Prohibitory Act threatened the access of American merchants to their prewar British markets and overseas buyers in general. Prior to April 1776, governmental actions associated with the war thus virtually stifled American commerce, except for a small trade in war materials with the West Indies.[71]

After that date, the drift toward independence no longer justified American restraint, and the need for military supplies and foreign sales to finance their purchase prompted Congress to open American ports to the world and to give its own shippers free rein. As compensation for the loss of British markets, American merchants obtained access to the ports and markets of France and its cobelligerents as well as northern Europe, and American shipping received the protection of the French navy. In addition, a lucrative indirect trade with Europe, to include illegal exchanges with Great Britain, developed in the Dutch West Indian port of St. Eustatius. Until 1782, moreover, when the Royal Navy launched a devastating assault on American commerce, the British forces had too few ships and North American bases and too many other responsibilities to conduct an effective blockade or attempt the seizure of all American ships on the high seas. Risks and insurance rates nevertheless rose even as American merchants established new markets and alternate patterns of trade. Despite all those difficult adjustments, the war's overall effect was probably to produce a modest, though perhaps not serious, decline in American overseas trade.[72]

For that decline America's merchants found several compensations. Privateering—the use of privately owned and armed ships to seize enemy merchant ships—flourished, as both an alternate source of scarce imports and of income from the sale of prizes. Throughout the war Great Britain lost over 2,000 vessels with goods worth eighteen million pounds sterling to the some 550 vessels holding Continental authorization to privateer. American merchants also found new customers among the armed forces of the United States, France, and (illegally) Great Britain. Like farmers and manufacturers, American merchants thus found ways to surmount wartime dislocations and to draw profit—in some cases fortunes—from the war.[73]

The war also had a more subtle influence on merchants. Prior to the Revolution, trade and economic ties joined colonial ports and merchants not to one another but to Liverpool and London. English banks and trading houses also provided the credit for a currency-scarce colonial economy. In contrast, wartime trade forced American merchants to look to the national government and to one another. It created personal, intra-American business contacts. In addition, Continental paper money and debt instruments, the new Bank of North America, and foreign loans—all results of the war—provided alternative sources of credit. As Thomas Cochran discovered, the war with Great Britain became the "force that was to create an Atlantic coast business world within a single generation."[74]

Despite the gains by other economic groups and the wartime scarcity of labor, American workers seem to have drawn little profit from the war. Skilled workers, those employed in powder and grist mills, iron furnaces and foundaries, shipyards and ropewalks, print shops, or arms and munitions production, did benefit by exemption from militia service and drafts for Continental troops. Scarcity and inflation, moreover, brought higher wages—dramatically so in the case of Maryland's 2,500 percent boost between 1777 and the end of 1780. Prices, however, tended to run ahead of wages, leaving workers few real gains except from acquiring better jobs or more steady employment. That meals often constituted a part of a worker's compensation and that employees often successfully demanded payment in specie or goods also helped circumvent the negative effects of price inflation.[75]

As skilled workers benefited from military exemptions, indentured servants found enlistment a route to early release from bondage. The war further disrupted servitude by temporarily halting the flow of immigrants to the United States. The Revolutionary idealism that helped spark the wartime attack on slavery failed, however, to enhance the postwar legal position of indentured servants, whose contracts continued to make them the virtual, if temporary, personal property of their masters. Then, in the 1780s, importation of servants resumed, if under new laws requiring the maintenance of slightly more humane and healthy conditions aboard ship and more careful registration upon arrival. Only between 1817 and 1831 did indentured servitude decline and disappear.[76]

Granted that the war wrought modest material changes in the status of various economic groups, its most important function may have been educational: creation of a new outlook among American businessmen. To compensate for wartime dislocations and to profit from war's opportunities, businessmen developed new lines of trade, new techniques, and a speculative fever for gain equal to the challenges and risks involved. As explained later, the various debt instruments left by the war created a domestic pool of capital, and the wartime interest in banking suggested another new way to finance business. In addition to reduced dependence on London, the personal contacts and national outlook necessary to wartime business also resulted in a greater sense of community among businessmen and in more group investments, especially for privateering, spreading maritime insurance risks, and providing military supplies. That outlook led in turn to the increased postwar use of the joint-stock company as a vehicle for both investment and more specialized management. During the entire period before 1775, the colonists had received only six charters of incorporation, one of the forms taken by group investments. Yet, eleven more corporations were established between 1781 and 1785, twenty-two in the next four years, and over a hundred between 1791 and 1795. The Congressional creation of the Bank of North America, the first charter of incorporation granted under purely American sovereignty, thus initiated a still immature trend away from the merchant capitalism of the colonial period and late eighteenth century. By the end of the Revolution, America possessed, wrote Thomas Cochran, "all the elements from which the mighty business system of the United States was to be built."[77]

The Politics of Mobilization

The wartime economy also provided a political education. As noted, American farmers, who, prior to the war, exported food to the British empire, continued to produce and even to prosper. American manufacturers and home producers increased their supply of goods to civil and military customers. American merchants, who had quickly discovered ways to circumvent the

British blockade, found new overseas customers for American agricultural staples and continued to import manufactures to help compensate for shortages in domestic output. Privateering provided a less certain source of foreign goods, but America's French ally furnished critically needed war materiel. The war thus did minimal harm to the economy, and contemporary observers, in fact, uniformly noted America's wartime prosperity. Benjamin Franklin, for example, expressed amazement at the "extravagant luxury" of Americans, who apparently spent their profits from wartime business on "tea, . . . gewgaws and superfluities."[78]

Despite such luxury, the American army starved, and its soldiers wore rags. The sufferings at Valley Forge in 1777-1778 have become a national legend, but Baron de Kalb declared that those who had not also "tasted the cruelties" of the 1779-1780 encampment at Morristown "know not what it is to suffer." In that winter, soldiers ate roasted shoe leather and dined on their pet dogs.[79]

While those winters marked the extremes, and in emergencies the country sometimes supported its forces well, privation dogged the army throughout the war. "Would to God that, in a land blessed with the best food in abundance," complained Colonel Timothy Pickering, "the army were not served with the worst! that the sick were not left to perish for want of wholesome diet, or with the cold for want of proper clothing." George Washington and a host of contemporary observers agreed. "The country does not lack resources, but we the means of drawing them forth," lamented the Commander-in-Chief.[80]

Despite transportation problems, the failure to supply the army was less economic than political; American governments lacked the ability to mobilize the nation's considerable resources. Although sufficiently rich and populous to keep in the field and, with a minimum of foreign material assistance, adequately supply an army far larger than any Britain might have maintained in North America, the United States consistently failed to do so. As a result, the American Revolution became a long war in which the decisive victory at Yorktown depended as much upon the land and naval forces of France as those of the United States. And George Washington, wrote John Miller, suffered the final humiliation of "seeing the cause of America, in America, upheld by foreign arms."[81] A short description of the means used by Congress to finance the Revolution and Washington's army will help account for that final humiliation and explain how the war educated Americans in the problems of political economy.

When Congress in 1775 decided to create and supply a national army, build a navy, and dispatch diplomats abroad, it also elected to mobilize the necessary resources by purchasing them with a new Continental paper currency. Congress simply determined the dollar amounts needed, ordered the money printed, and paid its delegates to certify, by signature, the bills' authenticity. Various government agents then obtained the resources needed to carry on the war by purchase from citizens who voluntarily surrendered their goods and services in return for paper dollars. The Continental notes had no backing except the expectation that the state governments would eventually withdraw them from circulation through taxes and land sales and then return them to Congress as their contribution to the war's expenses.[82]

If such creation of money seems as questionable as alchemy, Congress had little choice. It had no authority to tax individuals or to levy duties on trade. The country had no banks to lend it money. Until 1778 it had no allies, and foreign loans, while helpful, could never suffice. Because the nation suffered a chronic shortage of specie (gold and silver coin), raising money through loans by domestic creditors remained difficult. To obtain men and supplies by drafting citizens and seizing their goods seemed not only unwise but inefficient and potentially unjust. Such a policy might have made Congress appear a bigger despot than the British tyrant Americans were struggling to overthrow.

Earlier in the eighteenth century, moreover, Americans had frequently and successfully used such paper money to finance the various colonial wars, during which the provincial governments had paid their citizens for goods and services with either paper money or interest-bearing certificates. Though backed by a pledge of the governments' future revenues, the payment of taxes and other obligations usually took those notes out of circulation with ease and in the meantime maintained their value. Because of the colonists' lack of both specie and a banking system that could provide notes or credit, Americans grew to like such paper money, which deferred the tax burden of war, facilitated trade, and otherwise stimulated colonial economic development. As a means to finance—without heavy taxes—a revolution begun in protest against taxation, Congress at first found paper extraordinarily appealing.[83]

Much as in the colonial wars, the Continental paper money worked well during the war's first two years. In 1775 Congress issued a total of only $6 million and, by pledging each state to redeem its share of the issue between 1779 and 1786, helped maintain confidence in the Continental bills. In the next year Congress made further emissions, bringing the total in circulation to $25 million. Several factors nevertheless maintained the special value of the notes. Cut off from the credit formerly provided by British merchants and with less than $12 million in specie circulating domestically prior to the war, those modest issues provided a much needed medium of exchange and meant that Americans could carry on business without reliance on barter, commodity money (tobacco was often used), or other instruments that lacked the status of legal tender for payment of debts. Enthusiasm for the war still ran quite high in 1776, and despite Washington's defeat in New York, his retreat through New Jersey, and the miscarried invasion of Canada, the performance of the American army still seemed to promise ultimate military success. Unfortunately the states had done little to redeem the Continental notes and return them to Congress.[84]

The national government therefore had to choose between further emissions of paper currency, which might destroy the value of its notes, and giving up the war. As indicated in Table 1.2, the government continued to print money—even in the face of less favorable conditions: further military failure and increased wartime demand that tended to bid up prices and increase the need for more paper currency.

Table 1.2
Emissions of Continental Currency, 1775–1779

Year	Amount
1775	$6,000,000
1776	19,000,000
1777	13,000,000
1778	63,400,000
1779	124,800,000
Total	$226,200,000

Source: *The Power of the Purse: A History of American Public Finance, 1776–1790*, by E. James Ferguson. Copyright 1961 The University of North Carolina Press. Published for the Institute of Early American History and Culture.

Because the states had also resorted to paper money (collectively in excess of $200 million), each new emission further inflated prices. By 1779 the amount of Continental paper money required to buy $1.00 in gold or silver began to climb sharply, as shown in Figure 1.2. By early 1781, Continental bills passed 150:1 relative to specie and virtually dropped out of circulation. State paper issues often fared even worse, their ratio to specie varying between 40:1 and 1,000:1. The Congress and the states had in effect taxed all those who held the depreciating and ultimately worthless paper money.[85]

Despite that collapse, Congress tried to defend both its currency and its ability to finance the war. Its monetary requisitions on the states, which had been expected to levy war taxes payable in Continental notes, totaled some $95 million by late 1779. Rather than help take the depreciating notes out of circulation, however, the states had complied only to the extent of some $3 to $12 million of the requested sum. After 1776, Congress also tried to absorb its notes in exchange for interest-bearing loan certificates. When after September 1777, Congress began to pay that interest in specie, sales increased

**Figure 1.2
Depreciation of Continental
Currency, 1777-1781
(Currency Required to Purchase $1.00 Specie)**

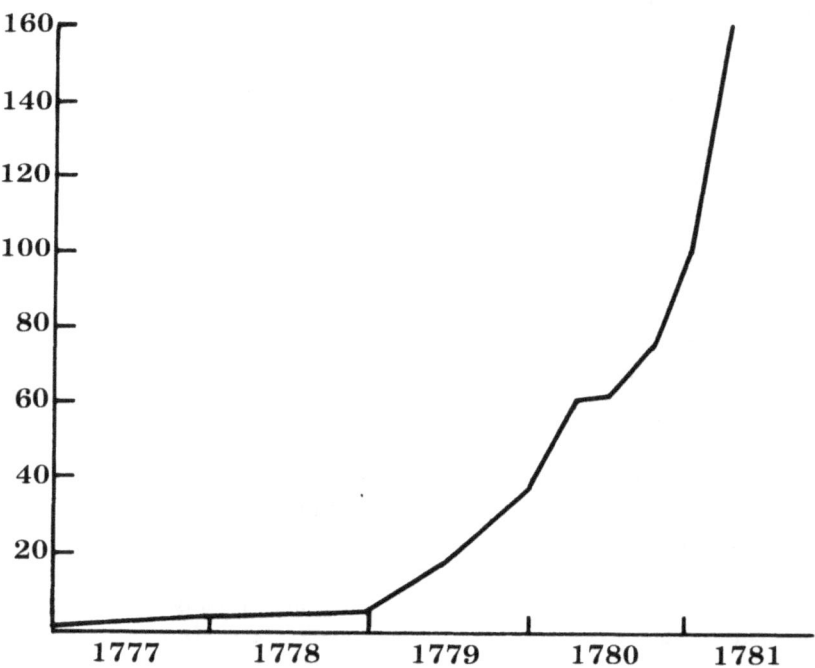

Source: *The Power of the Purse: A History of American Public Finance, 1776-1790,* by E. James Ferguson. Copyright 1961 The University of North Carolina Press. Published for the Institute of Early American History and Culture.

dramatically. Unfortunately, lack of funds and inflated prices forced Congress to put the $63 million it collected back into circulation, and the loan certificates, which began to circulate as a somewhat more valuable alternative to paper currency, only hastened the depreciation of the Continental bills. In an effort to limit future issues by controlling prices and thereby enhancing the buying power of its paper currency, Congress also supported futile attempts by the states to set limits on the rise of wages and prices. Foreign loans presented yet another alternative to issuing more virtually worthless paper, but with the American economy and military effort bordering on collapse by 1779, Congress found few overseas creditors willing to lend large sums. Congress could of course dispense with money altogether by directing military supply officers to seize needed items and issue certificates representing a monetary claim on the government to the victims of impressment. A useful expedient, more widely used as the war progressed, such seizures nevertheless angered their victims and seemed a confession of financial failure. Nor was impressment an adequate substitute for a sound currency.[86]

Pushed to the wall by 1779, Congress virtually abdicated responsibility for financing the war. Hoping to circumvent rising prices and unable to get the states to provide it with tax money, Congress began in that year to ask them for goods rather than cash. The resulting system of "specific supplies" left to each state government the problem of financing their purchase and provided the army with a lot of shoddy merchandise located far from the theater of war. In a related program, Congress also turned over to the states responsibility for paying their own soldiers serving with the Continental army—including the back pay owed them by Congress.[87]

Congress nevertheless considered attempts to shift the war's financial burdens from the national to state governments and to support the armed forces without further emissions of the old paper money mere expedients to cover the period during which the national government put its financial affairs in order. To that end, it ceased issuing the old currency and devalued it to 40:1 relative to specie, still well above a Continental's market value. Congress also called upon the states to support a new series of notes, valued at 20:1 relative to the old ones, by imposing taxes at the rate of $15 million per month for the next thirteen months. When the states, already engaged in withdrawing their own worthless paper currency, failed to honor the Congressional request, the Continental notes quickly became worthless and virtually passed out of circulation.[88]

The Political Consequences of War

Although some members of Congress predicted that the states would prove unequal to the responsibilities thrust upon them in 1779 and 1780, those delegates, later known as Nationalists, still lacked the votes to implement their alternative to Congressional disability: augmenting the powers of the national government and reforming its administrative agencies. To appreciate fully the doubts of those who opposed surrendering the management of the war to the states requires a brief description of the structure and powers of the new state governments and the assumptions and politics that guided their formation.

In many respects the state constitutions written in haste in 1776 reflected the colonial political tradition. In the previous century and a half, particularly during the political struggle preceding the Revolution, Americans had cast their less competent or unpopular provincial governors in the role of enemy and despot. Generally appointed by the King and often representing British or personal interests harmful to the colonists, those officers sometimes embodied the twin threats of tyranny and misgovernment. In contrast, the colonists had gradually come to acknowledge the lower houses of their legislatures as the guardians of colonial interests—or at least those of the local elites that controlled the assemblies. By 1763 those lower houses had everywhere acquired wide control over colonial administration: the membership and conduct of their own legislative sessions; lawmaking; taxation; provincial finances; and the appointment and salaries of local and provincial officials. The colonial assemblies had in effect achieved the ability to dominate both the provincial governors and the members of their administrations. In that light, Great Britain's post-1763 program of reforms represented to the colonists a threat to the powers of the provincial assemblies and everywhere forced colonial elites to begin considering independence as an alternative to a loss of legislative preeminence.[89]

With that experience and perspective in mind, the makers of America's state constitutions generally reduced their state governors to virtual impotence. Ten states limited their terms to one year, and seven added restrictions on the governor's reelection. The legislatures themselves elected the chief executive in nine states and in two others played some role in his selection. The new governor also generally lost the authority to appoint state and local officials and thus to control administrative agencies. In eleven states the governor could not veto legislation and had to seek legislative approval even to use many of his own limited powers. Pennsylvania and New Hampshire so feared executive tyranny that they vested the governor's powers in a council whose president could act only with the approval of his councilors.[90]

Paying only lip service to the modern concepts of the separation of powers and balance among the branches of government, the state constitution makers not only confirmed in the legislatures the powers garnered in the colonial period but made those bodies virtually supreme. Early in the war the legislators fully exploited their new authority, accompanying each legislative enactment with detailed instructions that left governors with neither discretion nor flexibility. In most cases the legislatures also exercised a similar control over state judges. Serving limited terms and threatened with impeachment for unpopular decisions, the judges had to yield to legislators with authority to drive them from office by reducing their salaries and fees.[91]

Despite making such a wide grant of legislative authority, the constitution makers also showed that even the lawmakers were suspect. The new lower houses of assembly contained many more members, and one-year terms became the norm. In no branch of government was the individual accumulation of power—or the development of continuity and experience—facilitated.[92]

Along with colonial experiences, a widespread belief in the virtues of democratic government also shaped those early constitutions, whose form most often reflected the influence if not the absolute control of popular politicians. Sometimes known as Radicals, these men intended to insure that a majority of the people—as determined by the votes of delegates representing districts of roughly equal population—shaped legislation and controlled provincial governments. Similarly, Radicals sought to enfranchise all adult white males, lower the qualifications for officeholding, and limit the ability of governors, judges, and members of the upper houses of the legislatures—offices previously held by men of wealth and influence—to check the wishes of the people as expressed in the popular branch of the assemblies.[93]

Though the Radicals among the Revolutionaries generally failed to achieve their goals, the new constitutions did offer more equal representation to Westerners, did lower the property requirements for voting and holding office, and did drop many religious restrictions on political activity. As a consequence the state legislatures contained an increased proportion of members who were farmers and other men of middling wealth and social position. Although hardly demonstrating the occurrence of an internal social or political revolution, the new constitutions did permit a determined and united popular majority to overcome all obstacles to its control of the state governments.[94]

Unfortunately, many of the new governments designed with that goal in mind also impeded effective conduct of the war. Weak state executives or executive councils, sometimes further restrained by detailed legislative instructions or a requirement to consult special bodies of councilors, often failed to provide the forceful and flexible leadership required to rouse the public and meet the often unforeseen problems of a revolutionary war. Without full control over state officials, neither could the governors effectively direct the actions of agencies whose coordinated efforts were essential to success. The powerful legislatures, even when in session during a crisis, remained more suited to deliberation and debate than the kind of decisive action demanded by the war. Because political parties, in a modern sense, existed in only a few states, the governments found it difficult to sustain and coordinate policy, and the public found it impossible to fix individual responsibility for the legislatures' shortcomings.[95]

Despite those weaknesses, the state governors, as the only executives within the American governmental system, rendered valuable wartime service. By the skillful use of propaganda and personal example they often helped sustain morale during the war's darker moments. They assisted the recruitment of Continental soldiers and, when national forces operated in or near their states, called forth the local militia and advised Continental commanders on strategy and supply. The state governors also became the links between the Continental Congress and the state legislatures.[96]

Detailed studies of the state governments in the Revolution nevertheless reveal that a "series of wartime shocks" taught Americans that "their legislatures were much too strong, their executive departments too weak." While the respect with which wartime governors honored both legislative supremacy and the constitutional limits on their own powers helped reassure Americans about the benevolence of executive power, the "painful experience" of war also served to convince many that "a committee could not win a military campaign nor an impotent chief executive feed starving soldiers." Although Americans did not immediately alter their state constitutions, legislatures passed laws expanding executive authority, and the public began to look more favorably on the vigorous use of executive power while becoming far more skeptical of legislative supremacy.[97] Although the idea would gain full force only in the postwar period, Americans like James Madison had also begun to perceive that "the accumulation of all powers, legislative, executive, and judiciary, in the same hands, whether one, a few, or many, and whether hereditary, self-appointed, or elective, may justly be pronounced the very definition of tyranny." That conclusion applied even when the all-powerful body was the popular branch of the legislature.[98]

By comparison even with the weak executives created by the state constitutions, the powers of the President of the Continental Congress were virtually nonexistent. Essentially only a figurehead, he presided over the sessions of the Congress, carried on much of its considerable correspondence, and performed such ceremonial duties as the new government required— receipt of foreign diplomats and entertainment of official guests. That fourteen different men held the position before 1789 impeded the effective use of expertise and precedent to enhance the informal powers of the office.[99]

The executive powers of the national government rested, at least initially, in Congress itself. Fearful of executive power and eager to maintain legislative control, the Congress in May 1775 began to create a series of ad hoc committees charged to investigate specific problems as a prelude to decisions by

the Congress as a whole. Special committees were thus formed to accomplish the following tasks:
- Draft a declaration for George Washington's assumption of command of the troops surrounding Boston
- Estimate the need for cannon and devise means to obtain them
- Contract for muskets and consider means to promote their manufacture
- Recommend policies for handling British prisoners of war
- Increase the national production of saltpeter (an ingredient of gunpowder)
- Furnish hospitals for the Continental forces
- Develop a network of spies
- Provide medical support to the army
- Investigate the health and discipline of the army
- Supply uniforms to the military forces
- Provide beef for the army
- Find salt to preserve the army's meat
- Improve the states' militia
- Furnish cavalry units to the army
- Prepare instructions for recruiting officers
- Raise battalions for the invasion of Canada[100]

In hindsight the procedure appears obviously unsound. Many of the functions either overlapped or required coordination by a single body. Most concerned matters too trivial for the sustained, direct attention of Congress. In mid-1776 Congress therefore began the creation of administrative boards with broad responsibility for the conduct of war, naval affairs, finance, and diplomacy. That system, like the ad hoc committees, still imposed on board members a heavy load of administrative functions that interfered with their deliberative and policymaking duties as members of Congress. In the war's first two years, when men of talent filled Congress and most delegates attended full time, the double burden could be sustained—barely. As delegates later left to assume state offices or to attend to personal affairs, the system virtually collapsed. The resulting dramatic increase in the turnover of board membership also produced a loss in the collective continuity and expertise of the boards. More and more the conduct of the war suffered as the burden of national administration fell on a few overworked men.[101]

Nowhere had the means of administrative control created more problems than in the national government's relationship to its suppliers. As already noted, the primitive state of military technology meant that the civilian economy already produced and supplied items that, slightly modified, became the tools of war. Moreover, the United States in 1775 comprised a number of rather isolated regional economies focused more on overseas markets than on one another. Although it had established neither administrative agencies nor a trained civil service, Congress had to integrate those regions and draw forth the necessary supplies.[102] Congress had little choice then but to call upon the nation's merchants, the only men capable of integrating the economy or experienced in handling the goods required for war. Reliance on civilian businessmen and the nonmilitary nature of the supplies required thus tended to blur the distinction between public and private affairs.

Colonial business practices further blurred that difference. In the eighteenth century, merchants commonly performed a variety of business functions: banker, manufacturer, shipper, wholesaler, retailer, and insurer. They often performed all those functions in the conduct of their own business and frequently performed some of them as local agents for other businessmen, usually those in another port or country. They kept their business relations secret, took and paid commissions on the functions performed by others, and maintained their informal network of business ties largely by their reputation for personal honesty. The era's ethical code thus permitted merchants freely to mix their own and others' business, providing only that they handled another's affairs as carefully as they handled their own.[103]

When the Congress called such men into government service, they regarded themselves as its commission agents and felt free to continue conducting their private businesses. In their public capacity as supply officers they bought for the government goods that in their private capacity as wholesalers they also sold to the government. They shipped private goods in public vessels and in wagons hired by the government—and vice versa. They used public funds to make the government in effect a partner in their private business ventures and gave government business to their friends and associates. While dishonesty did not taint all or necessarily most transactions, the conflicts of interest were legion. The public everywhere suspected fraud. Many in Congress believed that its agents raised the cost of the war to their own immense personal profit. Aside from lingering popular distrust of the business community, the war had by 1789 produced a determination to create a business system that separated public and private business. The new Federal Government the next year wrote conflict-of-interest laws for its Treasury officials, and the army subsequently supplied itself by contract rather than direct purchase by government agents.[104]

In the midst of war, however, Congress had little opportunity to reform in relations with private business, however unsatisfactory and destructive they were of the public welfare. Still struggling to create an adequate executive that would not also threaten legislative supremacy, Congress in mid-1777 removed its own members from the boards and staffed them with a small number of full-time commissioners (usually three). Within a year, however, Congress supplemented those commissioners with two more from among its own delegates. Although an improvement over earlier systems, those new, semiprofessional boards still provided administration by committee, which slowed decisions and failed to fix responsibility for either success or failure. Congress, moreover, continued to control its servants less by careful supervision than by dividing and limiting their authority. The result was neither efficiency nor control.[105]

After almost six years of administrative experimentation, one consequence of which was the 1779–1780 decision to thrust responsibility for support of the war at least temporarily on the state governments, Congress in 1781 responded to Nationalist demands and reassumed control of national affairs. In that year Congress created true executive departments headed by a single individual, not a member of Congress, with some expertise in the affairs of his department and a wide grant of authority for independent decision and action. Perhaps the archetype of the new national executive, Robert Morris became the head of the Department of Finance. The equally competent but less controversial Robert Livingston, and later John Jay, directed the Department of Foreign Affairs, while General Benjamin Lincoln assumed control of the War Department. After six years of frustrating experimentation, the demands of a nation at war had finally prompted Congress to create an effective national administrative system and, unknowingly, to lay the groundwork for the cabinet departments of the post-1789 Federal Government.[106]

The administrative reforms of 1781 became one part of a more general program to strengthen the central government. Until ratification of the Articles of Confederation in 1781, the Continental Congress had no formal grant of power, causing experts on its development to describe its initial status as a "council of ambassadors" or an "advisory body to the states."[107] The reasons for such weakness seem obvious. The colonists' differences with Great Britain made them fearful of the power of centralized and distant government, and they had begun their struggle with thoughts of sovereign independence for their own province, not for some "hazy and inchoate" national government.[108]

The war, however, soon forced the Continental Congress to assume many of the attributes of sovereignty. By 1775 it had raised an army, begun the creation of a national administration, and assumed direction of efforts to mobilize men and resources. Although at first seeking only to force Great Britain to recognize American rights, Congress had by 1776 discovered that effective coercion required foreign trade and diplomatic support that could only be obtained by a declaration of independence. The demands of war in that sense prompted both independence and the creation of a true central government.[109]

When wartime events demonstrated that the Articles of Confederation, written in 1777 and ratified four years later, impeded effective conduct of the war, the advocates of the administrative reforms of 1781 also sought to increase the powers of Congress. Because the state governments had failed to satisfy Congressional requests for men, money, and supplies, the reformers wished to give Congress the power to tax, initially with a duty on imports, and to coerce state governments, by military force if necessary, when they failed to honor its requisitions. Through pensions and improved administration, the reformers also wished to secure the loyalty of the Continental army— the new nation's only other national institution.[110]

Financial affairs, however, remained the focus of their program. The proposed tariff on imports would provide the national legislature an independent income; the creation of a national bank would become a source of loans to the central government and a means to finance and facilitate national commerce. National assumption of the entire war debt, and plans for its eventual payment, would win for the Congress the loyalty of all citizens who held its paper obligations. More likely than not men of wealth and influence in their local communities, those same citizens might see in their support of a stronger national government a means to control state legislatures too often under the influence of popular leadership.[111]

Although the collapsing war effort of 1779–1780 had enabled those reformers of a national and conservative outlook to win wide public support and thus control of Congress, even in 1781, the Radical opponents of strong national government retained sufficient strength to block any reforms, like the taxes on trade, requiring approval by the states. The triumph at Yorktown in October 1781, moreover, seemed to signal victory in the long struggle with Great Britain, and it consequently undermined support for programs designed to facilitate the conduct of the war by strengthening the national government. The Nationalists therefore achieved little more than the introduction of more effective administrative agencies and the creation of America's first commercial bank.

The desire to rewrite the Articles of Confederation, to create a stronger central government with coercive powers, and to grant that body control over national finance and commerce nevertheless survived the return of peace. The Nationalists of 1781 in fact rehearsed the reforms advocated by the Federalists of 1787. As John Miller explained: "The movement toward a more perfect union which reached its consummation in the Federal Constitution of 1787 began during the Revolutionary War." In contrast to the Revolutionaries' original desires and expectations, the long military struggle that had begun as an attack on the centralizing reforms of the British Empire ended with independence and the subsequent establishment in America of a potentially strong central government with power to coerce both the states and their citizens.[112]

The war also influenced the formation of such a government in two other ways. On the one hand, Revolutionary service in either the army or other national institutions like the Continental Congress and diplomatic service created a cadre of Americans with a cosmopolitan outlook and a commitment to creation of a strong central government. The war had opened to them new opportunities for national service and then shaped the outlook of those who seized them. "Intimate experience with the war effort," wrote Stanley Elkins and Eric McKitrick, "convinced such men as Washington, Madison, Hamilton, Duane, and Wilson that something had to be done to strengthen the Continental government."[113]

On the other hand, a change in political theory—also prompted by the war—provided the intellectual justification for a stronger national administration. In 1776 most of the American Revolutionaries had assumed the existence of a single set of interests common to all the people. They had described colonial politics as a struggle between the people (represented by the legislative lower houses) and the rulers (ambitious individuals or groups who used the governorship or positions on provincial councils to advance private interests and corrupt the representatives of the people). To establish good government and serve the general welfare, the Revolutionaries had merely to achieve independence from a corrupt imperial administration and bring executive and judicial agencies under firm legislative control. The tyranny of a popularly controlled legislature seemed inconceivable; the people could not possibly harm their own interests. As the people were innately virtuous, or would become so upon elimination of the corrupting British influence, they would willingly set aside personal advantage in favor of the public good and refrain from any self-interested infringement of the rights of others.[114] Or so they thought.

Even an easily won independence might in time have challenged such notions; war quickly demonstrated their error. Americans had not willingly sacrificed personal gain to the public need. After the *rage militaire* of 1775, they generally refused to serve in the armed forces. Farmers would rather exchange grain and livestock for British specie than sell it to the Continental army for depreciating paper currency. Townsmen regularly charged the farmers with inflating their prices or holding food supplies off the market to the detriment of urban dwellers. Merchants also traded with the British and abused governmental offices in pursuit of private profit. Everywhere those who profited from wartime prosperity spent their new wealth on a most unrepublican display of luxury while avoiding payment of taxes and refusing to subscribe to the government's war loans. Independence and republican ideology had unexpectedly failed to transform American society and create a nation of virtuous, public-spirited citizens.[115]

The wartime behavior of Americans had in fact shown the "people" to consist of a collection of competing interests in need of protection from one another. Government must therefore become sufficiently strong to compensate for popular shortcomings and to ensure, by coercion if necessary, public support for the common good. Any agency of government, including the legislature, being capable of misuse by a self-interested faction, Americans must devise constitutions that would check the possible abuse of power by any governmental branch or officeholder. That meant creating an independent judiciary, returning the governor's power of appointment and legislative veto, strengthening upper houses of the legislature, and setting the fundamental law of a constitution above legislative statute. To the same end, a strong central government, so large and distant as to be beyond the control of faction, would provide additional protection for minority rights. The war thus convinced a majority of Americans that they must devise new governments that did not rest on an assumption of public virtue, governments designed to moderate the selfish struggles for advantage among elements of the society rather than to control a contest for power between the rulers and a homogeneous public.[116]

Wartime dislocations and widespread participation in the struggle for independence had thus created a more fluid sociopolitical structure and made it possible for groups outside the elite to advance—provided they had given active support to the Patriot cause. Sometimes Revolutionary leaders had to gain that support through coercion or through creation of more representative and democratic institutions of government.

Wartime economic conditions also furthered the advance of some formerly disadvantaged groups. While the war brought economic hardship to a few merchants, some farmers, many laborers, and most soldiers and others on fixed incomes, it also gave many individuals an opportunity to acquire vastly increased wealth, which they then readily converted into social prestige and political power.

For groups who failed to support the war, it often brought near total ruin. Americans, intolerant of those who opposed the war for political or ethical reasons, threatened the civil rights and liberties, the property, and even the lives of Loyalists and pacifists, and used all forms of social, economic, political, and military pressure to convert the merely indifferent into at least reluctant Patriots.

The war also tested institutions and values. The widespread failure of American governments to mobilize the nation's resources and achieve a quick victory led to a greater respect for executive power and a strong central government. The failure of individual Americans to behave as virtuous, self-sacrificing citizens led in two directions. The Radicals, who rested their political theories on the existence of such citizens, redoubled their efforts to educate Americans on the requirements of republican citizenship. The Nationalists, convinced by the war that the public comprised many competing, self-interested groups, devised political structures designed to deflect the pursuit of private interest into channels that would serve the public good. Conservatives, threatened by the Revolutionary governments' more democratic features, and businessmen, who emerged from the war with a new national outlook, supported the Nationalist cause, which eventually converted wartime experience and programs into the Constitution of 1787 and the next decade's Federalist administration.

War, like independence, had served as a powerful solvent of social, economic, and political institutions. And like independence, war shaped the course taken by the new nation as it faced its future. The consequences of the American Revolution were indeed the result of a war for independence.

2
THE CIVIL WAR

Through our great good fortune, in our youth our hearts were touched with fire.

Oliver Wendell Holmes, Jr.[1]

In his 1884 Memorial Day address, Oliver Wendell Holmes, Jr., former Union officer become Supreme Court Justice, spoke of the Civil War's psychic effect on those who had fought. Determined to act greatly, Holmes and his youthful companions had committed themselves "with enthusiasm and faith" to a "long and hard" war, "without being able to foresee exactly where [they would] come out." From that experience, he claimed, they had emerged forever changed—a generation set apart from other Americans.[2]

At the distance of two decades, Holmes' memory may have attributed to Union soldiers too much nobility of purpose. He surely knew that the war's effects were more than psychic and hardly limited to those who, like himself, had served in the Union armies. Institutions as well as individuals had emerged from the war much altered. Nor had such results been unforeseen. During the first year of the war, an officer on the staff of Confederate general John B. Gordon warned that "war is an omelet that cannot be made without breaking eggs, not only eggs in *esse*, but eggs in *posse*."[3] Although the nature of the changes lay beyond prediction in 1861, four years later there emerged from the fire of war a new American nation.

A full appreciation of that wartime transformation requires, first, an examination of war-induced economic and political developments. A grasp of group and institutional changes in those spheres will in turn inform understanding of the war's impact on those whose "enthusiasm and faith" committed them to action on fronts remote from the field of battle. The totality of those economic, political, and social consequences will in the end reveal that the fire of the Civil War touched far more than the soldiers' hearts.

The Northern Economy at War

In 1861, secession, war, and early military reversals had a nearly ruinous effect on an economy just recovering from the financial panic and subsequent business depression of 1857. Midwestern farmers lost Southern customers, while closure of the Mississippi River threatened access to international markets. Northeastern manufacturers similarly faced ruin, particularly those who relied on Southern cotton or produced ready-made clothing or shoes for the South's slave laborers. During the resulting business slump of 1861, the North experienced some 6,000 business failures—half again as many as in the panic year of 1857.[4]

The outbreak of war also imperiled the nation's banks, and with them the entire system of commercial credit and exchange. Internationally, the war stemmed the prewar influx of foreign investment while it also eliminated income from the sale of exported cotton. As a result, gold left American banks in payment for imported goods. Domestically, the war cast doubt on the solvency of Midwestern banks that had invested heavily in Southern state bonds and Northeastern banks and businesses that held some $300 million in uncollectible Southern debts. That led stockholders to unload their shares and depositors to further drain specie from the banks as they exchanged their paper money for gold.[5]

To the North's wounded bankers, the new administration's Secretary of the Treasury almost delivered the coup de grace. With secession and the business slump reducing Federal revenues (and expenditures rising in response to the military build-up), Secretary Salmon P. Chase negotiated three $50-million war loans with Northeastern bankers. Rather than accept payment in the form of bank deposits on government account, upon which the Treasury could draw by writing checks, Chase insisted on a reserve-threatening delivery of gold. To rebuild their reserves, the bankers had to depend on prompt public purchase of the bonds given them by the government and deposit by manufacturers of the proceeds of their government sales. Bad military news and the threat of war with England, however, caused Northerners to hold onto their gold. Bankers consequently became unable to exchange their bank notes for gold, forcing the Treasury, too, to suspend specie payment.[6] By the end of 1861, the Union government consequently lacked funds and its economy a means of exchange. Both developments portended further harm to the conduct of business.

Despite that dismal beginning, within a year the Northern economy had begun to boom. Agriculture led the way when three bad harvests in Europe (starting in 1860) created more than enough new customers to replace the farmers' loss of Southern markets. At the same time, the railroads and canals linking the Midwest to Eastern ports replaced the Mississippi River as the farmers' link to world markets. Both developments enabled Northern agricultural exports to rise dramatically as indicated in Table 2.1. (The increased sale of Northern wheat in Europe may also have helped discourage any European intervention on behalf of the South.) Domestic farm sales also surged as the army's contractors bought beef cattle, hogs, and grain to feed hungry soldiers and wool and leather to make their uniforms, shoes, and equipment. To supply the wool, American growers doubled the sheep population, but the army demand for meat, draft animals, and cavalry horses caused slight declines in the numbers of other livestock.[7]

Table 2.1
Annual Export of Pork, Beef, Corn, and Wheat Products, 1860–1865

Year	Amount
1860	$28,458,558
1861	83,405,566
1862	108,565,722
1863	127,660,780
1864	94,159,130
1865	81,548,290

Source: Paul W. Gates, *Agriculture and the Civil War* (New York: Alfred A. Knopf, Inc., 1965), p. 227. Copyright 1965 by Alfred A. Knopf, Inc. Reprinted by permission of the publisher.

The increased demand for agricultural products, which doubled the average prices that farmers received for their crops, brought prosperity to the countryside. Between 1862 and 1864 the total value of farm goods leapt from just over $700 million to more than $1.4 billion. With high demand, rising prices, and easy money, farmers paid off their old debts and in many cases borrowed to purchase more land and equipment with which to increase their output and, they hoped, boost their future incomes.[8]

The army's demand for manpower, which took one-third of the prewar farm labor force, made machinery purchases particularly significant. Greater efforts by wives, children, and aged parents could only partially compensate for the enlistment of a husband, son, or hired hand, and the resulting wartime shortage of hands hastened the acceptance of labor-saving agricultural implements developed in the prewar decade. Between 1860 and 1865, American farmers tripled the amount of machinery in use and within the decade produced a 13 percent increase in output per farm worker.[9]

Using improved seeds and fertilizers and putting more land into production could also expand agricultural output. Accordingly, the government took several steps with those ends in view, steps facilitated by the secession of Southern States whose representatives and sympathizers had previously blocked the necessary legislation. In 1862 the Republicans passed the Homestead Act, granting a 160-acre farm to any man able to pay a ten-dollar fee and willing to work his homestead for five years. To further the spread of agricultural science, the new administration created a Department of Agriculture and approved the Morrill Act. The latter gave the states public lands whose sales would endow agricultural and mechanical colleges as centers for research and the education of a future generation of farmers as well as engineers.[10]

The Civil War also bequeathed farmers several less positive legacies. The end of the war and resumption of more bountiful harvests in Europe reduced demand just when the opening of new homesteads and wartime expansion had increased American supplies. Prices also fell with the end of wartime inflation, bringing farm prosperity to an abrupt end. Farmers who had borrowed to purchase more land and machinery soon considered their war-induced debts a crushing burden. That experience prompted farmers gradually to abandon their old Jacksonian distrust of paper money and strong government; rural Americans increasingly looked to the Federal Government, as they had during the war, for favorable farm legislation and an expansion of the money supply designed to boost prices and ease repayment of debts.[11]

The war brought mixed blessings to those businessmen engaged in commerce and transportation, and it dealt a mortal blow to the merchant marine. The latter industry immediately lost the South's cotton-export business, which had employed half the deep-sea fleet. Later, Confederate commerce raiders, like the storied *CSS Alabama*, captured or destroyed 239 ships totalling 105,000 gross tons—5 percent of the 1860 fleet. To escape the raiders, American shippers used foreign-flag vessels, and American shipowners sold a thousand ships totalling 800,000 tons to other nations, whose neutral status protected the vessels from the depredations of the small Confederate fleet. Although the merchant marine's decline had begun before 1860, the Civil War dramatically accelerated the pace. Between 1860 and 1864 the portion of US foreign trade carried in American-owned ships fell from 63 to 25 percent, and it "recovered" to only 31 percent by 1869, before commencing a new decline.[12] Except for temporary, wartime naval construction, which helped increase the navy to more than ten times its prewar size, the decline of the merchant marine might have forced a similar fate upon American shipbuilders between 1861 and 1865.[13]

Despite the loss of cotton exports and the Union's initial overseas purchases of arms and equipment, the North's international trade account, as Table 2.2 indicates, remained in rough balance because of the surprising increase in agricultural exports reinforced by a governmental effort to limit imports. New tariff schedules, which probably account for most of the decline

Table 2.2
US Imports and Exports, 1860–1865
(Millions of Dollars)

Year	Exports	Noncotton Exports	Imports	Trade Balance
1860	400.1	208.3	362.2	+ 37.9
1861	249.3	215.3	335.7	− 86.4
1862	227.6	226.4	205.8	+ 21.8
1863	268.1	261.5	252.9	+ 15.2
1864	264.2	254.3	329.6	− 65.4
1865	233.7	226.8	248.6	− 14.9

Source: Emory R. Johnson, et al., *History of Domestic and Foreign Commerce of the United States*, 2 vols. (Washington, DC: Carnegie Institution of Washington, 1915), 2:55. Reprinted by permission of the publisher.

in imports, also resulted from secession and war. The departure of Southern Congressmen facilitated, and the North's wartime need for revenue and taxes on domestic manufacturing justified, a significant increase in levies. By 1865, the Republicans had raised the average prewar rate by 47 percent and doubled the tariffs on some items. While initially motivated by a need for revenue and a desire to be fair to domestic manufacturers burdened with heavy wartime taxes, the Republicans left the barriers in place after 1865, thus reversing several decades of American tariff history and committing the nation to protectionism.[14]

Although the merchant marine languished and foreign trade barely held its own, the Civil War probably brought the nation's railroads and canals their best years. With the Mississippi closed, Midwestern farmers made greater use of rail and water links to the East, while increased grain sales to Europe via Northeastern ports also boosted traffic. As the army grew in size, so did its need to ship men and supplies. The business recovery in 1862 also added to the traffic as increased shipments of raw materials and finished goods placed new demands on the transportation system. The Pennsylvania Railroad, for example, supplemented its passenger business by the movement of almost a million soldiers between April 1861 and December 1865. During the same period, its annual freight business jumped from 1.5 to 2.8 million tons. As a result of the war, the North's previously overbuilt rail network enjoyed unprecedented prosperity (many lines paid their first dividends), and as a group railroad stocks more than doubled in value.[15]

The Civil War also affected the railroads in other ways. It illustrated the advantages of the four prewar trunk lines connecting the interior to the Atlantic coast, which in turn encouraged further consolidation, the connection of terminals within cities, bridge building, and the establishment of a standard track guage. Although the construction of new track fell to only 4,459 miles during the war years, heavy wartime use required the replacement of many older, inferior rails. Wartime profits, war-induced interest in transportation, and the 1862 passage of the Pacific Railway Act also prompted the laying of 52,922 miles of new track in the five postwar years.[16]

The situation in manufacturing also produced a mixed, though generally favorable report—with the difficulties of New England's cotton textile mills providing the principal loss in a record dominated by general wartime prosperity. Though the mills had an unusually large supply of cotton on hand in 1861 (and subsequently received small shipments from the occupied South, loyal border states, and overseas growers), by 1863 fewer than half the spindles in Northern cotton mills remained in use. Considering that the mills had lost their principal supply of raw material, New England experienced less distress than might be imagined. Some owners converted to the production of woolens—an industry that boomed as army contracts helped push annual consumption of wool from 85 to 200 million pounds. Some of the dismissed workers joined the army or took the places of soldiers leaving jobs in other industries, and by 1864 cotton deliveries from army-run plantations and seizures in the occupied South allowed an increase in cotton production.[17]

The loss of Southern markets might similarly have hurt the manufacturers of readymade clothing and shoes—except for the almost insatiable demands of an army eventually numbering nearly one million men. Government contracts not only rescued those two industries but also encouraged a greater use of sewing machines and the factory system of mass production.[18]

Supplying the armed forces also brought fat contracts and prosperity to existing arms and munitions makers and stimulated the growth of such relative newcomers as meat packing and the commercial canning of fruits, vegetables, and milk. The government purchases that brought prosperity to American farmers also indirectly benefited the manufacturers of farm machinery, as suggested by the figures of Table 2.3 on the wartime sales of reapers and mowers. The ability to harvest a larger crop in turn led to new interest in machinery for planting and cultivating—and a wartime doubling in the annual number of applications for agricultural patents.[19]

The Civil War brought less obvious benefits to mining and heavy industry. Output in both areas grew during the war—coal by 36 percent and pig iron by 23 percent—but the decennial rates of growth for the 1860s in many such industries fell behind those of the immediately preceding and postwar decades. As Figure 2.1 suggests, heavy industry experienced a period of slow wartime growth followed by five years of rapid expansion.[20]

From the perspective of twentieth-century wars, that slow growth seems a surprising result. It should not seem so. However modern in many respects,

Table 2.3
Sales of Reapers and Mowers, 1862–1865

Year	Quantity
1862	33,000
1863	40,000
1864	80,000
1865	80,000

Source: Paul W. Gates, *Agriculture and the Civil War* (New York: Alfred A. Knopf, Inc., 1965), p. 233. Copyright 1965 by Alfred A. Knopf, Inc. Reprinted by permission of the publisher.

the Civil War placed few demands on heavy industry. The services required relatively few cannon, and the navy had only several dozen iron ships—despite the publicity given the historic battle between the *Monitor* and *Merrimack*. Slow-firing, muzzle-loaded weapons used relatively small quantities of iron for shot and shell, and small-arms manufacturers imposed similarly limited demands on the iron industry, even though they may have required more metal of a consistently high quality. The manufacture of rails continued to use a large portion of the industry's output, but during the war most went to the maintenance of more heavily used existing lines rather than to the laying of new track.[21]

Overall, the nation's national product, which had reached $3.8 billion in 1860, grew to $4 billion in 1864, despite the war and the loss of eleven Confederate states.[22] Although the North's economy thus passed the test of growth, a more important aspect of the war's impact concerns the possibility of subtle wartime changes in economic structure, business attitudes, and political environment, changes that may have contributed to the nation's dramatic postwar economic expansion.

While not greatly affecting output in the short run, the war, for example, apparently encouraged the consolidation of American industry. In 1861 the army's quartermaster general, Montgomery C. Meigs, tried to spread government contracts among the nation's thousands of firms—both small and large. Many of the former, according to Allan Nevins, unfortunately proved "inexpert or unreliable," forcing Meigs to concentrate his orders on the few larger manufacturers. They in turn used their war profits to expand and mechanize their facilities and to buy out smaller competitors.[23]

The wartime tax structure, which levied each stage in the production of an end item when undertaken by a series of independent manufacturers, also encouraged such consolidation. Vertical integration of an industry, which kept all stages of manufacture within a single firm until sale of the final product, enabled integrated businesses to avoid payment of all but the last

Figure 2.1
Production of Pig Iron and Rails, 1860-1870

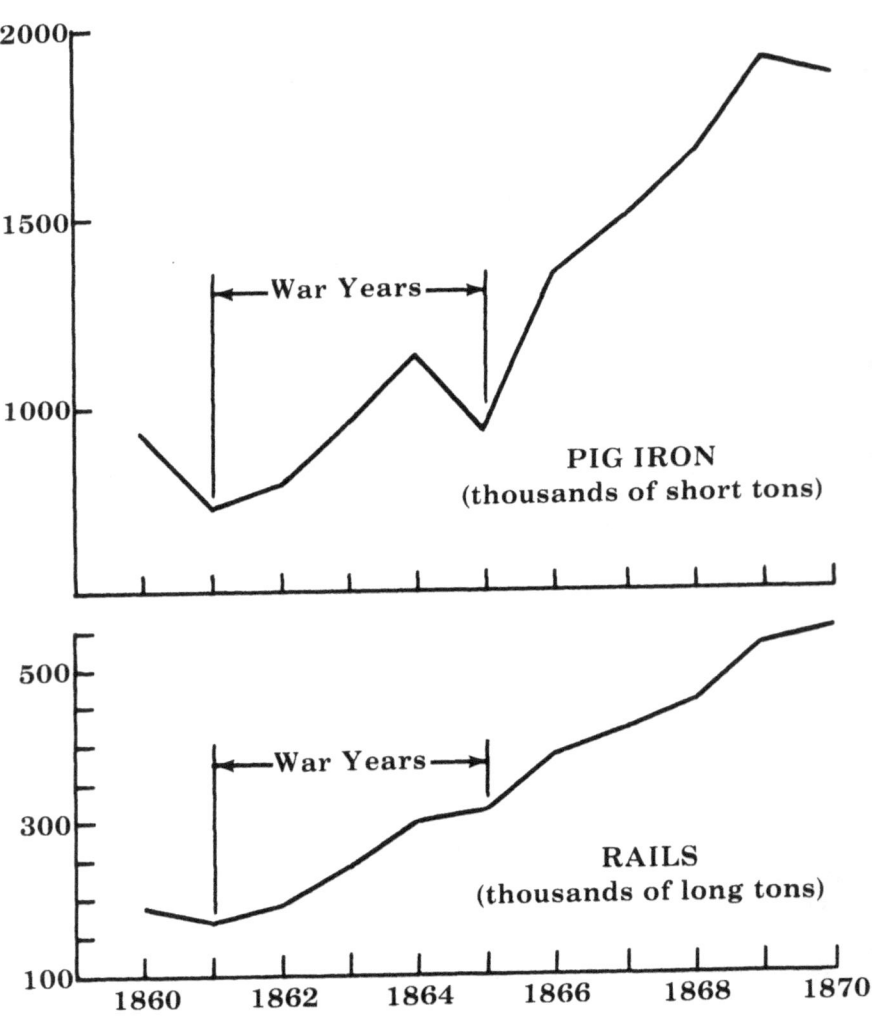

Source: Ralph L. Andreano, ed., *The Economic Impact of the Civil War*, 2d ed. (Cambridge, MA: Schenkman Publishing Company, Inc., 1967), pp. 226-29. Reprinted by permission of the publisher.

tax and gave them an economic edge over competitors subcontracting earlier phases of the work to small, independent firms.[24]

The war, in other words, laid the foundations for postwar expansion. It gave businessmen experience in handling large orders and an incentive to build facilities capable of large-scale production for a national market. Wartime inflation helped them repay old debts, and war profits gave them capital for further expansion. A Republican administration increasingly friendly to business promised high tariffs and an improved banking system, which meant high profit margins and ample credit to finance trade and growth. Northern businessmen consequently emerged from the war filled with optimism and self-confidence and prepared for the aggressive pursuit of profits in the postwar period.

Whatever the combination of reasons, the postwar period showed a remarkable advance over the trends established in the prewar decade. Among heavy industries, pig-iron production, which had grown by 50 percent between 1850 and 1860, doubled in the eight postwar years. Mining showed similar gains. Bituminous coal output, which had doubled in the prewar decade, increased by 145 percent between 1865 and 1875. In the same years, new railroad trackage also doubled. As summarized in Table 2.4, the North's economy quickly resumed and then increased the prewar rates of economic growth. Successfully passing the test of war also pushed per-capita Northern commodity output ahead of that of the South. Whereas the latter region had slightly led the rest of the Union in 1860, by the end of the war Southern per-capita commodity output had fallen both relatively and absolutely and through 1880 remained at less than 60 percent of the levels reached elsewhere in the United States.[25]

Table 2.4
US Output and Decennial Rates of Change, 1849–1889

Year	Output		Decennial Rate of Change	
	Total (Millions)	Per Capita	Overall	Per Capita
1849	$1,657	$71	52%	11%
1859	2,686	85	62%	20%
1869	3,271	82	23%	−4%
1879	5,304	105	62%	29%
1889	8,659	137	63%	30%

Source: Adapted from Ralph L. Andreano, ed., *The Economic Impact of the American Civil War*, rev. ed. (Cambridge, MA: Schenkman Publishing Company, Inc., 1967), p. 212. Reprinted by permission of the publisher.

The Collapse of the Southern Economy

For the Southern economy, the war was an almost unmitigated disaster, especially so for the region's agriculture and foreign trade. The Union blockade of Southern ports—reinforced for a time by a near universal agreement to hold cotton off the market as a means to pressure France and England to recognize and aid the Confederacy—cost the South the income from its principal export crop and left it with a cotton surplus for which it had little use. Prodded by Southern governments, the planters consequently began conversion of their operations from cotton and tobacco to production of the livestock and grain needed by the Confederate army and a population previously dependent in part on imports from the border states and Ohio Valley. As Table 2.5 shows, those efforts met some success. Athough that conversion probably produced enough food to feed the Southern population, maldistribution created severe shortages both in urban areas and the armed forces.

Table 2.5
Southern Agricultural Production, 1860–1866

Year	Cane Sugar (Millions of Pounds)	Cotton (Thousands of Bales)	Tobacco (Millions of Pounds)	Wheat	Corn	Potatoes
				(Millions of Bushels)		
1860	n.a.	3,841	404	24	196	36
1861	459	4,491	n.a.	45	350	50
1862	87	1,597	n.a.	35	300	40
1863	78	449	n.a.	55	350	60
1864	10	299	n.a.	n.a.	n.a.	n.a.
1865	18	2,094	n.a.	n.a.	n.a.	n.a.
1866	41	2,097	316	n.a.	n.a.	n.a.

Source: Paul W. Gates, *Agriculture and the Civil War* (New York: Alfred A. Knopf, Inc., 1965), pp. 104, 371. Copyright 1965 by Alfred A. Knopf, Inc. Reprinted by permission of the publisher.

Conversion to unfamiliar crops also accounted in part for the 70 percent decline in Southern agricultural output between 1859 and 1866. Other wartime developments, however, caused most of that collapse. Inefficiencies and labor shortages developed as younger men left to join the Confederate forces, robbing the small farms of their principal workers and the plantations of those experienced in supervising slave labor. Unlike the North, the Confederacy had no farm-equipment industry to permit substitution of machinery for labor. In fact, the South could not even keep its existing agricultural tools in good repair. The army further disrupted production by stripping Southern farms of draft animals and wagons and devouring livestock faster than it could reproduce. Finally, as the Union armies advanced, they either occupied or ravaged much of the countryside upon which the Confederacy depended for food. As Figure 2.2 suggests, the war caused a decline in all the important measures of rural wealth.[26]

Figure 2.2 also reveals that it took Southern agriculture almost fifteen years to recover its prewar capital investment. Output remained similarly low. During the five postwar years the average harvest of every major crop generally reached only 40 to 60 percent of prewar levels. The loss not indicated in Figure 2.2—the war's emancipation of slaves worth perhaps $3 billion—helps explain that low output and slow recovery. No longer driven in gangs by often brutal overseers, the ex-slaves consumed a larger share of their output, freed women and children from work in the fields, and used more of their time as leisure—which reduced overall regional production. Unable without Federal help to buy their own homesteads (as the ex-slaves desired) and unwilling to work as contract laborers (as their former masters preferred), the South's blacks generally entered into sharecropping or tenancy agreements. Agriculturally inefficient and unresponsive, those arrangements also contributed to the South's slow recovery. Given the attitudes of the Federal Government, the ex-slaves, and their former masters, as well as the South's lack of credit facilities, sharecropping and a steep decline in agricultural output may have been the inevitable consequences of the war and emanicipation.[27]

Like passengers on a rollercoaster, Southern railroads rode a dizzying cycle of boom and bust. They experienced initial prosperity, then almost total deterioration and destruction, followed by rapid postwar recovery. Smaller and less complete than the Northern rail net with its several trunk lines, the Southern "system" consisted of over one hundred small companies operating short lines with inferior equipment. The entire South had less rolling stock than the four largest Northern lines, and it had little capacity to replace or maintain what it had. The first rush of prosperity due to the movement of military forces and supplies soon collapsed as the Southern railroads faced the loss of experienced workers to military service, a destructive wartime inflation, and the deterioration of its equipment. Then in 1864 and 1865, Union forces advancing deep into the South destroyed all the lines and equipment they did not need. Postwar recovery nevertheless came quickly as the occupying Union army rebuilt many of the former lines and Northern capital became readily available to finance reconstruction.[28]

By contrast, blockade running remained a growth industry almost to the end. Unfortunately, far too many of the swift vessels that slipped in and out of the long Southern coastline brought luxury goods that drained the South of its scarce specie and contributed little to the war but dissension as the lower classes objected to the high life style of some Confederate leaders. Only late

Figure 2.2
Southern Agricultural Capital, 1850-1880

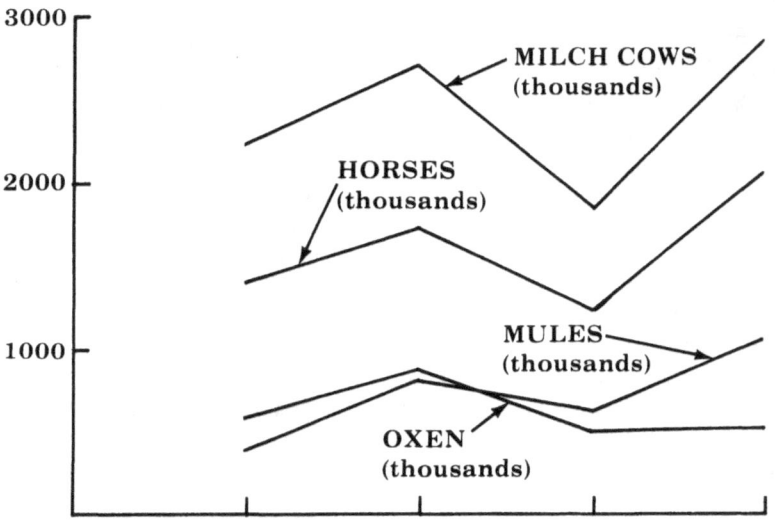

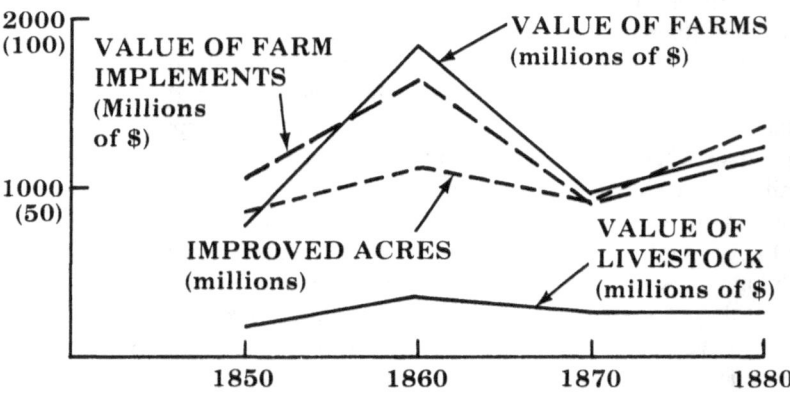

Source: Eugene M. Lerner, "Southern Output and Agricultural Income, 1860-1880," in *The Economic Impact of the American Civil War*, 2d ed., ed. Ralph L. Andreano (Cambridge, MA: Schenkman Publishing Company, Inc., 1967), p. 111. Reprinted by permission of the publisher.

in 1863 did the Confederacy move to control private blockade runners by requiring them to devote a portion of their cargo space to government-approved goods. State governments often helped circumvent that requirement, however, by investing in the vessels, thus making them public ships and exempt from controls. By 1864, the Confederate government extended its control by requiring a license for the export of staples, prohibiting the import of luxuries, centralizing European and domestic transactions relating to foreign trade, and even establishing its own fleet of blockade runners. Despite the resistance of some governors and the captains of private vessels, the system worked well—though it came far too late to affect the outcome of the war.[29]

Southern industry experienced a fate much like that of the railroads. Accounting in 1860 for only 8 percent of the American output of manufactured goods, facing a wartime demand for arms, munitions, clothing, and equipment, and supported by large profits and governments willing to grant subsidies and other aids to expansion, Southern industry experienced an initial period of rapid growth as it provided military essentials sufficient to sustain the South in its struggle with the more industrialized North. Had the Civil War been more modern in its demands on heavy industry, the end for the South would have come much sooner. As it was, home manufactures, the establishment of new powder mills and arsenals, and the efforts of establishments like Richmond's Tredegar Ironworks kept the army minimally supplied until late in the contest. Even so, the Confederate soldiers often lacked shoes and wore rags, even if they usually had powder and shot.[30]

As the war progressed, however, Southern industry showed signs of strain. It could not replace the many Northern craftsmen and managers who had returned home in 1861, and it lost other skilled personnel to the Confederate military forces. Later, worn machinery, which the South lacked the ability to repair or replace, began to collapse just as the Union blockade began effectively to deny the South access to its foreign suppliers. The insufficiency of the rail system also precluded the timely movement of raw materials even before the invading Union forces seized or destroyed both industrial facilities and rail lines. By the war's end, wrote Victor S. Clark, the South's manufacturers had consequently fallen "far behind the position they had acquired in the promising earlier period of their development, during the decade which closed with the panic of 1857."[31]

Southern industry nevertheless quickly revived in the postwar period, even if—as Table 2.6 shows—its position relative to the North began to decline, reversing several prewar trends. The South's postwar demand for almost every type of manufactured goods, and its great natural resources and wartime experience, account for that rapid revival. The war had nevertheless burdened the South with a mighty and enduring industrial handicap.

Table 2.6
Indicators of Southern Manufacturing, 1850–1880

Indicator	1850	1860	1870	1880
Number of Establishments	123,025	140,433	252,148	253,852
(Percent of US Total)	(13.7)	(14.7)	(12.3)	(11.5)
Industrial Capital (millions)	$55.3	$96.0	$98.7	$133.3
(Percent of US Total)	(10.4)	(9.5)	(4.6)	(4.8)
Number of Laborers	88,390	110,721	144,252	171,674
(Percent of US Total)	(9.2)	(8.4)	(7.0)	(6.3)
Cost of Raw Materials (millions)	$40.8	$86.5	$116.2	$151.8
(Percent of US Total)	(7.4)	(8.4)	(4.7)	(4.5)
Value of Products (millions)	$79.2	$155.5	$199.0	$240.5
(Percent of US Total)	(7.8)	(8.2)	(4.7)	(4.5)

Source: Eugene M. Lerner, "Southern Output and Agricultural Income, 1860–1880" in *The Economic Impact of the American Civil War*, 2d ed., ed. Ralph Andreano (Cambridge, MA: Schenkman Publishing Co., Inc., 1967), p. 112. Reprinted by permission of the publisher.

Southern Mobilization

As the preceding sections indicate, the Confederacy commenced the Civil War at a relative disadvantage. Expressed as simple ratios, the Union had three times more railroad trackage; four times more total wealth, population (excluding slaves), and merchant vessels; six times more real and personal property (excluding slaves); and ten times more annual manufacturing output.[32] To have a good chance of success in even a defensive struggle, the South had either to obtain the generous support of foreign allies—such as the United States had had in the War for Independence—or achieve the maximum mobilization of its limited supply of men, money, and productive capacity.

Philosophically, however, the South found such a mobilization extremely difficult to achieve. Deeply committed to individualism and hostile to powerful government, many Southerners inevitably regarded a centrally directed mobilization as intolerable regimentation and the antithesis of what they had hoped to achieve by secession. Georgia Governor Joseph E. Brown, for example, claimed he had become a rebel to contribute his "humble mite to sustain the rights of the states and prevent the consolidation of the Government," and he announced his willingness to oppose even the Confederate leadership should it threaten those objects.[33] Although the Confederate government in many ways ultimately went much further than the Union in attempting the control of men, money, and facilities, such attitudes rendered many of its initiatives too little and too late and, once begun, obstructed their implementation.

Efforts to raise military manpower provide an excellent illustration of that point. The Confederacy in 1862 established America's first system of *national* conscription and used that draft to ráise about a third of its total military force. To maintain essential war production and administration, it also exempted, for example, railroaders, ferrymen, printers, ironworkers, telegraphers, certain skilled craftsmen, and factory owners. Even while taking such steps toward a system of modern selective service, the Confederacy established other exemptions that caused dissension or invited abuse. By excusing one white man for every plantation with twenty slaves and permitting conscripts to hire a substitute (who usually demanded at least $500), the Confederacy seemed to make its struggle a rich man's war but a poor man's fight. When it also exempted state and national officeholders, the Confederate government made it possible for draft opponents like Governor Brown to excuse men from service by commissioning them in his state's militia, a body that he refused, along with the governors of Mississippi and Louisiana, to let serve beyond the state's borders. Judges and local officials unsympathetic to the draft also readily accepted counterfeit exemption papers or used habeas corpus writs to release men from the army.[34]

Nor did the Confederacy ever fully centralize its military supply methods. In the course of twenty months it moved from a "system" requiring each soldier to supply his own uniforms to one in which the national government undertook to clothe all *enlisted* men. Throughout the war, however, the Confederacy had to battle governors who demanded the right to supply their own troops. The lack of full central control led to such absurdities as North Carolina Governor Zebulon B. Vance, another states' rights zealot, having in his warehouses some 92,000 uniforms at a time in 1865 when General Robert E. Lee's army literally wore rags. Vance also commandeered his state's entire output of textiles, and both North and South Carolina banned out-of-state shipments of food. Meanwhile Confederate soldiers starved.[35]

Some of the army's misery also resulted from the Confederacy's failure to develop a fully centralized command system and integrated national bureaucracy. Until the last two months of the war, no one short of President Jefferson Davis had authority to shift troops and supplies from one of the army's thirty-eight semiautonomous departments or districts to more threatened areas. Nor did adjacent regional commanders voluntarily cooperate, even when facing a common enemy. Although victory in the struggle with the more powerful Union depended upon complete efficiency in the use of every human and material resource, little interagency cooperation characterized the operations of even the national government. While the Confederate bureaucracy grew from 10,000 civil servants in 1861 to some 45,000 by war's end (excluding employees of government arsenals and mills), the national administration never developed agencies for interdepartmental coordination—another example of an incomplete centralization of authority.[36]

In the control of industry, however, the Confederacy went very much further than any previous American national government. On the one hand, it quickly seized the region's few textile mills and joined state governments in encouraging the creation of new factories. It established government powder mills and arsenals—the latter using equipment seized at Harper's Ferry—and subsidized through no-interest loans the creation or expansion of privately owned war plants. To insure a fair price, the Confederate government also limited the profits of those receiving its subsidies. To regulate other war-related industries, it threatened to use its control of the railroads and the military draft to deny raw materials and laborers if plant managers refused to cooperate. On the other hand, the Confederacy limited its controls essentially to industries that supplied or supported the army, and it made little effort to manage the economy generally. Moreover, to control even war industries via drafts on their labor and threats to their transportation was to employ clumsy and not always effective tools.[37]

In a story reminiscent of the American experience in the Revolutionary War, the Confederacy similarly moved too slowly and ineffectively in the mobilization of its financial resources. In the best of circumstances the South would have found it difficult to raise money to finance the war. Its agricultural economy relied on credit—much of it formerly supplied by the North—and the total amount of specie in circulation in early 1861 did not exceed $30 million. Heavily invested in land and slaves, the South's wealthy men could not easily make their capital available to the government or investors. Heavy taxes, moreover, would have been unpopular, and their collection would have required creation of the kind of large central bureaucracy that was anathema to many Southerners. Nor, with the Union navy blockading the South's ports, was an indirect tax via high tariffs on imports a practical solution.

Treasury Secretary Christopher Memminger convinced the Confederate Congress to impose only a few modest taxes. In 1861 it levied a small property tax on slaves, business inventories, securities, and money loaned at interest—collectible by the state governments. All but one, however, raised its share of the tax by confiscations of Northern property, bank loans, or bond issues. An 1863 act increased revenues by imposing income taxes, license fees, a tax on money, and excises on manufactures and farm and forest products—sometimes payable in goods rather than money. Then, in each of the next two years Congress raised the rates in each category. Resenting even that modest taxation, Southerners justified widespread evasion by describing those levies as evidence of despotism and a too-strong central government. In the end, the Confederate government financed but 5 percent of the war's cost through taxation.[38]

Memminger had somewhat more success with the sale of bonds. An 1861 issue permitted Southerners to buy bonds with specie, military stores, or pledges of the profits on future sales of the output of farms or businesses. When cotton prices fell, however, planters fulfilled few of those pledges. Later the Treasury paid for war supplies with bonds, using them much like interest-bearing paper money. In similar circumstances, the Continental Congress had made decisively important foreign loans and bond sales. Denied diplomatic recognition, however, the Confederacy obtained no intergovernmental loans and attempted only one $15 million private bond sale in Europe. Altogether the Confederacy financed only one-third of its war costs with loans.[39]

The only alternative was to continue issuing more paper money than could be withdrawn from circulation through taxes or bond sales. That led, inevitably, to runaway inflation. By January 1864 the Confederacy's stock of money had risen by 1,100 percent and begun to circulate with great velocity as citizens sought to divest themselves of the rapidly depreciating notes. In that month, for example, sixty-one Confederate dollars bought only one dollar's worth of gold, and prices had risen between 90 and 100 times prewar levels. Those who grew their own food had some protection, but urbanites claimed that inflation had produced a revolution of sorts: "You take your money to market in a basket and bring home what you buy in your pocket book." By the 1864 Funding Act the Confederacy sought to pull large amounts of its paper money out of circulation by repudiating any note of $100 or more not exchanged for Confederate bonds and offering to swap new notes for the smaller old bills at the rate of two for three.[40]

The forced bond sale and one-third devaluation did little to restore confidence in the currency. Hoarding, speculation, and barter had already become rampant. With inflation destroying the buying power of their higher salaries, workers insisted that employers pay a part of their wages in food or other goods. Soldiers' families, if forced to live on their provider's wage of $11 per month, faced starvation at a time when a week's groceries cost over $68. According to General Joseph E. Johnson, such a prospect weakened military morale by leading to desertion as soldiers chose "between their military service and the strongest obligations they knew—their duties to wives and children." Price controls, imposed by the government in each year after 1863, roused cries of despotism from some citizens and brought little relief for others as farmers and manufacturers held their goods off the legitimate market. Such hoarding led the government to make wider use of impressment after 1863, which meant that those nearest the scene of military operations and lines of communication bore a disproportionate share of the war's burdens.[41]

Southern Politics

As the preceding section illustrates, by 1865 the Confederacy had gone quite far, at least in a legislative sense, toward transforming the South, wrote Emory Thomas, "from a states rights confederation into a centralized national state." That state had created a national army, written America's first national conscription law, attempted to control international commerce and domestic railroads, subsidized, built, and controlled war industries, seized goods required for war purposes when monetary purchase failed, impressed slaves to work on military roads and fortifications, passed national income taxes, and established a large civil service and central bureaucracy to administer those efforts.[42] All of those actions directly challenged the Southern political tradition. While they might have thus prepared Southerners to accept the more centralized national state that emerged with the reconstructed Union, they were in the main also adopted slowly and grudgingly—and in the face of political opposition that often nullified their effect.

That shortcoming implied no inherent constitutional defect; the Confederacy's fundamental law closely followed the Constitution of 1787, except for a formal declaration of state sovereignty and a few minor adjustments only slightly related to the war effort. Nor did the Confederacy adopt an administrative structure much different from that of the Union. In other words, the Confederate government possessed the potential for the same kind of wartime centralization successfully accomplished by the administration in Washington.[43]

The Confederate political failure lay, instead, in attitudes and in informal systems and arrangements. The Congress, which had grudgingly supported Davis early in the war, turned against him after the 1863 elections, forcing the Confederate president to use some thirty vetoes. Except for the provisional body of 1861–1862, the Confederate Congresses contained few talented men because Southerners seemingly preferred military to political glory. The same lack of talent weakened the Confederate cabinet, which experienced rapid, disruptive turnover in several key departments. Davis had, for instance, three secretaries of state and five secretaries of war. Several of the governors and his own vice president thwarted Davis at every turn—preaching disaffection and, as previously noted, subverting both the conscription act and the regulation of blockade runners and impeding efforts to procure supplies for the national army. Nor, except in three strictly limited circumstances, did Congress permit Davis to suspend the writ of habeas corpus in order to crush those whose obstruction had moved beyond legal opposition—to prevent, for example, court-ordered release of conscripts, deserters, and hoarders or those suspected of using the press or secret societies to spread disloyalty and subvert the war effort.[44]

Do not conclude, however, that only rabid states' rights fanatics inhabited the Civil War South. That region contained men and women at all levels who would have supported early and effective centralization—at least as a temporary war measure. Yet, Davis never molded them—indeed, never tried to mold them—into an integrated political force capable of controlling Congress and the state governments and thereby able to write timely, effective legislation or see to its implementation by national and local officials. The South, in other words, lacked a party system. It could not, therefore, unite leaders at all levels behind a common program. It had no effective instrument for mobilizing public opinion and swinging it behind the war effort or against Davis' equally disunited opponents. Nor did Davis make effective use of patronage either to build a political party or even to fill the government with men committed to waging a centrally directed war—the only approach with even a chance of success. Describing as evidence of democracy such qualities as Southern individualism, great sensitivity to any limits on personal liberties, and an almost unreasoning commitment to states' rights, David Donald has written that the South "died of democracy." Perhaps. It might equally be said to have died of its failure to develop a party system capable of giving direction to the efforts of the central government, achieving cooperative intergovernmental relations, and uniting the majority of Southerners behind a reasonable wartime regimentation, centralization, and limitation of individual liberties.[45]

Northern Politics

Whereas the prewar collapse of the party system in the South reduced all politics to the issue of secession, the war revived party competition in the North and, according to Eric McKitrick, helped account for the Union victory. While Southern men of talent left politics for the army, President Abraham Lincoln drew first-rate men of his party's divergent wings into his often contentious but generally stable cabinet. Although not all Republicans accepted each of Lincoln's war aims or approved all of his methods for conducting the struggle, as members of a political party they had to moderate their public criticism or risk losing their new party's recently won control of the national government.

Replacing almost 80 percent of those who held office in 1860, the new President made skillful use of patronage to unite his young party and build solid support for its programs. He also reached out to the Republican governors and state party organizations, seeking their advice on appointments to the war-induced expansion of the federal bureaucracy and sustaining them in their struggle with local Democrats. When Indiana Governor O. O. Morton, for instance, lost control of the state legislature following the 1862 elections,

Lincoln made available a quarter million dollars in Federal funds so that Morgan might govern his state without calling into session a legislature likely to undermine his support for the war. If the Republican governors' efforts had been responsible for Lincoln's election in 1860, four years later the new President had created a vital national party responsive to his leadership and able to unite a majority of Americans and most state administrations behind the Federal war effort.[46]

The Republican victory in 1864 both established the political revolution begun four years earlier and commenced a period that Leon Friedman considered the "darkest in the history of the Democratic party." Between 1860 and 1884 the previously dominant party of Jefferson and Jackson would elect no presidents, win a majority in only four of the twelve sessions of the House, and control the Senate for but two years. Of 300 gubernatorial elections outside the deep South, the Democrats would win only 70 as the Republicans threatened to make themselves a permanent majority party. If the initial Republican advantage rested on secession and war (and subsequently on the party's control of Southern Reconstruction), it depended finally on the influence of the war's Union veterans.

United in the Grand Army of the Republic, begun in 1866 as a fraternal organization, former Union soldiers gradually became a political force. The G.A.R. advised its members, "Vote as you shot!" It also made service in the Union army a prerequisite for election or appointment to Federal offices and equated the Democratic party with treason and sectional conflict by "waving the bloody shirt" during the election contests of the next two decades. In return, the G.A.R. won Republican support for its major goal, "cash for veterans," which by the 1890s had become a Federal pension program annually dispensing $156 million at a total cost of over $4 billion at the death of the last Union veteran.[47]

Still, the war had not enabled the Republicans to reduce their opponents to lasting impotency. In fact, the three postwar decades became a period of stalemate in which neither party achieved a clear edge until the Republican triumph in 1896. Even during the war, Democrats had played a decisive role. Those who supported the war, though perhaps not the emancipation of slaves, considerably broadened the consensus seeking a Union military victory. Some of those war Democrats either became Republicans or, beginning in the border states in 1861, united with them to form the Union party—a device also used by Lincoln in 1864 when war Democrat Andrew Johnson became his vice-presidential running mate. The majority of Democrats, however, maintained their independence and the viability of the two-party system. While supporting the war, they objected to making emancipation a war aim, criticized many of Lincoln's methods, and often opposed economic legislation unrelated to the sectional struggle.[48]

Unrealistically advocating a compromise peace and voluntary reunion, another faction of Democrats took a more extreme view. Those peace Democrats became the party's dominant faction for a time after 1862, when it appeared that public discontent with the lack of military success coupled with the votes of Northerners sympathetic to the South might enable Democrats to gain control of both state and national governments. Sometimes called Copperheads (poisonous snakes that strike without warning), those most venomous of Lincoln's opponents drew support from several diverse groups. They included New York merchants, with Southern business connections; workers and poor farmers threatened by inflation, the military draft, and a possible postwar influx of ex-slaves; citizens of the loyal border (slave-owning) states; and Southern-born residents of the Ohio River Valley—the area with the strongest political antiwar movement. As the prospect of electoral victory faded after mid-1864, however, a minority of peace Democrats shifted from loyal opposition and sought to block the war effort with illegal subversion and sabotage.[49]

By 1864 the Lincoln administration had several years' experience dealing with such opposition. Faced in April 1861 with Baltimore mobs disrupting the movement to Washington of Union soldiers, food, mail, and telegraph messages, the raising of secessionist militia units in eastern Maryland, and the imminent meeting in that state of a special convention to consider an (illegal) act of secession, Lincoln promptly suspended the writ of habeas corpus along the rail route between Washington and Philadelphia. He also authorized military officers to seize and hold without trial any individuals suspected of subverting Federal authority. In contrast to Davis' feeble efforts to suppress dissent, Lincoln gradually extended the areas over which he suspended the writ, and a September 1863 proclamation directed the army's seizure and the appearance before military commissions of all those anywhere in the United States suspected of being deserters, spies, or saboteurs, of aiding the Confederacy—even in speech—or of committing such offenses against the military forces as counseling draft evasion or desertion. Altogether the Union at one time or another held between thirteen and thirty-eight thousand individuals and closed for varying periods some 300 newspapers.[50]

As some peace Democrats began to oppose the war by illegal means, they faced the full force of a government armed with potentially dictatorial powers. That government had, moreover, infiltrated the secret antiwar organizations—Knights of the Golden Circle, Order of American Knights, and Sons of Liberty—used by peace Democrats to counsel draft resistance, mutiny, or desertion, provide protection to deserters, and organize violent attacks on bridges, railroads, and telegraph lines.The government also quickly disrupted a secret paramilitary group in contact with Confederate agents in Canada. This group planned a fantastic scheme to release and arm Confederate prisoners of war, use them to seize governments in the Midwest, and, after creating a northernwestern confederacy, to secede and make peace with the South.[51]

Although that plot unquestionably lay outside the law, the Lincoln administration or its military agents also proscribed other activities protected by the Constitution and frequently used methods unable to withstand peacetime legal scrutiny. James G. Randall correctly called attention to the resulting paradox. "Lincoln, who stands forth in popular conception as a great democrat, the exponent of liberty and of government by the people, was driven by circumstance to the use of more arbitrary power than perhaps any other President has seized." Usually willing to grant pardons to those who would pledge future loyalty and moderate in the use of sweeping Presidential powers, Lincoln realized the anomalous nature of his actions and once asked rhetorically: "Must a government, of necessity, be too strong for the liberties of its own people, or too weak to maintain its own existence?" Lincoln's Democratic rival, Stephen A. Douglas, may, however, have more nearly captured the feelings of most Americans: "There can be no neutrals in this war, *only patriots—or traitors.*"[52]

Lincoln's suspension of the writ of habeas corpus along the route to Washington, an action the Constitution seemingly made the prerogative solely of Congress, was not the President's only assertion of his office's wartime supremacy within the Federal Government. In the period between April and July 1861, sometimes called his "eleven-week dictatorship," he unilaterally committed the nation to war with the Confederacy, censored telegraph traffic leaving Washington, declared a blockade of Southern ports, proclaimed martial law in several areas, increased the size of the regular army and navy, and spent money not appropriated by Congress. Later in the war, he similarly made it a crime, punishable by military tribunals, to discourage enlistment, and in 1863 he "freed" all slaves living in areas still in rebellion against the United States. Finally, with the end of the war in sight, Lincoln ignored the will of Congress as expressed in the Wade-Davis bill and implemented his own plan for reconstructing the South. If he often left Congressmen spluttering their outrage, he also left them little option but grudgingly to give their retroactive approval, submit to the claim that he had merely exercised the Constitutional war powers of his office, or accept legally questionable acts justified by the Lincolnian analogy that "often a [Constitutional] limb must be amputated to save a life [the Union], but a life is never wisely given to save a limb."[53]

On a few occasions, however, Congress attempted, unsuccessfully, to limit the President's powers. In December 1862 a group of thirty Senators urged him to eliminate the moderates from his cabinet, fill it with men determined to wage vigorous war against the South, and submit his own judgment to the consensus in the cabinet—acts that would have given that Senatorial bloc effective control of his administration. Lincoln outmaneuvered the Senators and in so doing exposed Treasury Secretary Chase, who had been involved in the plot to oust the Radicals' chief antagonist, Secretary of State William H. Seward. Two years later, Lincoln similarly finessed the Radicals' effort to impose a punitive reconstruction on the South. He pocket-vetoed their Wade-Davis bill, announced his objections, proposed giving the South a "choice" between his generous version and the Radicals' harsher proposal, and then simply went his independent way in reconstructing governments in occupied regions of the Confederacy.[54]

A third challenge appeared to come from what Louis Smith, following the lead of an older generation of historians and political scientists, described as "perhaps the most powerful and unusual investigative body ever established by the legislative branch." Smith argued that the so-described joint Committee on the Conduct of the War used its 1861 mandate "to inquire into the conduct of the present war" as a license to interfere ruthlessly with matters properly within the President's sphere by attempting to set policy, select military commanders, and shape administration much as had the Continental Congress almost a century earlier. The Committee, Smith wrote, "constituted an attempt to destroy the independence of the President and make the executive branch an arm of the legislature." More careful studies of the Committee reveal, however, that Lincoln let it exercise only such influence as he found useful, and War Secretary Edwin M. Stanton maintained a useful relation with it throughout the war. Lincoln's goals did not differ from those of the Committee's members, and their advanced positions on policy usually meant that they, unlike Lincoln, had no need to unite both moderate Republicans and war Democrats behind a common program. In that effort, he more often used the Committee's "pressure" to push ahead the reluctant members of his coalition than he yielded to the Radicals' demands.[55]

Despite Lincoln's great wartime powers and independence of Congress, he never acted as a legislative leader in ways common to twentieth-century American Presidents. On only a few occasions, concerning minor matters having little to do with the war, did he offer such leadership. In contrast, he acquiesced in several early Congressional assaults on slavery (in the District of Columbia, the territories, and occupied areas), even though he felt that those acts undermined the border states' loyalty to the Union. On most important issues, moreover, he acted alone—usually basing his policy on his war powers and denying the necessity of legislation.[56]

More significantly, few of the new powers with which Lincoln endowed his office were assumed by his immediate successors, who let the prestige of the Presidency slip to the level of the late antebellum Presidents. If Lincoln's use of Presidential power ranks with that of Washington, Jefferson, and

Jackson, there is hardly even a Polk among his nineteenth-century successors—at least until William McKinley in 1897. Clinton Rossiter seems correct in both of his claims: Lincoln did raise "the Presidency to a position of constitutional and moral ascendancy that left no doubt where the burden of crisis government in this country would thereafter rest." Yet the postwar reassertion of Congressional authority temporarily enfeebled the Presidential office in the continuing ebb and flow of power between the two bodies. In that sense, the war permanently enhanced the powers of the Presidency only by setting a precedent for any of Lincoln's successors facing a grave national crisis and by establishing a benchmark from which they would measure their own growing authority.[57]

The 1857 *Dred Scott* decision colored the wartime relations between Lincoln and the Supreme Court. That decision, in which the majority overturned the forty-year-old Missouri Compromise and denied citizenship to American blacks, discredited the Court in the eyes of most Northerners. Accordingly, a cloud of disapproval hung over Chief Justice Roger B. Taney as he approached his first contest with the President. The occasion was the army's arrest and imprisonment of John Merryman, a pro-Southern agitator who had conspired to raise a secessionist militia company in Maryland. Although Taney ordered Merryman's release in a stinging condemnation of Lincoln's suspension of the writ, the President ignored the order, and the full Court—perhaps sensing the public's attitude—took no action.[58]

The Court similarly sidestepped the army's 1863 arrest and court-martial conviction of Clement L. Vallandigham, an Ohio Congressman and peace Democrat. In the same year, however, it did accept the *Prize Cases*, a challenge to the constitutionality of Lincoln's unilateral announcement of a Union blockade of the Confederate coast. By that year, two deaths and a departure due to secession enabled Lincoln to place three of his own appointees on the Court—all of whom joined in the five-man majority that sustained the President's action.[59]

Public support for the President, Lincoln's new appointments (he made a fourth when Congress expanded the Court and a fifth when Taney died), and judicial recognition of the government's need to take drastic action in a crisis seem to have rendered the Court relatively impotent during the war years. With the return of peace, however, the Court, like Congress, reasserted its authority and overturned the army's arrest and conviction of Lambdin P. Milligan for illegal antimilitary activity on the grounds that Indiana's civil courts had been in operation and fully competent to handle the case.[60]

Mobilizing the Union for War

Lincoln's use of the Presidency's war powers to augment the authority of that office vis-a-vis Congress and the Court also represented a temporary but precedent-setting growth in the power of the central government. The latter, however, also benefited from wartime legislative and administrative measures that, though designed as aids to mobilization, endured into the postwar period.

In addition, Southern secession permitted Congressional action on several important bills unrelated to the war. In July 1862 Congress passed the Pacific Railway Act and thus determined that the nation's first transcontinental railroad would follow a central route west from Omaha to Sacramento and San Francisco. As that act represented the first *Federal* corporate charter since 1816 and probably the first Federal land grant to a *private* company, it also hinted at the relationship to come between government and business and initiated a shift in the burden of supporting internal improvements from the state to Federal level.[61] The absence of Southern Congressional opposition also facilitated the previously mentioned passage of legislation creating a Department of Agriculture, granting free farm homesteads, and establishing agricultural and mechanical colleges in each state—thus redefining the Federal Government's relation to another group of America's businessmen: its farmers. The purpose of this section, however, is to give attention to the significance, of war-mobilization measures.

Having far greater wealth than the Confederacy (and with more of that wealth in relatively liquid forms), the Union more easily mobilized its financial resources. As described earlier, however, Secretary Chase's fumbling efforts in 1861 had caused suspension of specie payment and created considerable financial chaos. Lacking a medium of exchange and an adequate national income, Chase, like Memminger, also turned to the printing press and won Congressional approval for the issuance of $450 million in paper notes known as Greenbacks. That increase in the money supply had the usual inflationary influence, at least until military success raised public confidence in the government and new taxes and bond sales created a demand for the notes (and started them flowing back into the Treasury). Even at its lowest point, for a brief period in 1864, a Greenback dollar would buy 35 cents in gold, and as Table 2.7 indicates, the North avoided the ruinous wartime inflations of the South and the American Revolution.[62]

The modest size of the North's inflation stemmed in part from its greater use of taxes and bond sales to finance the war. Whereas by late 1864 paper currency had covered about two-thirds of the Confederate expenditures, Greenbacks paid for only 13 percent of the Union's war costs. Intentionally so, because Chase had never considered the Greenbacks as anything but a

Table 2.7
Average Annual Prices, 1861–1865
(Gold, Cost of Living, and Wages in Terms of 100 Greenback Dollars)

Year	Gold	Cost of Living	Wages
1861	100	103	100
1862	113	112	101
1863	145	129	112
1864	203	156	130
1865	157	168	150

Source: Arthur Nussbaum, *A History of the Dollar* (New York: Columbia University Press, 1957), pp. 102–3. Reprinted by permission of the publisher.

stopgap until new taxes and bond sales began to refill the government's coffers.[63]

To a large degree his expedient worked, and taxes soon paid almost a quarter of the war's costs, versus only 5 percent in the Confederacy. The list of new revenues included excises on bank capital and deposits, tobacco, spirits, sugar, and a host of luxury goods ranging from yachts to silver plate. In July 1862 Congress imposed a stamp tax on legal, business, and financial instruments and required that liquor dealers buy licenses. Every manufactured article and the gross receipts of railroads, ferryboats, steamships, and toll bridges also became the objects of new taxes, and in addition Congress raised tariff rates an average of 47 percent. By enacting the nation's first Federal income and inheritance taxes, Congress established a precedent for the twentieth century and initiated a new relation between citizens and their national government. The tariffs, excises, and income taxes raised over $650 million during the war, which created a demand for paper money among citizens eager to pay their government debts with depreciated Greenbacks rather than gold.[64]

The sale of bonds also served to maintain the Greenback's buying power, contain inflation, and finance about 60 percent of the war, versus 30 percent in the Confederacy. That success came despite the fact that in the war's early years the United States had neither a system for the large-scale marketing of its bonds nor many eager buyers—that is, until the Treasury offered financier Jay Cooke a commission on each bond he sold. With the help of advertising that appealed to patriotism, a host of local committees, small-denomination bonds, and banks as sales agents, Cooke launched a sales campaign aimed at average citizens rather than bankers. He thus established a pattern repeated during America's twentieth-century wars. Inflation lent a hand to salesmanship when buying a bond with depreciated Greenbacks dramatically raised its effective interest rate. In mid-1863, for example, with Greenback dollars worth 60 cents in gold, an investor could buy, for the equivalent of $600 specie, a $1,000 bond with interest and principal payable in gold—a truly fabulous bargain! Whatever the reason, between October 1862 and July 1863 Cooke's sales totaled $157 million and before the campaign ended six months later reached $362 million.[65]

By that time Secretary Chase and the Congress had taken a far-reaching action that also created a new market for government bonds. The National Banking Act of 1863 and several wartime amendments made Federal charters available to private banking associations—the first since the 1816 second Bank of the United States, which the Jacksonians had subsequently discontinued. Those banks had to deposit with the Treasury at least one-third of their capital in the form of government bonds, thus creating a demand for Federal securities. In return, the Treasury would issue (to 90 percent of the bonds' value) United States notes, which supplemented the Greenbacks and gave the United States a truly national paper money. To encourage withdrawal of the notes issued by state-chartered banks (the prewar source of paper money), Congress later imposed a crippling 10 percent tax on such issues. The Federal Government then extended its modest degree of control over the nation's banking system by resuming the practice of depositing Treasury funds with selected national banks and requiring that all meet reserve requirements based upon deposits and currency in circulation.[66]

The Civil War consequently had a profound financial and economic impact. As a war measure, the government had created a national banking system that survived into the twentieth century and gradually substituted Federal for state control of banks. A national legal-tender paper currency thereafter slowly replaced the $200 million in notes of uncertain value issued by over 1,600 state-chartered banks. The Federal Government also placed its first taxes on individuals and businesses and, though they were dropped shortly after the war, initiated the shift in Federal revenue from customs and land sales to income taxes. Along with the wartime protective tariff, which was not dropped, such measures gave to the Federal Government a new influence over the nation's economy and finances.[67]

Being better financed and building upon a diversified industrial and agricultural base far stronger than the Confederacy's, the Union government could also rely upon the market rather than extensive governmental control to complete its economic mobilization. With very few exceptions, industries required no extensive conversion to war production, and the Northern economy could produce adequate quantities of the goods required by the still technologically quite primitive armed forces. The government had simply to outbid civilian competitors for the output of the North's farms and factories. Only in the case of the railroads did the government bring businessmen into a close economic relationship, and after overcoming problems of the war's chaotic first year, the Union avoided the corruption of the Revolutionary era by excluding businessmen from government posts and contracting openly in a competitive market.[68]

Despite the absence of direct governmental regulation of industry and commerce, the war still produced a five-fold increase in the Federal bureaucracy, which reached 195,000 members in 1865. Although the War Department, which created the world's first large, unified logistical system and, in 1864, America's first modern command structure, accounted for most of the increase, all the executive departments grew rapidly as the Federal Government increased the range of its responsibilities.[69]

One of the most important of those new tasks was mobilizing the North's manpower. The Union began as the nation always had: summoning the states' militia and relying upon the governors and prominent individuals to raise regiments of volunteers. In addition to commissioning the officers of the units thus raised, the states provided the new regiments with weapons, uniforms, and equipment. Not only did those actions reveal the Union's initial lack of a national system for mobilizing manpower, they provided the army with units possessing a variety of weapons and sometimes exotic uniforms and contributed to much of the confusion, waste, and corruption of 1861 as state and national governments competed with one another for the small stock of military goods on hand at the outbreak of hostilities.[70]

By the end of the war, however, the states had lost—never to recover—the majority of their military responsibilities. In 1862, the War Department established Federal standards for arms, uniforms, and equipment and centralized their purchase. That eased resupply of the field army while eliminating the competition between state and national governments that plagued the Confederacy throughout the war. In that same year, the Federal Government established a recruiting service and issued a new call for volunteers—backed up by a Federal bounty for enlistment and a threatened militia draft with an unprecedented Federal involvement in what had previously been a state responsibility. The intervention did not become immediately necessary, however, and new War Secretary Stanton unwisely cancelled the proposed recruiting service.[71]

The Federal Government took the penultimate step in March 1863, when Congress passed a Federal conscription law giving the Union the power to conscript soldiers without the states' assistance. Although the Federal law raised only 46,347 conscripts because 202,912 recipients of a draft call exercised their option of hiring a substitute or paying a commutation fee to avoid military service, it reduced the governors to Federal recruiting agents who struggled to fill the ranks of their states' volunteer regiments rather than see their citizens drafted. The decision, in May 1863, to create a Bureau of

Colored Troops and raise, under Federal authority, volunteer regiments from among the nation's black population became the final indication of the extent to which the Civil War had achieved the federalization of a military responsibility formerly shared with the states.[72]

Although Federal assumption of responsibility for the wartime mobilization of men and material worked a relative gain in the power of the national government, few in 1861 would have predicted that outcome. As the year opened, secession sent the national government reeling with a challenge to its very existence and to the "leadership" of James Buchanan, one of the weakest of American chief executives. To face down the Confederacy after his inauguration, Lincoln had only an insignificant regular army, a minuscule national bureaucracy, and a depleted treasury. In contrast, the governments of the loyal states were for the most part politically stable, financially sound, and eager to fight to preserve the Union. They possessed, in their militia, complete if somewhat creaky military organizations and recent experience (the Mexican War) in raising volunteer units to wage America's wars. Except for an aversion to secession, the Northern governments had a commitment to states' rights comparable to those of the South. Within two years, however, the Federal Government assumed the supply burden initially thrust upon the states, managed the mobilization of manpower, extended martial law to control political dissent, established its financial supremacy, became the source of economic favors, and began even to sustain Republican governors unable to maintain their political control. The Civil War had thus not only settled the theoretical question about the locus of sovereignty and the right of secession, it had also bound together the state and Federal governments in a true national union under the latter's leadership. By January 1865, observed Civil War historian William Hesseltine, "states rights were dead."[73] Although the nation would have less occasion to use the Federal powerhouse in the postwar decades, the war years had suggested its potency.

Civil War and American Society

Attention to the more measurable economic and political effects of the Civil War should not obscure its more subtle and indirect social consequences. Most of those in social categories whose predecessors had felt the impact of the War for Independence had a similar experience during the Civil War, which gave new vitality to Revolutionary-era advances that had often stalled in the antebellum decades.

American women, for instance, had emerged from the Revolution with feelings of self-confidence and an expanded political role, even if still denied equal citizenship. Despite the efforts of a few feminists and suffragists to extend that small advance, they achieved little in the next half century. Women, in fact, probably suffered a relative decline as Jacksonian democracy brought political rights to the "comman man" and the professionalization of medicine and law closed those fields to women. By the 1830s, moreover, a cult of true womanhood asserted woman's innate purity, piety, and domesticity—justifying a sexual double standard, confining middle-class women to home and church, and demanding that they focus all their energies on being wives, mothers, and homemakers. Men claimed that political activity, like any sort of professional work, exceeded a woman's intellectual capacity and threatened her emotional stability. Marriage and school teaching offered the only real choices open to middle-class women. Necessity, which compelled the wives and daughters of the working class to accept employment—usually in the expanding textile mills or domestic service—only served as another sign of their inferiority, even among women.

Although the Civil War dictated that reformers subordinate the pursuit of women's rights to the cause of black emancipation, that conflict enabled women to reverse the antebellum trend and to make gains in other respects. Their loyalties everywhere dividing along state lines, women supported their section's decision to fight, encouraged husbands and boyfriends to enlist, and willingly shouldered responsibility for running farms and businesses. In rural areas, where most Americans lived in both North and South, a Civil War song claimed that women told their husbands:

> Just take your gun and go;
> For Ruth can drive the oxen, John,
> And I can use the hoe!

Inspired by their section's cause, some 400 women even masqueraded as men to serve as soldiers, and many more took grave risks as military spies and couriers. At least in the North, women also entered the political arena in a direct way by following reformers Susan B. Anthony and Elizabeth Cady Stanton into the National Woman's Loyal League and undertaking to gather one million signatures on petitions in support of the Thirteenth Amendment abolishing slavery.[74]

Volunteer war work provided another outlet. Through 7,000 local societies joined in the US Sanitary Commission, Northern women raised $50 million and provided soldiers many of the services now offered by the Red Cross, United Services Organization, and the army's Medical Department. A woman who widened her sphere by doing such work, claimed Eleanor Flexnor, "could never be quite the same person afterwards." Confederate women established similar soldiers-aid societies but failed to unite them in a "national" association—another indication of the less organized nature of Southern society. For the women, however, wartime volunteer work undoubtedly prompted feelings comparable to those felt by their Northern counterparts.[75]

Going beyond hometown volunteer work, some Northern women answered the appeals of the Sanitary Commission, Dorothea Dix (reformer turned army Superintendent of Nurses), or private organizers like Clara Barton (future founder of the American Red Cross) and became nurses in Civil War hospitals. Though generally banned during the antebellum period from becoming doctors and midwives, that wartime service kept the medical profession open to women and, according to Barton, put women "at least fifty years in advance of the normal position which continued peace . . . would have assigned" them.[76]

Improving employment in other fields sustains at least the economic dimension of her claim. With many men leaving for military service, women achieved a dominant position within elementary and secondary education as their share of teaching posts began its rise from 25 percent in 1860 to 60 percent two decades later. While educated women left the mills for teaching jobs (and men left all sorts of industrial work for the army), some 100,000 women got wartime factory work and over half that number held onto their jobs in the postwar industrial expansion. Women also took advantage of a precedent established by the Patent Office in the 1850s and obtained clerical jobs in the growing government bureaucracy. Clerical work of a different sort also opened in retail sales as men departed for the army.[77]

Although the South provided fewer industrial or governmental opportunities to its women, they nevertheless followed the advice one Georgia soldier gave his wife: "You must be man and woman both while the war lasts." That experience, concluded Bell Wiley, "loosened conventions," and Southern women "departed considerably from the [prewar] clinging vine stereotype," even when husbands returned to resume their dominant position within the family. Wartime work and their husband's loss of caste due to military defeat nevertheless weakened Southern patriarchy and increased a wife's influence within the family.[78]

As in the Revolution, women filled the economic gap created by men leaving for the armed forces and in so doing developed their self-confidence and demonstrated their intellectual, physical, and emotional ability to do men's work. The war, according to Mary E. Massey, acted as "a springboard from which [women] leaped beyond the circumscribed 'woman's sphere' into that . . . reserved for men."[79]

As the spread of the cult of true womanhood hampered the efforts of American women to build on gains made during the Revolutionary War, the growth of antebellum nativism reversed the relatively easy assimilation of new immigrants characteristic of the early national period. During the new republic's first three decades, it received fewer than a quarter million immigrants, a number so small as almost to escape notice and surely pose no threat to working-class jobs or American mores. The situation began to change in the 1820s, and as Table 2.8 indicates, immigrants became a significant portion of the national population in the two decades preceding the Civil War.[80]

Table 2.8
United States Immigration, 1820–1860

Period	Immigration	Year	Total Foreign Born	Total Population
1820–1830	154,000	1830	n.a.	12,866,020
1831–1840	598,000	1840	n.a.	17,069,453
1841–1850	1,713,000	1850	2,244,000	23,191,876
1851–1860	2,598,000	1860	4,103,764	31,443,321

Source: US, Department of Commerce, Bureau of the Census, *Historical Statistics of the United States, Colonial Times to 1970*, Bicentennial ed., 2 vols. (Washington, DC: US Government Printing Office, 1975), 1:8, 14, 106.

Still, growing hostility to the foreign born had more complex origins than a simple increase in the rate of immigration. The English, whose immigration increased dramatically in the 1840s and soon made them the third most populous group of America's foreign born, nevertheless had little to distinguish them culturally, and they quickly became quite indistinguishable among the general population.[81]

Small numbers probably facilitated the assimilation of other groups, even when culturally distinct from most Americans. Although the Scots emerged from the Revolution with a reputation tarnished by their loyalty to the British King, mistrust vanished as fewer than 10,000 arrived in the years before 1850, and the solid middle-class background of the larger number arriving after 1852 made them desirable citizens. America also scarcely noticed its 18,000 Scandinavians, a situation that changed little even as their number rose by 10,000 per year after 1852—despite the fact that language and culture set them apart from other Americans. Foreign-born residents of French, Dutch, Polish, and Italian origins entered the United States in yet smaller numbers, and even their Catholic religion did not significantly hamper their assimilation. Nor was Jewishness an issue, despite a subtle undercurrent of anti-Semitism. The 130,000 Jews in America in 1860 had become respected businessmen, dispersed throughout the country, and adopted Reform Judaism, as a religious accommodation to American culture.[82]

The prewar hostility to immigrants focused instead almost entirely on those born in Ireland and Germany, whose numbers in the United States had reached 1.6 and 1.3 million respectively by 1860. Although their predecessors from both areas had won acceptance during the Revolution, the nativism of the 1840s and 1850s began to change attitudes. Viewed as alien groups, with foreign connections (usually Catholicism), and unable or unwilling to adopt American culture, the Germans and Irishmen came to be seen by many native-born citizens as a threat to the very life of the nation. For those recent arrivals the Civil War offered an opportunity to win acceptance anew.[83]

Political expediency probably suggested the wisdom of ending nativist attacks on America's diverse German-born population. The Republican party, although drawing support from the nativists of the collapsing Know-Nothing movement, did not wish to drive away the German Forty-eighters. Liberal refugees of Europe's failed revolutions of that year, their political views, their vociferous attacks on slavery, and their general freedom from the taint of Catholicism made them natural Republican allies. Unlike the cosmopolitan Forty-eighters, the mass of German-Americans lived in the rural Midwest. When the consequences of the proslavery Kansas-Nebraska Act and the appeal of Republican support for a homestead act weakened their loyalty to the Democratic Party, many Republican nativists also learned to overlook foreign birth and the minority who professed Catholicism.[84]

Overwhelming German support for the war removed any lingering doubts. Perhaps 200,000 German-born residents enlisted in the Union army, a number well in excess of their proportion of the total population. At one time, many Americans also felt that the Germans of St. Louis had saved Missouri for the Union, and German citizens produced a number of popular if not too successful generals, among them Franz Sigel and Carl Schurz. By the war's end, according to Kathleen Conzen, "the German service record had won the group an unquestioned place in the nation's regard"—at least until World War I raised new doubts about its loyalty.[85]

Having also won acceptance by their predecessors' participation in the Revolution, the Irish immigrants who came to the United States in small numbers early in the nineteenth century met little hostility. Being for the most part relatively prosperous ex-farmers, professionals, artisans, or merchants from Ireland's Protestant north and east, those settlers had a knowledge of English and a desire to rise. They quickly assimilated and soon showed a very American contempt for the next famine-inspired wave of Irish immigrants, who after 1835 typically came from Ireland's uneducated, unskilled rural peasantry and brought with them both Catholicism and an apparently Irish love of strong drink and riotous behavior. Arriving in large numbers (almost 800,000 between 1841 and 1850 and over 90,000 per year in the next decade), they congregated in Northeastern cities and roused the nativist fears of many American Protestants. The Catholic Irish also became zealous Democrats and opponents of both abolition and blacks, whom they regarded as competitors for the low-paying manual labor available to the Irish. With not a little irony, the latters' cry was often: "Down with the Nagurs! Let them go back to Africa, where they belong!"[86]

Although the Irish thus made poor recruits for the Republican party, the firing on Fort Sumter converted them to eager defenders of the Union. Some 170,000 Irish-born soldiers ultimately served in the Union army, and Irish units and Irish officers were among the war's most heroic. As with the Revolution, wrote William V. Shannon, participation "submerged" many "old hatreds," and nativism "never again flared in the open violence that had been almost habitual in the generation of 1830-1860." Due to participation in the war, Americans "welcomed" the Irish "as partners in the common cause of saving the Union."[87]

Most Irish workers retained, however, their great hostility to blacks, and to anything that might increase the latters' numbers in Northern cities. Wartime developments such as Lincoln's Emancipation Proclamation and the Conscription Act, which forced Irishmen to fight an abolitionist war, consequently produced widespread antiblack riots, most notably the one in New York City in July 1863. While the Civil War Irish laborer never lost that hostility to blacks, the enlistment of ex-slaves apparently moderated the racism of Irish soldiers. A refrain from a camp song popular in the Union's famed Irish brigade, for instance, claimed that:

> The men who object to Sambo
> should take his place and fight.[88]

Within the Confederacy the immigrant population showed an only slightly different response to war. Except for the Germans, the immigrant groups resident in the South overwhelmingly supported their section, and the most numerous Irish provided the Confederacy with some of its best fighters. The Germans, the only other group with significant numbers, divided. Some supported the Confederacy, while an aversion to slavery and secession drove others to opposition and even emigration. Despite that instance of immigrant opposition, foreign-born participation in the war and a postwar need for industrial labor changed Southern attitudes toward immigration. After 1865, at least eight of the former Confederate states established bureaus seeking to encourage European migration into the South.[89]

Throughout the reunited Union, then, ethnic Americans' support for and participation in the war, wrote John Higham, "completed the ruin of organized nativism by absorbing xenophobes and immigrants in a common cause." In every case, America's foreign-born citizens had joined the Union army in greater numbers than their proportion of the population, become Americanized by that service, demonstrated to the native born their equal loyalty and devotion to the nation, and thus helped to overcome the tensions arising from the unusually strong flow of immigration during the quarter century preceding the war. By the close of the war, moreover, immigration, which had fallen below 100,000 per year in 1861 and 1862, regained its strength, reaching 248,120 in 1865.[90]

Among the socially disadvantaged, however, America's black population gained most from the war, even if those gains remained far less than justice demanded and were eroded by postwar developments. As neither a peaceful secession nor a quick military victory could have done, a long civil war, wrote Peter Parish, "redefined and intensified the slavery issue.... It shifted the spotlight from slavery where it might exist, in the territories, to slavery where it already existed in the Southern states." In the prewar period, one could hate both blacks and slavery and consistently oppose the extension of either into territories desired for the free labor of whites. During the war, however, opponents of slavery who proposed the emancipation of blacks, as either a moral imperative or a means of militarily weakening the Confederacy, significantly heightened the race hatred of those who despised blacks and feared their postwar migration to the North.[91]

Before 1790 few Americans expected ever to face such a dilemma. With independence won, the Northern States had gradually begun to abolish slavery within their borders (even Virginia seriously considered emancipation), and the new Federal Government blocked the further importation of slaves. With slavery apparently limited by climate, geography, and economics, many Americans—North and South—expected its confinement to a small area and eventual disappearance. An effective cotton gin, however, revived the faltering institution, and as it spread to new regions, Southerners suppressed an earlier acknowledgment of the inherent evil of slavery and began to describe it as a positive good—both for the allegedly inferior African race and the South's supposedly superior civilization. From the racism that accompanied such arguments, blacks everywhere suffered. The four million held in slavery received harsher treatment, and the states of the South and Midwest multiplied the political and legal disabilities of America's half-million free blacks. The Revolutionary era's impulse toward greater liberty thus suffered an almost overwhelming reverse.

In those circumstances, the North's 252,000 free blacks immediately perceived the war as a means to revive the Revolutionary trend. Although barred from enlistment in the Mexican War, blacks expected that the sectional conflict would enable them to fight for both emancipation and full citizenship. "Once let the black man get upon his person the brass letters, U.S." predicted ex-slave and abolitionist Frederick Douglass, "let him get an eagle on his button, and a musket on his shoulder and bullets in his pocket, and there is no power on earth which can deny that he has earned the right to citizenship."[92]

That grant of full citizenship was, of course, exactly what most people in the border states (which Lincoln had to hold within the Union) and many throughout the North (whose support for the war was essential to victory) wished to deny America's blacks. For almost two years, the Lincoln administration consequently fought simply to preserve the Union. Although the President allowed Federal commanders to enroll blacks in labor details, he refused black combatant enlistments and overturned the unauthorized efforts of a few Union commanders to raise black regiments. At the same time, he struggled in vain to convince the loyal border states to support the compensated emancipation and colonization of their slaves. The Congress, meanwhile, ended slavery in the District of Columbia and the territories and passed two confiscation acts that freed runaway slaves and permitted their use as labor auxiliaries to the Union army.[93]

The end of 1862 nevertheless found Lincoln ready to adopt a new policy. With the loyalty of the border states secured, and military reversals raising the prospect of a long war, he came to see emancipation as a means to weaken the South and the enlistment of black troops as a way to strengthen Union arms. Early in the new year, he accomplished both. By mid-1863 Congress had prompted the War Department to reverse its earlier decision and authorize Federal commanders to form black units in occupied areas of the South. Federal authorities also began to assist the earlier efforts of some Northern governors to raise black regiments in their states including permission to recruit ex-slaves within Union lines, and the War Department established a national bureau to recruit blacks directly into Federal service. Blacks responded with enthusiasm, and by 1865 Afro-American enlistments reached at least 178,000. About one-tenth of the Union army, that figure excludes black teamsters, wagoneers, and laborers. In two years of fighting, black soldiers participated in 39 major battles and 410 other engagements, suffered 68,000 casualties (over 37,000 deaths), and won 17 Congressional Medals of Honor. Accepted by the navy since the war of 1812, black enlistments in that service created controversy only in regard to the acceptance of escaped slaves. Black sailors eventually numbered 30,000—about one-quarter of the navy's strength—and four black sailors also received the nation's highest award for valor.[94]

For blacks, participation in the war meant many things. Negro soldiers, concluded Dudley Cornish, "proved that the slave could become a man," and for the remainder of the nineteenth century, black veterans "enjoyed wide respect and some equality of treatment and consideration throughout the North." Six Northern states eliminated the black laws that had limited prewar black citizenship, and several states and cities integrated their schools, transportation systems, or public accommodations. The Federal Government recognized black citizenship (thus overturning the *Dred Scott* decision), opened the Supreme Court bar to black lawyers, and permitted blacks to testify in District of Columbia courts and to carry mail throughout the nation. When Congress reorganized the land forces in 1866, it granted blacks their first opportunity to serve in the peacetime army by creating four black regiments of infantry and two of cavalry. The Civil War also necessitated the Thirteenth Amendment ending slavery throughout the nation, and black military service encouraged the passage of the Civil Rights Act of 1866 and the Fourteenth Amendment to insure black rights in the former Confederacy. Despite his colorful language, Union General Ben Butler came close to the truth when he wrote that America's black soldiers, "with their bayonets," had "unlocked the iron-barred gates of prejudice, and opened new fields of freedom, liberty, and equality of right."[95] Surely he can be forgiven his failure to foresee that other forces would gradually roll back many of those political and legal gains.

The war also brought benefits that lay beyond the grasp of postwar racism and political failure. Almost half the 500,000 ex-slaves who fled the South during the war learned to read and write in army schools, and many had their first experience working for wages as military laborers or growing cotton on government-run plantations in the occupied South. For a time, a few even owned or leased their own small farms. From such activities, as well as military service, blacks learned self-confidence, independence, and racial pride.[96]

Even blacks who remained in the South discovered that the war improved their condition. The absence of white overseers and owners made plantation life easier, and the shortage of labor often took slaves off the plantation and permitted them to work with the Confederate army as teamsters, cooks, hospital attendants, medical corpsmen, and laborers while also opening new positions in Southern industry. Blacks comprised, for example, half the labor force at Richmond's Tredegar Ironworks, the South's largest industrial establishment. So great was the black contribution to the war effort that Jefferson Davis later acknowledged that "much" of the Confederate military success was "due to the much-abused institution of African servitude." While thus sustaining the Confederacy, the wartime work of Southern blacks nevertheless prepared them for life as free men and women.[97]

In sharp contrast to the improved status of women, blacks, and ethnic Americans, the Civil War—like the Revolution—was a disaster for the Indians. Although pushed into the trans-Mississippi West in the antebellum years, Native Americans nevertheless found it impossible to avoid involvement in the war.

Confederate efforts to defend Arkansas, threaten the Rocky Mountain region, and sustain a grandiose plan to seize New Mexico and Arizona and join with Southern sympathizers on the Pacific coast prompted rebel forces to invade the Indian Territory (modern Oklahoma) in 1861. Several of the Territory's tribes looked with favor on that Southern advance. As former residents (until the 1830s) of the Southeastern states, the Five Civilized Tribes felt bound to Southern culture by links of blood, marriage, and custom. Tribal members of mixed blood had brought slavery and cotton culture with them to the Territory. Southern agents had handled the Territory's trade, and Southern institutions invested tribal trust funds. Fearful that the new Republican administration might open the Indian Territory to white settlement, the Indians became alarmed by the Union's failure to appoint new local agents and continue payment of the annuities due the tribes. With such advantages, skilled Southern diplomats quickly won the support of the five tribes—except for dissenting factions within the Seminoles, Creeks, and Cherokees. The resulting war, which pitted Gray against Blue and the Indians against each other, devastated the Territory and wrecked three decades of improvements. With defeat, the tribes also lost land, and the Confederates' allies suffered Reconstruction. As a consequence, the Five Civilized Tribes became an easier target for later white expansion.[98]

Uncoordinated uprisings elsewhere in the West hurt white settlements in the Minnesota, Dakota, Colorado, and New Mexico territories without bringing any long-term advantage to the Indians. Observing the withdrawal of regular-army garrisons (or anticipating the Confederate invasion of New Mexico) and hearing of Union defeats in the East, many of the Western tribes thought they saw an opportunity to redress old wrongs or drive out white settlers. In some respects, the resulting battles merely opened the struggle for the Far West that would occupy the postwar army until the 1890s and, for the Indians, end in ultimate defeat and assignment to reservations. For the four territories, however, the uprisings represented only a temporary slowing in population growth and a brief decline in prosperity.[99]

Elsewhere in the West, development progressed as before—perhaps sustained by the arrival of deserters and draft dodgers—or even advanced more quickly due to the civil conflict. Land sales recovered after 1861, to be boosted again after 1865 as the Pacific Railroad Act and Homestead Act—themselves facilitated by secession—began to take effect. The shift of the overland mail and telegraph routes into the central region brought employment, business, and prosperity to those along its route—especially the residents of Utah and Nevada. The wartime demand for grain and scarce metals similarly contributed to the prosperity of farmers and miners. War conditions also prompted considerable territorial reorganization in the West and, to Nevada, Nebraska, and Colorado, an offer of early statehood—which the latter rejected. Left to their own devices by the war, the territories for the most part prospered.[100]

If the war only slightly altered life in the territories, it had a profound impact upon American pacifists. During the Revolution that designation applied only to the members of a handful of peace sects opposed to war as a matter of church doctrine. Although proportionately less significant by 1861, those sects still survived. But in their opposition to war—any war—they had, in the early nineteenth century, received reinforcement from another quarter.

Following the War of 1812, Americans began to form private volunteer societies that sought to promote international peace. Usually referred to as the nonsectarian or secular peace movement, to distinguish it from the peace churches, its opposition to war nevertheless drew inspiration from a belief in nonviolence as a duty to one's brothers in Christ as well as from secular or Enlightenment views concerning the irrationality and barbarism of war. That union of Christian and secular pacifism also reflected America's civil religion: the belief that the United States had a divine mission to bring republicanism and peace to the world, whether through the arrival of the Christian millennium or the workings of inexorable human progress.[101]

The main strength of that movement lay in the North, but sectional conflict and Civil War tore apart the secular peace societies and, according to Peter Brock, made "a mockery of what they had been preaching year in, year out over the previous half century." Some secular pacifists justified their willingness to fight for the Union by describing the conflict as domestic rather than international and therefore not a war. Others who had always maintained the acceptability of defensive war, emphasized the Confederate attack on Fort Sumter. For the most part, however, the secular pacifists were also abolitionists. When their two ideals clashed, they willingly compromised by accepting the lesser evil—a war to end slavery.[102]

The peace churches, on the other hand, maintained their witness, though a few antislavery Quakers did waver. By the time of the Civil War, the states' militia (North and South) had long permitted religious exemption in return for paying a commutation fee or hiring a substitute. The North's 1863 conscription law created no religious exemption but retained those two ways of avoiding military service until an 1864 amendment also offered noncombatant duty in hospitals or among the freedmen. As most members of a peace church could accept one of those options in good conscience, and Lincoln liberally granted furloughs and pardons to those who could not, Northern religious pacifists suffered little from the war.[103]

Although the South had few religious pacifists, it was sorely pressed by a lack of manpower and suspicious of the antislavery views and hostility to secession common to most peace churches. Southern nonresistants—when they did not pay the commutation fees or flee to the North—therefore suffered considerable harassment, occasional brutality, and infrequent imprisonment before winning exemption.[104]

The sectional crisis and Civil War showed America's principal churches to be far less unified and consistent in their witness. By 1860, a dispute over the morality of slavery had divided all but the Roman Catholics, Episcopalians, and Lutherans—who sought to maintain through official silence a sometimes artificial unity. Thus divided, churchmen in each section greeted the outbreak of war by announcing God's support for that section's particular cause. In the South, clergymen described slavery as divinely established with the same enthusiasm and conviction that Northern churchmen characterized an abolitionist war as serving the cause of both God and humanity. The existence of that logical impossibility seemed to bother few church leaders in either section.[105]

By settling the slavery issue, the Civil War in the end allowed the churches to move on to other work. In the North, they developed a "social gospel" that for a time put the churches in the forefront of efforts to counter the worst efforts of industrialization. Thrown on the defensive, the former Confederate churchmen devoted themselves to the less inspiring task of preserving Southern civilization—which included encouraging ex-slaves to establish their own churches.[106]

Although Roman Catholics maintained their formal unity during the sectional crisis, individual clergymen were found on all sides of the slavery issue—usually condemning it in principle but accepting it in fact and working vaguely for its amelioration. During the war, the church supported its communicants on both sides and quieted their racial fears by doing little to recruit black Americans.[107]

However much the Civil War had shaken American churches, it produced only evolutionary changes in the nation's civil religion. Protestantism continued its undisputed influence over American culture. Even if not active in a church, the nation's citizens typically regarded religious faith as a civic duty and themselves as adherents—generally believing in the existence of God, a life hereafter, the reward of virtue, the punishment of vice, and—in the grip of extreme religious tolerance—paying little heed to denominational differences. But the Civil War also introduced a new theme. The Founding Fathers suffered a decline in national esteem because they had preserved the sin of slavery, which required their sons to wage a Civil War that chastised yet purified the corrupted nation. The sons, who had fought the Civil War and preserved the American experiment in free government, thus became heroes in their own right and had less need of the paternal Washington. The assassination of the Christ-like Lincoln on Good Friday in 1865 reinforced the transition. His life and martyrdom seemed a new testament of American freedom, one that reinforced, yet partially eclipsed, the ancient faith.[108]

Organizing the Nation

The very concept of civil war suggests the existence of potentially irreconcilable differences among a nation's citizens and the disruption of at least its national institutions. Secession and the outbreak of war in 1861 represented, indeed, the climax of divisive forces within American life. Four years of internecine conflict, which might logically have deepened those divisions, paradoxically produced a reunited nation prepared for a more organized, centrally influenced national life.

That new unity resulted, in part, because the war seemingly resolved two paramount issues of the antebellum period: the locus of governmental sovereignty and the future of slavery in the United States. In any subsequent dispute over the rights of the national versus state governments, the latter had lost their ultimate weapon—secession—and must know that a national institution—most probably the Supreme Court—would in the end determine the relative authority of the two levels of government. Similarly, the very length of the war caused the Federal Government not simply to block slavery's extension but to decree its extinction, and Northern military victory insured that the Union's views would prevail. Unexpectedly metamorphosed in the postwar period, the debate over slavery became a struggle to determine the character of America's multiracial society. That future conflict over race, however, had an increasingly less sectional character even as the Federal Government retained the ultimate power to shape the outcome of events by its intervention on behalf of black Americans (and later any minority) persecuted by state government or denied its protection against the private oppression of powerful individuals or groups. The war-induced decision to use Federal power to secure the rights of black citizens—itself a new and positive role for the Federal Government in the area of civil rights—in time made the national government the ultimate resort for any disadvantaged group.

The war also set other political precedents. Lincoln's vigorous Presidential leadership, his use of war powers to justify virtual temporary suspension of parts of the Constitution, and the increased responsibilities that the war thrust upon a much strengthened Federal bureaucracy all foreshadowed the ways in which Americans would respond to future events they might regard as grave national crises. Although initially placing only major wars in that category, Americans eventually accepted more ambiguous, slow-developing challenges, such as those resulting from industrialization or economic collapse, as worthy of an expansion of Federal power.

In the Civil War no Yorktown temporarily arrested the progress of centralization two years before the formal close of hostilities. In both the Union and the Confederacy, Americans continually strengthened their central governments as a means to mobilize both resources and the citizenry in pursuit of common purposes. Although the South acted first (and in some respects more extensively), both governments assumed the right to draft their citizens for military service. Through ownership, subsidies, controls on profits, and threats of retaliation, the Confederacy also sought directly to control its war industries. Placing relatively smaller demands on its far stronger economy, the Union, in contrast, relied on the market to mobilize its section's resources. The Federal Government nevertheless achieved an indirect but lasting influence over economic development through such war measures as the National Banking Act and the introduction of protectionism. The Union was also more successful in both the suspension of the writ of habeas corpus and the use of its vigorous party system to control the war's opponents and rally the nation for the long struggle toward victory.

If almost a half century would elapse before Americans again politically exploited their Federal powerhouse, they more quickly grasped the war's economic implications. Despite the fate of the merchant marine and the cotton textiles industry, the inflationary reductions in both the real wages of laborers and the resources of those on fixed incomes (especially soldiers' families), and the decline in the growth rate of heavy industry, the Northern economy successfully met the challenge of war. From sustaining an immense army engaged on widely scattered fronts, wartime businessmen gained an appreciation of the requirements for supplying a national market: large-scale production in highly mechanized factories making standardized products out of resources drawn from widely scattered areas and sold to customers throughout large regions, even the entire nation. To build and coordinate operations on that scale, postwar businessmen had the assistance of wartime improvements in financial institutions and communications systems and a more friendly central government supplying them with such aids as protective tariffs and land grants.

In contrast to the growth in the Northern economy (despite war and the loss of eleven states), emancipation and four years of conflict sent the Southern economy into decline. Although its industries rather quickly returned to prewar levels, they produced a relatively smaller proportion of the national output, and poverty haunted the region's agriculture for the remainder of the century. Southerners also lost their prewar parity in per-capita output.

If the South in general suffered, participation in a great national endeavor brought benefits to several disadvantaged social groups. Reversing several prewar trends, black Americans won their freedom, the foreign born gained acceptance as antebellum nativism collapsed, and women experienced a further slight expansion in the sphere that confined them still. All Americans, even those in the South, lost much of their localism and felt the centralizing, organizing forces at work in politics and the economy.

For such changes Americans paid a fearful price: 635,000 dead (more than the combined total of all the nation's other wars) and the expenditure of some $8 billion (for the nineteenth century a truly awesome figure). Such numbers, however, fail to convey the war's costs as well as a simple, even personal, wartime memoir, like the scene observed by writer Rebecca Harding Davis while interrupting a wartime journey at one of Pennsylvania's small-town railroad stations. "Nobody was in sight but a poor, thin country girl in a faded calico gown and sunbonnet. She stood alone on the platform, waiting. A child was playing beside her. When we stopped, the men took out from a freight car a rough, unplaned pine box and laid it down, baring their heads for a moment. Then the train steamed away. She sat down on the ground and put her arms around the box and leaned her head on it. The child went on playing."[109] In ways quite unlike those imagined by Justice Holmes, their lives, too, had been "touched with fire."

3
WORLD WAR I

War is the health of the State.

Randolph S. Bourne[1]

Bitterly disappointed by the support American liberals had given Woodrow Wilson's April 1917 call for a declaration of war on Germany, Randolph Bourne, one of the new century's young radical intellectuals, warned that intervention in a European war would defeat all their plans. War would transform the decisions and policies of a fallible government, which Americans had previously felt free to criticize, into the military needs of a mystic and all-powerful state, which would brand all criticism disloyal. To further silence opposition and justify authoritarianism, those who controlled the government would also force a mindless patriotic conformity upon the American people. Worse yet, he predicted, the upper classes would use the war to seize control of the government and, with heightened wartime patriotism protecting them from close scrutiny, defeat the liberals' program of reforms and fasten a thoroughly reactionary regime on an unsuspecting public.[2]

Bourne's predictions, popularized by opponents of the recent war in Vietnam, contained an element of truth. The scope and power of wartime government did increase dramatically as the administration struggled to mobilize both the economy and public opinion behind the war effort. Reorienting the economy indeed gave to businessmen a prestige and access to government they had often been denied in the progressive era, and rousing popular support for the war produced a degree of conformity and repression that challenged the nation's democratic traditions.

In other respects, however, Bourne's predictions fell far short of wartime reality. A whole range of groups—most of them neither conservative nor a part of the ruling class—also used the wartime government to advance, with some success, their particular interests. And if conformity temporarily restrained social conflict, wartime experiences also seemed to prepare the way for the severe social clashes of the immediate postwar period. Upon closer examination, even the government's enhanced powers—acquired for the most part in a piecemeal, confused fashion—yielded perhaps too quickly to demands for a return to normalcy.

America's World War I transition to the modern era was thus filled with contradiction—expectations only partially realized, democratic war aims pursued with occasionally autocratic means, success too easily surrendered, triumph that bore the seeds of defeat, and a temporary unity that concealed the roots of discord. To penetrate that paradox requires a brief description of the means whereby the government mobilized the nation's human and material resources, the circumstances in which it acted, and the economic, social, and political consequences of its endeavors.

Neutrality: Prelude to Mobilization

The August 1914 outbreak of war in Europe initially dealt a sharp setback to the American economy, which still suffered from a twenty-month depression begun in 1913. As Europeans hastened to sell their American securities, convert the proceeds into gold, and ship the precious metal to Europe, they sparked a 23 percent decline in American stock prices, a six-month closure of the stock exchange, and a modest banking crisis. Expectations of a short war that would disrupt international commerce also depressed commodity markets and caused American exports to fall 41 percent below their level of August 1913. Industrialists followed suit and cut their output; the production of steel ingots, for example, fell 35 percent between March and November 1914. Industrial stagnation also meant trouble for both the nation's work force, as unemployment rose to perhaps 11 percent, and its railroads, which experienced a 4 percent decline in ton miles of freight handled in 1914 and again in 1915.[3]

Meanwhile, however, the French army held along the Marne, frustrating the German plan to encircle and destroy it in a short, decisive war of maneuver. Soon the trench line ran from Switzerland to the English Channel, and the opposing forces settled down to an exhausting and brutal effort to dislodge one another in massive frontal assaults that squandered both lives and materiel on a scale theretofore unknown in the history of war.

The resulting military stalemate entirely reversed the war's impact on the United States. Europeans, unexpectedly facing a long war of attrition, developed a craving for American goods. Gold returned to the United States to pay for the resulting exports, industry and employment boomed, and full economic recovery was underway by June 1915.[4]

That surge in America's economy first appeared as an increase in exports, which leapt upward in the two-plus years before the United States became a belligerent. (See Table 3.1.) Despite the collapse of its trade with Germany, which fell from an annual rate of $169 million in 1914 to just over $1 million in 1916, America's exports forged ahead, paced by a four-fold increase in shipments to the Allied powers during the same period. The United States also made gains in Latin American and other markets that the European powers could no longer supply.[5]

Table 3.1
American Foreign Commerce, 1913–1921
(Millions of Dollars)

Year	Exports	Imports
1913	$2,466	$1,813
1914	2,365	1,894
1915	2,769	1,674
1916	5,483	2,392
1917	6,234	2,952
1918	6,149	3,031
1919	7,920	3,904
1920	8,228	5,278
1921	4,485	2,509

Source: US, Department of Commerce, Bureau of the Census, *Historical Statistics of the United States, Colonial Times to 1970*, Bicentennial ed., 2 vols. (Washington, DC: US Government Printing Office, 1975), series U187–200, 2:884.

To pay for the exports, France and Britain shipped over $1 billion in gold to the United States, liquidated 70 percent of their citizens' investments in American securities, sold government bonds to American investors, and obtained short-term credits from American banks. America's $4 billion prewar net debt to foreigners, already being gradually diminished by its modest annual trade surplus, became a net credit of comparable size in about three years; that credit jumped to $12.5 billion as a consequence of intergovernmental loans made when the United States became a belligerent.[6]

Soon the entire American economy responded to the stimulus of increased exports. Raw materials producers increased their output, farmers brought new land under the plow, and manufacturers put idle capacity to use. The Dow-Jones stock averages rose by 81 percent during 1915, and as Table 3.2 shows, the gross national product registered impressive gains.[7]

Although American industry for the most part met the outbreak of World War I by expansion along already well-established lines, the European war

Table 3.2
Gross National Product (GNP), 1914–1918
(Billions of Dollars)

Year	GNP (Current Prices)	GNP (1914 Prices)
1914	$38.6	$38.6
1915	40.0	38.3
1916	48.3	41.3
1917	60.4	41.6
1918	76.4	46.7

Source: Based on data in US, Department of Commerce, Bureau of the Census, *Historical Statistics of the United States, Colonial Times to 1970*, Bicentennial ed., 2 vols. (Washington, DC: US Government Printing Office, 1975), 1:224.

produced several important exceptions to that generalization. Denied access to former German suppliers, the United States developed a domestic capacity to produce dyes, chemicals, and drugs from coal. The companies in that field rose quickly from five to 98, and they dramatically increased the range and sophistication of their products. Among infant industries, aircraft production also leapt to significance during the war years, annual output jumping from under $2 million before 1916 to some $175 million two years later, and electronics received a boost from a war-inspired interest in radio. Supplying the Allied powers with rifles, shells, powder, explosives, and gun carriages also created—well before the United States became a belligerent—the nation's first armaments industry, which before 1914 had consisted of only a few shipyards, some small-arms manufacturers, and several government arsenals. In addition to those relatively new industries, the war sometimes prompted expansion well beyond prewar trends. Aluminum capacity, for example, doubled during the war, and American shipbuilding, a $100-million industry that temporarily rose to $1.4 billion by 1919, experienced a virtual resurrection.[8]

In the main, however, and well in advance of America's rearmament and declaration of war, the nation's economy expanded along established lines. Industries responded to the Allied demand for increased exports of food and munitions, the chance to make new overseas sales in markets formerly dominated by European suppliers, and the desire for consumer products in a domestic market suddenly returned to prosperity. Textiles, which had been in the doldrums in 1914, did not boom but nevertheless benefited from increased domestic demand for cotton goods, woolen sales to Latin America, a change in fashion that favored silk, and, much later, American military purchases. Again, even before the United States entered the war, its meatpackers, canners, and millers prospered from increased sales to the Allies, just as did the producers of the motor transport, locomotives, and railroad rolling stock required to carry the vast quantities of military materiel needed by French and British armies engaged in the world's first truly modern war. The manufacture of rolling stock and the construction of new warehouses, wharves, piers, ships, military cantonments, and the trench systems of the war zone also revived the lumber industry, which flourished with later American intervention.

Like the booming munitions business, most of those industries also required iron or steel, as a raw material or for tools. Consequently, the iron and steel industry, which in 1914 had suspended dividends and operated at less than 35 percent of capacity, quickly felt the beneficial effects of war. Halfway through 1915, the industry reached 90 percent of capacity. Between January and December of that year, the level of pig-iron production doubled, reaching an annual rate of 38 million tons. Simultaneously, the price rose from $14.70 per ton to almost $20 before reaching $55 in 1916. Industry profits kept pace, rising by 7 percent in 1915 and 21 percent in 1916 with gains up to 55 percent going to the smaller producers.[9]

As indicated by the index numbers in Table 3.3, World War I thus brought a remarkable expansion in American industrial output. The numbers also reveal at least one other fact, whose significance must be discussed more fully later: The American economy had put virtually all its idle resources into production by late 1916 or 1917. In every category, the rate of expansion thereafter slowed—sometimes even declined—a development that posed special problems for the United States when its own military forces began to place heavy demands upon the economy after April 1917.

A detailed description of that mobilization, however, should follow a brief explanation of the situation on America's farms. Experts usually consider the two decades before World War I the "golden era" of American agriculture. With the best lands under cultivation and the farm population and number of farms holding steady, the rate of annual increase in farm output grew by only one-half percent between 1896 and 1915. Despite the declining export of American cereals (from 530 million bushels in 1897–1898 to 168 million in 1913–1914) the rapid growth of both the nation's urban population and per-capita real income maintained the demand for agricultural products and boosted prices by almost 90 percent in the twentieth century's first decade. Between 1911 and 1915 the per-capita income of persons employed in agriculture as compared to industry reached a peak it would not match until a second world war. With agriculture prosperous, farmers also found their land, buildings, and livestock increasing in value, both absolutely and relative to the growth of farm debt.[10]

Table 3.3
Indices of Industrial Production, 1914–1918
(1914 = 100)

Activity	1914	1915	1916	1917	1918
Industrial Materials					
All Commodities	100	110	127	132	127
Ferrous Metals	100	137	182	192	189
Textiles	100	111	124	127	123
Processed Food	100	103	111	110	118
Physical Production					
Mining	100	109	126	133	134
Manufacturing	100	117	139	138	137
Rail Transportation	100	107	124	136	142

Sources: Geoffrey H. Moore, *Production of Industrial Materials in World Wars I and II* (New York: National Bureau of Economic Research, 1944), p. 17; Charles Gilbert, *American Financing of World War I* (Westport, CT: Greenwood Press, 1970), p.205.

The outbreak of war in Europe reversed a number of those trends while bringing to American agriculture an unparalleled but almost fatal prosperity. The Allied powers lost access to both German sugar and Europe's old granary—Russia, Bulgaria, Serbia, and Turkey. By placing sixty million men under arms, Europe both cut its agricultural capacity and created a military demand for food in excess of peacetime needs. The wartime blockades and shortage of shipping then made it impractical to export extensively from New Zealand, Australia, China, or South America.[11]

The resulting wartime demand for North American agricultural exports hit farm markets in the United States with predictable results. Between 1913 and 1918, the value of American wheat and flour exports more than tripled (from $142 million to $505 million), and meat exports went up nearly ten times (from $68 million to $668 million). Because disease, bad weather, and overslaughtering restrained the growth of farm output, prices rose phenomenally. The increase for cereals ranged from 70 percent (oats) to 225 percent (rye). Livestock values went up from 34 percent (milk cows) to 130 percent (sheep). Cotton rose by 140 percent and wool by 264 percent. As indicated in Table 3.4, farm profits consequently rose rapidly.[12]

Farmers too behaved predictably. Although the value of land rose by 70 percent during the war, they added an average of 10 acres to the size of their farms and brought marginal land under the plow. Between 1914 and 1921 the land area devoted to crops increased by 40 million acres (13 percent). As Figure 3.1 shows, they also bought tractors and commenced the era of power-driven machinery on American farms. Because the purchase of land and

Table 3.4
Farm Profits and Production Index, 1914–1921

Year	Gross Profits (Millions)	Net Profits (Millions)	Volume of Agricultural Production (1914 = 100)
1914	$ 7,638	$ 3,518	100
1915	7,968	3,745	104
1916	9,532	4,687	100
1917	13,147	7,011	104
1918	16,232	8,674	109
1919	17,710	9,249	110
1920	15,908	6,778	111
1921	10,478	3,603	100

Source: Harold D. Guither, *Heritage of Plenty: A Guide to the Economic History and Development of U.S. Agriculture* (Danville, IL: Interstate Printers & Publishers, Inc., 1972), pp. 124–25.

machines cost money, farm mortgages also rose from an average of $117 per acre (1914) to $158 per acre (1918) to $245 per acre (1921), and farmers' short-term indebtedness increased from $1.6 billion (1914) to $2.5 billion (1918) to $3.8 billion (1921).[13]

As the indices in Table 3.4 reveal, however, the farmers' investment in land and equipment produced less than a 10 percent wartime growth in output, much of the "increase" in the value of farm production being mere price inflation. Table 3.5's figures on a few selected farm commodities make the same point. When the United States declared war in April 1917, it possessed, in agriculture as well as manufacturing, industries that were operating at near the short-term limit of their capacity.

Workingmen, Workingwomen, and the European War

The United States consequently faced a most difficult situation as it prepared to intervene in the European war. Because of the enormous amounts of military materiel that had to be made available to the armed forces, modern warfare laid a heavy burden on American industry. In a single campaign of World War I, for instance, the US Army used more weight in metal of shot and shell than fired by all Union forces throughout four years of the Civil War. To meet such requirements, the armed forces, which through 1916 had consumed one percent or less of the gross national product (GNP), demanded ten times that level in 1917 and almost a quarter of the GNP in the war's last year.[14] Yet, by 1916 American industry already operated at near its peak.

Unless the government achieved a dramatic reduction in civil consumption, only a rapid augmentation of the work force might in the short-term produce a sharp increase in the output of war materiel. Yet, just when industry

Figure 3.1
Tractors on American Farms, 1914-1920
(Thousands)

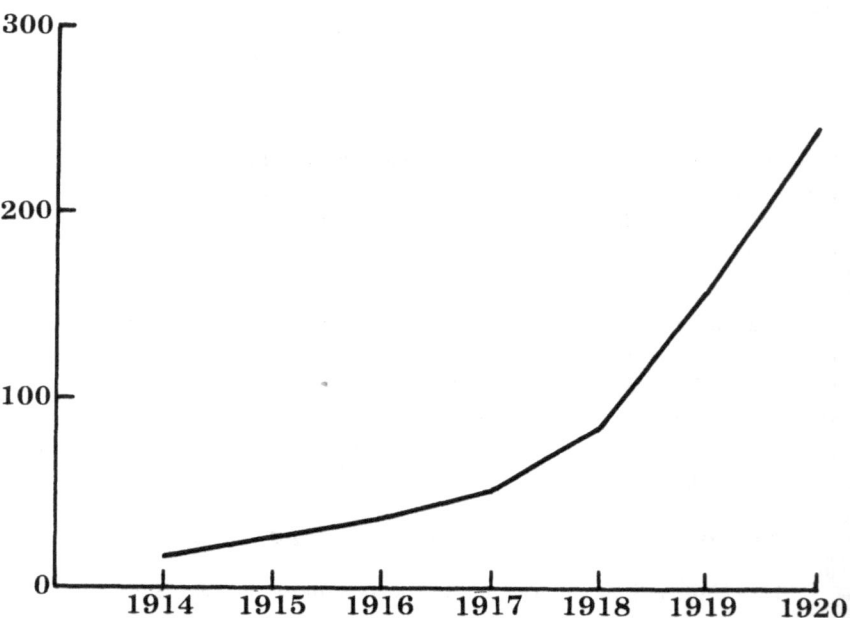

Source: Harold D. Guither, *Heritage of Plenty: A Guide to the Economic History and Development of U.S. Agriculture* (Danville, IL: Interstate Printers & Publishers, Inc., 1972), pp. 124-25.

Table 3.5
Production and Average Annual
Prices of Selected Farm Products, 1914–1918

Year	Cattle (Price) (Thousands of Head)	Hogs (Price) (Thousands of Head)	Wheat (Price) (Millions of Bushels)
1914	59,461 ($38.97)	52,853 ($10.51)	897 ($0.98)
1915	63,849 (40.67)	56,600 (9.95)	1,009 (0.96)
1916	67,438 (40.10)	60,596 (8.48)	638 (1.43)
1917	70,979 (43.34)	57,578 (11.82)	620 (2.05)
1918	73,040 (50.01)	62,931 (19.69)	904 (2.05)

Source: John T. Schlebecker, *Whereby We Thrive: A History of American Farming, 1607–1972* (Ames, IA: Iowa State University Press, 1975). p. 209. Reprinted by permission of the publisher.

needed every available worker, local draft boards issued the first draft calls that helped send some 16 percent of the male work force into one of the armed services. Manufacturers thus had to struggle merely to maintain production. In that effort, they exploited a development of the neutrality period—the increased industrial employment of women and black Americans.

A survey of almost five hundred firms at four key periods during the war (see Table 3.6) indicates the extent to which industries engaged in war work increased their employment of women. By 1918, some 10 million women were in the work force, a third of them in factories, and working at more occupations than ever before. In munitions plants, aircraft factories, and shipyards, women assembled equipment and ran such machines as lathes and drill presses. They handled baggage, operated elevators, and conducted streetcars—all jobs reserved to men before 1914. They entered other new areas when the wartime railroads hired them to maintain tracks, clean passenger cars, and work in the shops that repaired locomotives and rolling stock. Throughout war industries, women could also be found replacing men in the machine shop and the tool room and at the controls of heavy equipment in rolling mills.[15]

However dramatic those wartime developments in women's employment, they caused no significant fundamental change. Of the women workers in the war years, only 5 percent had joined the work force for the first time, and as the last column in Table 3.6 indicates, many—but not all—of the women in nontraditional work lost their jobs at the war's end. In the main, wartime employment of women had merely continued the prewar trend of employing more women as office workers, stenographers, typists, bookkeepers, accountants, cashiers, retail sales clerks, school teachers, and telephone operators and in unskilled and semiskilled manufacturing. The war, however, encouraged that last group of women workers (who had prewar factory

Table 3.6
Number of Women Per One Thousand Employees in 474 Firms Doing War Work, 1916–1919

Industry	1916	After 1st Draft	After 2d Draft	1919
Iron, steel, & their products	65	108	157	107
Other metals & their products	152	167	206	180
Lumber & its manufactures	31	45	114	71
Leather & its products	252	286	316	292
Chemicals & allied products	35	69	131	64
Automobiles	47	59	175	131
Electrical Machinery	114	62	233	156
Instruments	74	219	237	176
Other	144	182	237	197
Total	102	130	182	143

Source: US, Department of Labor, Women's Bureau, *The New Position of Women in American Industry*, Bulletin no. 12 (Washington, DC: US Government Printing Office, 1920), p.89.

experience in such traditional women's fields as textiles, clothing, shoes, gloves, food, and tobacco) to move at least temporarily to better paying jobs in war industries. In turn, women who abandoned domestic work and personal service in great numbers during the war—accelerating another prewar trend—took the places of those experienced women workers abandoning their traditional factory jobs. The vacancies in domestic work and the more menial jobs of cleaning in railyards and offices opened new, if temporary, opportunities for black women. In other words, the war did not so much permanently increase or change women's employment as move it along the path it had taken in the prewar years, and few of the women taking nontraditional jobs retained them when veterans returned in 1919 to resume their old positions.[16]

Black Americans, freshly arrived from the South, provided American industry its second source of new workers. Relatively few blacks had gone North at the end of the Civil War; the twelve Southern states that held 88 percent of America's blacks in 1860 retained 83 percent of a much larger Afro-American population a half century later. In 1910 the North's one million blacks, who had been increasing in numbers at the very modest rate of 16,000 per year since 1900, still constituted less than 2 percent of the region's population. Then in 1915, the wartime demand for labor pulled 400,000 blacks into the North within five years and initiated the next half century's new, higher rates of migration.[17]

Black leaders and some historians have attributed that migration to a desire to exchange Southern injustice for the North's freer environment. A verse from a contemporary song probably comes closer to the truth:

> Boll-weevil in de cotten,
> Cutwurm in de cawn [corn]
> Debil in de white man,
> Wah's [war is] goin' on.

Racial injustice—the devil in the white man—was, of course, no new discovery in 1915, even if Jim Crow had become more severe after 1890, and blacks knew that the North was not free of discrimination. Instead, blacks went northward pushed by low incomes (sometimes due to boll-weevil infestation) and drawn by better jobs and higher wages.[18]

The shifting of black Americans from Southern farms to Northern industries and women workers from domestic service to factory jobs might have compensated for the departure of young men to the army. But another loss—the wartime interruption of European immigration—insured that industry and agriculture would face a severe labor shortage. The migration that had brought over twenty million Europeans to the United States between 1880 and 1920 (and by 1914 produced over one million new arrivals each year) slowed to a trickle during the war. In 1918, for example, only 31,063 new immigrants arrived from Europe.[19]

At least in the short run, then, America's farms and industries could not readily expand output to meet the needs of its armed forces by making major additions to the work force.

Those who spoke for that work force, moreover, had very strong opinions about the war and American intervention. The Socialists, who hoped one day to use the government to sponsor radical economic reforms in the interest of labor, opposed both war and intervention and argued that America's workingmen and women had no interest in a capitalists' war. The International Workers of the World (IWW or Wobblies), who in theory advocated direct action by the workers to seize their factories, equally opposed war and intervention. After April 1917, however, they temporarily eschewed seizure while hoping to profit from American intervention by renewed efforts to organize unskilled workers in mass production industries.

Had either group had its way, the American government would have faced a work force hostile to the war effort. Both the Socialists and the Wobblies, however, were but minor spokesmen for American labor, which generally found their radicalism unappealing. The men who led the American Federation of Labor (AFL), and specifically Samuel Gompers, represented the majority of the nation's organized work force. And they defined a narrower and more realizable set of wartime goals.

The progressive era generally and the Wilson administration particularly had improved the position of working people. New state and Federal laws limited child labor and the working hours of all women, and men in certain industries. Similar prolabor laws in some of the states called for the periodic inspection of factories and mines, placed responsibility for industrial accidents on the employer, and established workingmen's compensation programs. The 1914 Clayton Antitrust Act had, moreover, declared that labor was "not a commodity or article of commerce" and exempted labor unions from the antitrust provisions the Act applied to business. The Act also limited the use of injunctions in labor disputes and indirectly legalized trade unions and recognized their right to bargain collectively and to strike.[20]

To protect such gains and to increase labor's influence within the Wilson administration, Gompers abandoned the pacifism he formerly shared with the Socialists and the IWW and led the largest of the labor organizations into Wilson's camp and support for the war. In return, Gompers expected the government to work with labor through the unions, which meant union representation on wartime boards and commissions. While pledging that labor would show restraint in the interest of winning the war, Gompers insisted on better wages, hours, and working conditions and retained labor's right to organize and to strike. The voters had provided a sympathetic administration, and the war had placed labor in a position of some power. Gompers intended to exploit both in the interests of labor and the AFL.[21]

In April 1917 his most pressing problem was a war-induced rise in the cost of living and the resultant wave of strikes. As indicated in Table 3.7, during the period of American neutrality, the money wages of industrial workers had increased, but only just enough to keep slightly ahead of the rise

Table 3.7
Industrial Wages and Living Costs, 1913–1921

Year	Average Annual Money Wages (All Industry)	Cost of Living Index (1914 = 100)	Index of Real Hourly Earnings (All Industry)	Index of Real Annual Earnings (All Industry)
1913	$ 578	99	100	101
1914	580	100	100	100
1915	568	98	103	100
1916	651	107	103	105
1917	774	129	97	104
1918	980	157	99	108
1919	1,158	178	101	112
1920	1,358	206	105	114
1921	1,180	177	114	115

Source: Paul H. Douglas, *Real Wages in the United States, 1890–1926* (New York: Houghton Mifflin, 1930; reprint ed., New York: A. M. Kelley, 1966), pp. 60, 205, 230, 239–40, 246. Reprinted by permission of A. M. Kelley Publishers.

in prices caused by the growing Allied and neutral demand for American goods. The surge of inflation induced by American intervention soon caused a real hourly wage loss only partially compensated by greater annual wages due to more regular work and overtime at increased hourly rates. During the neutrality period, workers had maintained the buying power of their wages largely by labor scarcity and an increased willingness to strike. As indicated in Table 3.8, employee strikes, employer lockouts, and the numbers of employees affected increased alarmingly between 1914 and 1917. On the eve of war, the American economy struggled, then, not only to overcome a shortage of productive capacity in industry and agriculture and a limited supply of labor but also to satisfy a work force demanding higher wages and better working conditions. The latter demands would only further raise the cost of the government's purchases of war materiel, increase the burden borne by American taxpayers, and—if strikes occurred—possibly disrupt war mobilization.

Table 3.8
Strikes and Lockouts, 1914–1919

Year	Strikes	Employees Involved	Lockouts	Employees Involved
1914	979	—	101	—
1915	1,246	468,983	159	35,292
1916	3,678	1,546,428	108	53,182
1917	4,233	1,193,867	126	19,133
1918	3,181	1,192,418	104	43,041
1919	3,253	3,950,411	121	162,096

Source: From *War-Time Strikes and Their Adjustment* by Alexander M. Bing. Copyright, 1921, by E. P. Dutton and Company; renewal, 1948, by Alexander M. Bing. Reprinted by permission of the publisher, E. P. Dutton, Inc.

As measured by wholesale prices, the inflation that had driven up industrial wages began only in late 1915. As Figure 3.2 suggests, until that time the employment of formerly idle resources met increased demand without a general rise in prices. A year later, however, prices had risen by 30 percent, reached 50 percent at the end of 1916, and topped 70 percent in the month the United States declared war.[22]

By that date, moreover, the government had done little to counter an inflation that rapidly gained momentum. The new Federal Reserve System, approved by Congress in 1913 but operational only in November 1914, had in fact been set up to counter quite the opposite problem in conditions that no longer existed. The purpose of the Federal Reserve was to create an elastic,

Figure 3.2
Price and Wage Trends, 1914-1921

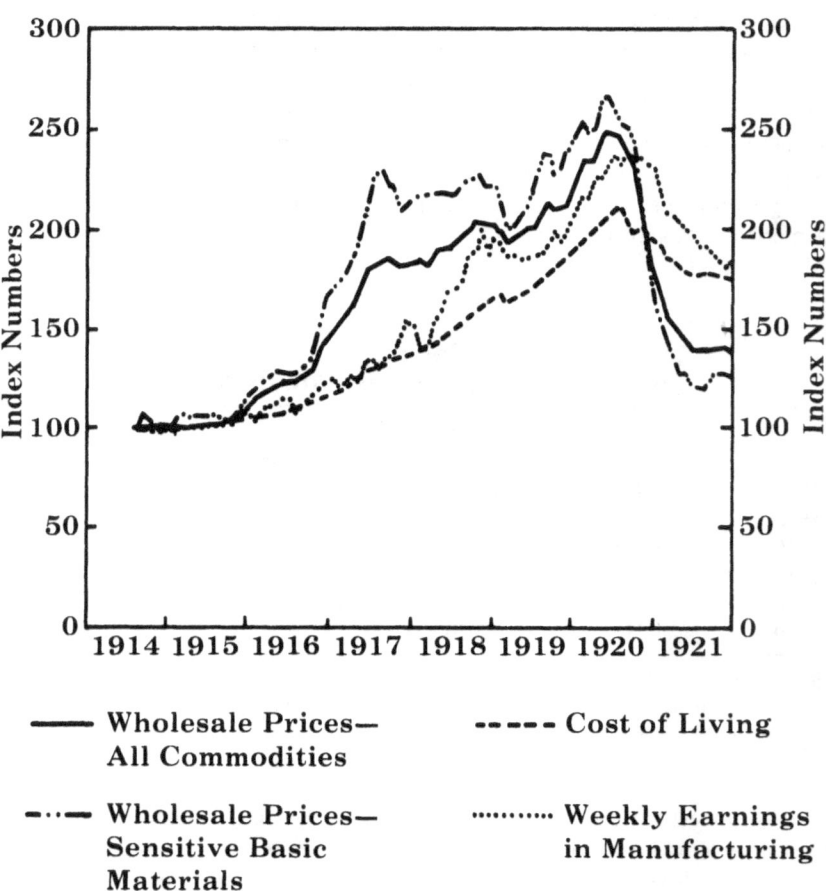

— Wholesale Prices—
All Commodities

–··– Wholesale Prices—
Sensitive Basic
Materials

----- Cost of Living

·········· Weekly Earnings
in Manufacturing

Source: Harold G. Moulton, *Can Inflation Be Controlled?* (Washington, DC: Anderson Kramer Associates, Inc., 1958), p. 101. Reprinted by permission of the publisher.

that is, growing, supply of money and to counter the financial panics that had plagued the United States whenever foreigners suddenly withdrew large quantities of gold from American banks. Yet, after 1915, gold and American securities flowed into the country in large quantities. It was then that the belligerents abandoned the international gold standard, which might have provided some automatic corrective to the sudden shift in commercial and financial relations. Simultaneously the Federal Reserve lowered the discount rate at which banks could borrow, and Congress later reduced their reserve requirements. That led to an increase in the banking system's ability to grant credit—to Allied buyers or American munitions manufacturers. It also caused an expansion of the nation's money supply, which increased by 46 percent between June 1914 and March 1917.[23] The government had thus fueled rather than dampened the inflation that would after April 1917 obstruct its ability to limit the financial cost of the war effort.

Mobilizing the American Economy

The war in Europe, developments in the period of American neutrality, and the decision to intervene thus placed the United States in a situation quite unlike anything in its experience. In the short term, its economy already operated at near full capacity. Yet, the needs of its allies and the armament and supply of its own armed forces demanded a sharp increase in war production.

Somehow the United States must drastically curtail its civilian consumption and then divert and convert the productive resources thus freed to war use. Yet, that task had become too large and the economy too complex and interdependent to expect the states to carry the burden. The loss of immigrant labor, only partially compensated by the increased industrial employment of women and blacks, and the need to raise an unprecedentedly large army without further disrupting the industrial and agricultural work force, indicated a need for some centrally directed manpower system. Yet, nothing in the American military past pointed to an effective or politically acceptable method. A bad crop year in 1916 had cut into US agricultural reserves just as the needs of the Allies and the American armed services increased the demand for food and threatened further price inflation that would hurt consumers and add to the cost of the war.

Clearly, the United States needed to give wise central direction to the mobilization it must achieve. Yet, no Federal agency had a comprehensive understanding of the needs of the armed services, of the productive capacity available to meet those needs, of the best methods to expand output and to reconcile civil, military, and Allied demands, or of the appropriate agencies to determine policy and supervise its implementation. The United States thus sailed into a sea of troubles with little knowledge of the best course to its destination. That uncertainty must be kept in mind in order to achieve a proper understanding of the gradual, hesitant, and often piecemeal efforts of the Federal Government to mobilize the nation's economy for war.

By the middle of 1918, a year after its declaration of war, the United States had created a reasonably effective group of over 5,000 mobilization agencies—a collection of boards, committees, corporations, and administrations with varying authority to allocate resources, set priorities, regulate prices, encourage war production, and oversee some facet of the American economy.[24]

The most general responsibility rested with the War Industries Board (WIB), an outgrowth of the 1916 Council of National Defense, its Advisory Commission (NDAC), and several subordinate agencies created to set standards for the production of munitions and coordinate purchases by the military departments. The Council had also established a set of committees that served as liaison with war industries—enabling the government to obtain data concerning the sources of supply and the costs of production, and providing manufacturers with information on governmental needs and contracts. By the spring of 1918, the WIB, and through it the committees (now commodity sections), reported directly to the President and sustained by his prestige and authority pursued six major goals: It sought to expand supply by creating new facilities and discovering new sources; convert existing facilities to war uses; and conserve resources and facilities. It also advised government agencies on the prices to be paid for purchases; determined priorities of production and delivery; and made purchases for the Allies.[25]

The war thus brought American industry into a new, if temporary, relationship with the government. By appeals to patriotism and veiled threats of punishment, the WIB in the name of the government influenced what businessmen would produce, to whom they would sell it, and how much they might charge. With considerable difficulty the WIB had also united government and Allied purchasing, enabling the Board to allocate resources and determine priorities among competing war needs and to insure that older purchasing methods did not bid up the prices paid by the government. In addition, the WIB encouraged firms in the same line of work to form trade associations that might represent the industry's point of view and supply information to the government.

Several areas, however, lay outside the specific authority of the War Industries Board, among them control of the food supply. The August 1917 Food and Fuel Control Act gave legislative sanction to the Food Administration established by President Wilson shortly after the declaration of war. The Act charged the new agency to control the supply, distribution, and movement of food and articles necessary for its production. It also had authority to punish those who profiteered or hoarded, to seize their food stocks, and to requisition food when needed for military or public purposes. It could become a dealer in wheat, flour, meal, beans, and potatoes and commandeer food processing plants, if necessary. Unlike the WIB, the Food Administration had the power to regulate the cost of food by setting certain prices or supervision of exchanges and trades.[26]

Although the Food Administration thus had coercive powers denied the WIB, that agency used them sparingly and relied largely on indirect and voluntary methods. To restrain inflation and make more food available to the Allies and the armed forces, Food Administrator Herbert Hoover launched a voluntary conservation program that pledged housewives to conserve and to insure their families observed the wheatless meal (daily), the wheatless day (Wednesday), the meatless meal (daily), the meatless day (Tuesday), and the porkless day (Saturday) decreed by his administration. By licensing middlemen and food processors, Hoover controlled the distribution of food to users and limited their profit margins, which also aided the government's battle against inflation. Although Congress and the President had set a price for wheat—a high minimum price designed to encourage production—Hoover established the US Grain Corporation to monopolize grain exchanges by consolidating government and Allied grain purchases and thereby insure that the minimum price also became the virtual maximum that farmers would receive. To influence retail prices, Hoover relied on the social pressures of local committees, appeals to the patriotism of small distributors and retailers, and ample publicity in those cases where the government had punished wholesalers, bakers, and manufacturers for violating the Food Control Act.[27]

Those activities established an entirely new, if temporary, relationship between the government and the food industry and a more enduring change in the attitudes of farmers. By the time the Food Administration dropped its wartime controls, it had weakened farmer resistance to governmental direction of their affairs. Having observed how the government could shape wartime food prices, farmers would expect it also to act in peacetime to maintain the prosperity of America's farms.[28]

The act creating Hoover's agency also established the Fuel Administration and charged it to encourage conservation and stimulate production to meet the growing needs of war industries, the railroads, and the merchant fleet. When demand outran supply, the administration could also control allocation and distribution of fuels and regulate prices, which required that it adjust labor disputes in the mines. In the end, the Fuel Administration virtually rationed coal to consumers, limited the nonessential use of electricity, required certain businesses to observe heatless Mondays, and managed coal supplies by licensing all distributors of coal and coke.[29]

The fragmented, highly competitive nature of the bituminous coal industry, the paradoxical fear of a "coal trust," and poor management in the Fuel Administration made this one of the least effective areas of wartime governmental management, resulting in a shortage of coal and a snarling of ocean and rail traffic of crisis proportions in the winter of 1917-1918. By relying more fully on the advice of mine operators and avoiding the creation of an adversarial relationship, the government might have prevented that tie-up, which resulted in a five-day industrial shutdown.[30]

That coal crisis also contributed to the complete governmental takeover of another major industry: the nation's railroads. The takeover, however, had deeper roots. Between 1907 and 1916 overregulation of the railroads by an Interstate Commerce Commission and state agencies favoring the interests of shippers over those of the railroads had reduced by 6 percent the railroads' average revenue per ton mile—by 20 percent compared to 1892. As a result, the railroads' return on investment fell. Finding it difficult to raise money, they cut spending on maintenance and new equipment by almost 70 percent between 1911 and 1916. By 1916, the number of miles of line in railroad receivership had set a record, and the stock market value of railroad shares had fallen to one-half 1906 levels.[31]

Although the war boosted traffic (from 289,000 ton miles in 1914 to 409,000 in 1918) and led to greater prosperity (a return on investment just over 6 percent), it also created a shortage of freight cars and impeded the railroads' ability to secure investment capital and obtain production priority for the 2,000 new locomotives and 150,000 freight cars they needed. Nevertheless, voluntary railroad committees operating under the Council of National Defense had eased some of the shortages by mid-1917. Cooperative pooling collapsed, however, in the face of developments beyond railroad control: extraordinary grain shipments in late 1917, Fuel Administration ineptitude that had delayed the shipment of coal into the fall and winter, severe weather, and mismanagement at the terminals, which prevented the timely unloading and return to service of scarce freight cars.[32]

The President therefore took control of the railroads in late December 1917, naming Treasury Secretary William G. McAdoo Railroad Administrator. The Federal Government, of course, easily raised investment money and gave the Railroad Administration the priority needed to speed the manufacture of new equipment. Unlike the railroad committees, a Congressional guarantee of each line's profitability during the takeover relieved the administrator of concern for the financial impact of his pooling arrangements. Unlike the private owners, the government could order a wartime boost in railroad rates and finance a favorable wage settlement that prevented a threatened strike. To extend the capacity to move essential traffic, the Railroad Administration also curtailed passenger travel, unified terminals, imposed more efficient loading policies on shippers, pooled maintenance facilities, and standardized the manufacture of railroad equipment—all actions quite beyond the private owners.[33]

Despite the sharp rise in rates that accompanied the higher wages, and only small increases in efficiency, some groups advocated permanent postwar nationalization of the railroads. That plan failed, but the war's unprecedented Federal operation of the nation's railroads gave the government and the owners a better idea of the needs and mutual interests of both the public and the railroads.[34]

Although the government also assumed wartime control of the telephone, telegraph, and cable companies, it held back from formal seizure of shipping and shipbuilding. Still, its varied controls and activities had almost that effect. A rise in shipping rates in excess of 1,000 percent, wartime losses, and the belligerents' unwillingness to see their shipping used for American exports that did not support their military effort created a shipping crisis for the United States over a year before its declaration of war. The resulting Shipping Act of 1916 established a Shipping Board authorized to regulate overseas carriers, and to construct, purchase, lease, and charter vessels for use in the American merchant service. The board could then lease such ships either to private US shipping companies or to a newly created government-owned shipping firm. The Emergency Fleet Corporation resulted from the latter provision.[35]

That corporation and several wartime amendments to the Shipping Act enabled the government, upon the declaration of war, to move promptly to meet its shipping needs. It seized almost 100 enemy ships interned in American ports since 1914, commandeered all steel ships over 2,500 tons under construction in American shipyards and all similar ships in operation by United States shipping lines, chartered all available foreign shipping, and commenced a shipbuilding program designed to produce 1,856 new ships totalling thirteen million tons.[36]

Although the government leased many of those ships back to private companies for their operation—on government business—the war gave the President virtual control of the American merchant marine. The government's ship purchases and wartime construction also boosted the US fleet from 1.8 million gross tons in 1914 to 12.4 million by 1923, making it second only to that of Great Britain and replacing its wooden sailing vessels with modern steel freighters. The war also shifted ownership—if not operation—of the American merchant marine to the Federal Government. As it had done with the railroads, however, the government quickly began returning that fleet to private control.[37]

By a variety of means, then, the Federal Government gradually assumed an unprecedented influence, and, in some cases, direct control over that part of American industry engaged in war work. Modern warfare and a modern economy had made such central direction desirable; only the means remained at issue. Effective regulation of industry, however, also required that the government take a stronger interest in the work force, whose efforts made production possible and whose wage demands influenced its costs.

Even during the period of American neutrality, the labor shortage and the workers' willingness to organize and strike had bid up industrial wages somewhat faster than the cost of living (see Table 3.7). Although the declaration of war threatened to exacerbate that trend, the government initially allowed market forces to determine where and on what terms workers accepted employment. Later in 1917, however, several Federal agencies, those that could not afford crippling strikes or the loss of skilled workers seeking better wages elsewhere, established boards to settle the labor disputes affecting government contractors. Often created by contract provisions binding employers to pay maximum wages on a periodically adjusted scale, such boards operated in shipbuilding, construction of military cantonments, and industries that supplied the army's quartermaster and ordnance departments.[38]

Despite the limited success of the piecemeal approach, the need for overall Federal direction had become apparent by 1918. Otherwise, workers might take jobs that made a lesser contribution to the war effort as employers bid up wages beyond the growth in living costs or the level of a living wage, thus stimulating an inflation ultimately ruinous even to the workers. In January 1918, President Wilson therefore set in motion studies that made his Labor Secretary the Labor Administrator and established a National War Labor Board and a parallel policymaking body. Aiming to settle without strikes or lockouts every labor dispute posing a direct or indirect threat to war production, the Board handled some 1,250 cases according to the following principles:

- Recognition of the workers' right to organize and bargain collectively and the employers' right to associate for the same purpose.
- Protection of workers from punishment for engaging in union activity and from coercion to join a union.
- Permission of unions to seek members but maintenance of status quo on union and open shops.
- Maintenance of existing health and safety standards.
- Establishment of the 8-hour day and 40-hour week with overtime paid for additional work.
- Granting to women equal pay for equal work.
- Right of workers to a living wage for themselves and their families.
- Respect for local custom in fixing wage rates and conditions of labor.

The membership of the Board, and the subordinate agencies it created to investigate, conciliate, or mediate, introduced yet another principle: mixed membership representing the unions, the employers, and the public. In mid-1918 the new policy board added yet another innovation when it prompted creation of the US Employment Service, which sought to match unemployed workers with vacant jobs.[39]

If by the close of 1918, the government reacted to possible strikes with threatened removal of a worker's draft exemption or a bar to further employment in war industry, it had also seized the Smith and Wesson Arms Company and Western Union when they challenged government labor policies. The war, moreover, had created a new—if temporary—relationship between government and labor and established wartime principles that labor would struggle to extend to peace during the next several decades. The government, in addition, had briefly committed itself to limiting business profits (in return for labor restraint) and considering intervention on labor's behalf in contract disputes—a change in attitude so rapid as to be almost revolutionary.[40]

While the Federal Government broke new ground in its wartime relations with industry, agriculture, and labor, its intrusion into finance moved along more customary paths. Even there, however, World War I drew it into new areas.

Although Treasury Secretary McAdoo used short-term borrowing to cover temporary shortages, he relied upon new taxes and loans to finance the war. He chose not to use unbacked paper money, as had his predecessors in the Revolution and Civil War, and he proposed covering a large proportion of the war's costs through taxes—another break with the past. Had he fully succeeded, the government might better have limited the rise in wholesale prices, which stood at 204 percent of 1913 levels in September 1918 and reached 246 percent by May 1920.[41]

Sustained by the new income tax law passed after the 1913 ratification of the Sixteenth Amendment, McAdoo initially sought to raise from taxes half the war's costs of almost $38 billion (through fiscal year 1920). To that end, Congress agreed to lower the prewar minimum taxable income from $3,000 to $1,000 but kept the 2 percent basic tax rate. To preserve the law's progressive character, it also lowered from $20,000 to $5,000 the point at which the surtax started and boosted the rate on the highest incomes to 63 percent! Together with higher corporate taxes and an excess profits tax, the new taxes raised revenues sufficiently to cover 36 percent of the war's cost—though the government collected perhaps one-third of that amount after the end of hostilities. By heavily taxing higher income groups, McAdoo forced them to bear a greater share of the war's burden but did little to reduce the consumer buying power that bid against the government for the products of American industry and agriculture and thus encouraged inflation.[42]

McAdoo's sale of war bonds, a conscious attempt to repeat the Civil War success of Jay Cooke's sales to average citizens, might have compensated for failure to cover more of the war's costs with taxes. Buyers oversubscribed each of the five Liberty Bond drives, which offered bonds in $100 and $1,000 denominations in order to reach lower income groups. With the same customers in mind, McAdoo offered Thrift Savings Certificates (25 cent stamps) and $4 War Savings Certificates. Despite McAdoo's hopes of thus siphoning off buying power and cooling inflation, individuals with modest incomes probably bought less than 20 percent of the bonds, and the certificates raised a pathetically small amount (under $2 billion net). Worse yet, McAdoo encouraged citizens to borrow from banks in order to buy bonds on installment. That did little to reduce the purchasers' buying power and added to the banks' credit base, another inflationary force.[43]

In addition, McAdoo turned the theoretically independent Federal Reserve System into a virtual arm of the Treasury. The "borrow and buy" program on bond sales, the lower discount rates, the reduced reserve requirements, a change in the basis for issuing Federal Reserve notes, and permission to issue those notes against holdings of Liberty Bonds and Allied loans sustained the growth in the money supply sparked by the earlier influx of gold. Between April 1917 and May 1920, the money supply grew another 49 percent and fueled the wartime rise in prices. Although McAdoo had issued neither Continentals nor Greenbacks, his policies caused an increase in bank deposits and credit and an issuance of Federal Reserve notes that had much the same inflationary effect—even if the new currency had a sounder backing.[44]

With the government making investment in Liberty Bonds a test of patriotism, some businesses had difficulties raising money for expansion. The Federal Government therefore assumed yet another new responsibility for regulating the economy when it attacked the shortage of business capital from two reinforcing directions. On the one hand, the new Capital Issues Committee exercised voluntary control over the issuance of new securities, discouraging investment in those firms not making a contribution to the war effort. On the other, a new War Finance Corporation encouraged bank loans or provided Federal monies to war industries seeking to expand their capacity or convert facilities to war work.[45]

The differential effects of the wartime inflation also deserve attention. For commodities whose prices were controlled by such agencies as the War Industries Board, the Food or Fuel Administrations, and similar bodies, the government achieved considerable success in slowing the rate of inflation and, during the war years, even rolling back some prices (see Figure 3.3).

WORLD WAR I 109

Figure 3.3
General Wholesale Prices and Prices of Selected Basic Commodities, 1914-1918

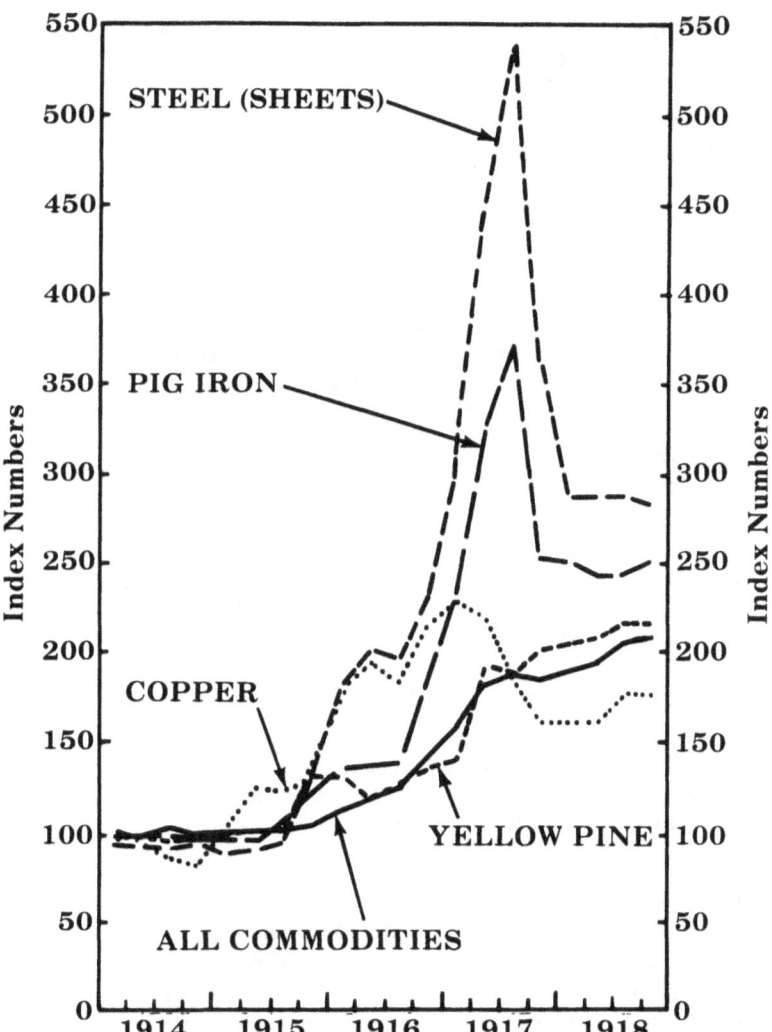

Source: Charles O. Hardy, *Wartime Control of Prices* (Washington, DC: Brookings Institution, 1940), p. 125. Reprinted by permission of the publisher.

For the vast majority of uncontrolled items, those purchased mainly by civilian consumers, the price rise continued throughout the war, and virtually everything resumed its rise in 1919. As with past wars, that inflation in effect redistributed income among various groups of Americans. The rise in farm prices boosted the farm sector's share of national income by about 5 percent, nearly matching the 1916–1918 drop in the share of nonfarm businesses. As already mentioned, the wartime taxes fell most heavily on the wealthy. Among the salaried, unionized labor engaged in factory work generally held its own, even gaining by 5 to 15 percent if the more regular employment, the overtime pay, and the entire 1913 to 1921 period weigh in the balance. The shortage of agricultural workers similarly benefited that group. As Table 3.9 shows, however, groups not engaged in war work, e.g., public school teachers and government employees, emerged from wartime inflation much injured. And individuals on fixed incomes suffered comparable harm.[46]

Table 3.9
Index of Annual Earnings in Selected Occupations, 1913–1921
(1914 = 100)

Year	All Manufacturing	Farm Labor	Public-School Teachers	Government Employees
1913	101	100	98	101
1914	100	100	100	100
1915	100	102	104	103
1916	105	104	100	99
1917	104	111	89	88
1918	108	114	78	77
1919	112	112	81	75
1920	114	116	81	70
1921	115	91	108	79

Source: Paul H. Douglas, *Real Wages in the United States, 1890–1926* (New York: Houghton Mifflin, 1930; reprint ed., New York: A. M. Kelley, 1966), pp. 187, 239–40, 246, 376, 382. Reprinted by permission of A. M. Kelley Publishers.

The high—and, for some, ruinous—rate of inflation suggests that America's mobilization effort, which caused Federal intervention in a host of areas theretofore believed to lie beyond the bounds of governmental interference, nevertheless fell short of success. The fact that the army of the "arsenal of democracy" fought the war with foreign weapons reinforces that conclusion. American troops used helmets and rifles of a British design and relied on light artillery supplied by the French. American industry completed only one antiaircraft gun before the armistice and delivered the first De Haviland planes (a copy of a British design) only late in 1918. None of the 23,000 tanks ordered by the War Department arrived before the armistice. The programs designed to build a "bridge" of ships and planes to Europe began to produce results only as the war ended. To a large degree, American troops and American supplies went to Europe on foreign ships.[47]

America's economic contribution was not for that reason negligible. The United States continued to supply the Allies with food and munitions without which the war could not have been won—at least by the Allies and in 1918. The American contribution had to be drawn, moreover, from an industrial base already at full employment and after April 1917 suffering the loss of workers to the armed forces. Having made virtually no advance preparation for war, government and industry took nearly a year to prepare for maximum support of the nation's forces—a preparation whose effect was being felt just as the war ended, unexpectedly, in November 1918.

At the same time, the philosophy with which the United States had approached its economic mobilization may have prolonged that preparation. The government avoided the expense and possible chaos of simply bidding in the market for the goods it needed—as in the Civil War. But its intervention—though unprecedented for the United States—fell short of that war socialism or dictatorial control described by some contemporary observers. Wishing to preserve the basic structure of the American economy (seizing industries only when no alternative seemed acceptable), the government relied upon the voluntary cooperation of its suppliers. To facilitate its dealings with industry, agriculture, and labor, the government encouraged creation of private economic associations. It then relied upon those organizations for essential information about the economy and for experts to staff governmental mobilization agencies, which blurred the line between public and private much as had the Revolutionary War—if for different reasons. Rather than use the power of government to commandeer or control plants, farms, and workers, the government chose to enter into cooperative relationships that gave private associations considerable influence on public policy.[48]

The groups affected by governmental action seemed to prefer that approach. The businessmen who staffed the War Industries Board and similar agencies wanted to show the benefits of business-government cooperation, which they hoped to use in peace as in war to maintain a stable, orderly economic environment free of conflict over antitrust issues. Those businessmen sought, in effect, corporate planning under government auspices.[49] As previously described, labor leaders too came to see the advantages of cooperating with a government that might intervene in its behalf. Farmers also lost much of their hostility to government intervention, which they would later expect (sometimes in vain) to maintain farm prices and income in peace as well as war. And in the system of farm and home agents, much strengthened by the war's demands, farmers discovered a government-financed network useful for making their needs known in Washington and for organizing the political pressures essential to gaining Federal support.[50]

A Divided Public

The American response to the outbreak of war in Europe and the social tensions of the neutrality period suggested that the nation might need to mobilize public opinion behind the war effort quite as much as the government strove to mobilize the various factors of production. Following that suggestion led the government into new areas and enhanced its powers, just as had its economic intervention.

The initial reaction to the events of August 1914 represented a blend of horror and relief. The Secretary of Agriculture, David Houston, recalled feeling "dazed and horror stricken," as though "the end of things had come." The *New York Times* concluded that "European nations have reverted to the condition of savage tribes roaming the forests and falling upon each other in a fury of blood and carnage to achieve the ambitious designs of chieftains clad in skins and drunk on mead." At least, felt Americans, the United States remained 3,000 miles away and uninvolved. "We have never appreciated so keenly as now," wrote one Midwestern editor, "the foresight exercised by our forefathers in emigrating from Europe."[51]

The strength of the reaction stemmed from more than relief at not being involved in a suicidal bloodletting. Also at work on the minds of Americans was the way the war—among apparently civilized nations—challenged the very assumptions of their cultural universe. Americans had confidently interpreted history as a story of inevitable human progress. The religious sometimes attributed that advance to the workings of a divine plan; the secular-minded traced it either to a sort of Darwinian cultural evolution or to the intelligent social engineering of progressive experts. Reinforcing that expectation was a belief in the existence of moral absolutes and unchanging social values. From that perspective, the war suggested that Europeans had gone berserk, denying their civilization and its values. In a Freudian sense, they were regressing, and their behavior made it difficult to believe in the underlying goodness of the social order and the fundamental decency of all mankind, or to anticipate the imminent arrival of either a secular or Christian millennium. At least until the United States intervened, however, Americans could cling to a belief in their nation's uniqueness and hope that by remaining aloof they might continue in the Western Hemisphere to create a just society of democracy and peace as an example to the world.[52]

Woodrow Wilson tapped that sentiment in 1917 by making American intervention—rather than continued neutrality—the means to accomplish that national mission. The United States, he claimed, fought to "make the world safe for democracy." He thus drew the support of the many idealists and reformers who would use the domestic wartime centralization to continue the reform of American society and the victory in Europe to improve world conditions—eliminating both at home and abroad the deprivations and injustices and the denial of popular government that caused war.

Wilson's stirring description of American goals aimed to inspire more citizens, however, than those concerned about social reform. For the neutrality period had also highlighted many deep divisions within American society.

Differences in ethnic background drew the first line that set some citizens apart from others. Although Americans initially had no clear opinion about the moral responsibility for World War I, and had once been favorably disposed toward Germany and its culture, several events quickly built sympathy for the Allied cause among a majority of Americans. The invasion of neutral Belgium, the destruction of Louvain, and the allegedly atrocious behavior of the Kaiser's troops created the earliest anti-German feelings. Closer to home, the crude attempts of the German and Austrian embassies to finance propaganda favorable to the Central Powers and their use of saboteurs to disrupt the manufacture and transport of munitions to the Allies struck most Americans as a further trampling on the rights of neutrals. And the German use of submarine warfare, especially the sinking of the *Lusitania*, seemed to confirm the tales of German barbarism being spread by the British.[53]

The 2.5 million Americans of German birth, their almost six million children, and uncounted others of more distant German background objected to such ethnic libels. They reacted not so much out of loyalty to the Kaiser, but out of fear for the ways that anti-Germanism or American intervention might adversely affect their own position in society. Moreover, the Puritanical Anglo-Saxon element that had taken a strong pro-Ally stance almost from the war's start had long been the German-Americans' principal political opponents in the prewar fight over prohibition, sabbatarian blue laws, and the closure of church schools—policies that challenged German-American customs and that group's pluralistic view of American society.[54]

Swedish-Americans, while like the German-Americans simply hoping to keep their new country truly neutral and uninvolved in the European war, also expressed sympathy for the German cause.[55] The German-Americans' principal ethnic supporters, however, acted out of hatred for one of the Allies rather than love for either of the Central Powers. By 1914, Americans born in Ireland or of an Irish-born parent were only half so numerous as German-Americans, but their intense hatred of England quickly aligned the two groups in efforts to counter Allied propaganda, end American munitions shipments, and keep the United States out of the war.[56]

As one-half the German-born Americans and most of the Irish were Roman Catholic, ethnic tension over the war spilled over into religious life. Prior to 1917, the Church, its nationally circulated journals, and probably most of its communicants gave genuine support to American neutrality. Many of its publications and some of its clergy, however, sympathized with Germany and condemned the propaganda spread by Protestant England and anticlerical France and Italy. Among Protestant churches, German Lutherans held to official neutrality while also trying to counter Allied propaganda and create sympathy for Germany.[57] Hatred of Russia's anti-Semitism, its domestic pogroms, and its support for attacks on Jews throughout Europe—in contrast to German leniency and removal of civil and political restrictions—caused many of America's four million Jews (80 percent of whom came from eastern Europe) also to take an anti-Allied stance, out of hatred of Russia.[58]

The American government thus declared war in April 1917 with some reason to believe that perhaps 15 percent of the population would oppose the sacrifices necessary for an Allied victory. Ethnic worries, however, extended even deeper and in the prewar period had focused on other groups as well. Between 1880 and 1920 over twenty million immigrants had arrived in the United States, and some 35 percent of the population was either foreign born or had a foreign-born parent (see Table 3.10). More significantly, immigration from southern and eastern Europe increased sharply in the 1880s (almost four times the number of the previous decade), surpassed that from northern and western Europe (the traditional sources) before the turn of the century, and added another six million by 1910.[59]

Table 3.10
Ethnic Americans in 1910
(Millions)

Country	Foreign Born	Both Parents Foreign Born	One Parent Foreign Born	Total
Germany	2.5	3.9	1.9	8.3
Ireland	1.4	2.1	1.0	4.5
England, Wales & Scotland	1.2	0.8	1.2	3.2
Russia & Finland	1.7	1.0	0.1	2.8
Austria-Hungary	1.7	0.9	0.1	2.7
Italy	1.3	0.7	0.1	2.1
TOTAL (includes unlisted groups)	13.3	12.9	6.0	32.2

Source: From THE GERMANS IN AMERICA by Theodore Huebener. Copyright 1962 by the author. Reprinted with the permission of the publisher CHILTON BOOK COMPANY, Radnor, PA.

Some native-born Americans feared those "new immigrants" because of their religion (most often Catholicism but also Judaism) or the radical political beliefs they allegedly brought to the United States. The principal source of prewar nativism, however, derived from theories identifying the new arrivals as culturally or racially inferior. Some nativist organizations, joined by prewar social workers, therefore advocated educational programs to insure the new arrivals quickly shed old ways and adopted "American" values and customs. Other nativists, however, regarded new arrivals from eastern and southern Europe as racially unassimilable and consequently worked for laws to restrict further immigration from those sources.[60]

Before 1914 the public showed little interest in the Americanization movement. But the ethnic tensions and fears that began to build during the neutrality period soon produced a narrow nationalism suspicious of all "hyphenated" Americans and demanding that they prove, in the words of one 1916 banner, "Absolute and Unqualified Loyalty" to their new country. Total conformity to American ways and American values, as defined by the nativist, became the only way to avoid ethnic persecution.[61]

The government's fear that disaffected citizens might undermine the war effort received nourishment from yet another source: the American peace movement, which combined at least four somewhat different lines of thought. Two of those philosophies derived from sectarian religious groups, traditional opponents of war but numerically insignificant in twentieth-century America. The non-resistants (for example, Mennonites) sought to withdraw from society and politics, regarded all governments as evil yet not to be resisted except when demanding such submission as the performance of military service. The second group, the Quakers, were also pacifist but politically active and sought through social reform to eliminate the injustices they believed caused violence. Following the American declaration of war, those sectarian pacifists continued their opposition to war and became the source of most of the conscientious objectors who defied the wartime military draft.[62]

From two newer sources, however, the pre-intervention peace movement drew its main strength. One of them, the secular peace societies, had collapsed during the Civil War but gained new vigor at the end of the century as the United States became increasingly involved in world affairs. Drawing upon the nineteenth-century faith in human reason, inevitable progress, Christian brotherhood, and cooperation among the great "civilized" powers, the societies attracted a large and influential following in the decade before World War I. Lawyers joined groups like the Inter-Parliamentary Union and the American Society of International Law to work for peace through international law and organization. Educators supported the World Peace Foundation and the Carnegie Endowment for International Peace, which hoped to end war through education and research into its causes. Politicians and businessmen joined the movement in large numbers, some hoping that free trade would spread prosperity and civilization and bring an end to war. Liberal Protestant clergy formed the Church Peace Union and sought world peace through the spread of Christian brotherhood. Never before had the peace movement such prestige and influence in American life.[63]

Through most of the neutrality period those peace societies battled the American preparedness movement, which rather than advocate intervention in the European war urged rearmament in preparation for the war's end. Whoever won, the movement claimed, the victor would emerge militarily strengthened. No longer restrained by the European balance of power, which had secured the United States in the nineteenth century, the winner would use its new strength to capture Latin American markets and possibly create a South American empire, actions that might involve the United States in a defensive war.[64]

If the clash between the peace movement and the preparedness campaign revealed another of the fissures in American society, the fourth spring from which the peace societies drew strength proved a source of division within the peace movement as well. The outbreak of war had increasingly drawn radicals, social-gospel clergymen, and the social reform wing of the progressive movement into the campaign for peace. Convinced that an unjust social order caused war, they sought world peace through social reform—at home and abroad—and fought the preparedness campaign through such societies as the Women's Peace Party and the American Union Against Militarism.[65]

Mobilizing Public Opinion

In April 1917, Woodrow Wilson, who only six months earlier had retained his grip on the Presidency through an implied promise to keep the United States at peace, thus led a divided nation into war, a struggle that would require a greater unity of national purpose and cooperative effort than any of its previous military struggles.

He and his administration immediately set about creating that sense of common national purpose. Gaining the support of the large pro-Ally and preparedness factions required no special effort; they had long chided the President for lack of boldness. Wilson's firm yet cautious approach nevertheless convinced them and many others that by March 1917 the United States had no honorable alternative to a declaration of war.

Certain of Wilson's war aims also helped him align former advocates of neutrality with the war effort. To German-Americans the promise of a "peace without victory" based upon the Fourteen Points seemed fair to Germany, and whatever their sympathies, they were above all loyal, law-abiding Americans. One German-American mother summarized their feelings.

> I love my Fatherland. Why shouldn't I? What I think personally about these things I keep to myself. But—my three boys, they are Americans. What must be, must be. I would be a bad mother if I did not teach them to love and live and die for their country, America.

With few exceptions and only occasional displays of reluctance, German Americans and the Lutheran Church dropped their opposition to intervention and gave the war effort their support.[66]

Irish-Americans, with the exception of a few extremist factions that wanted nothing to do with England, e.g., the Friends of Irish Freedom, also quickly dropped their opposition and gave Wilson their support. The Fourteen Points' espousal of the principle of national self-determination, which implied postwar freedom for Ireland, strengthened that support—until the President refused to put that subject on the agenda at Versailles.[67]

Wilson's war aims, and Germany's behavior in the two months before the declaration of war, insured that the Roman Catholic church acted in concert with the changing views of its two largest ethnic groups. Church leaders wishing to demonstrate that Roman Catholics were loyal, patriotic Americans soon threw their full weight behind the war effort.[68]

Jewish opposition, too, quickly melted. The revolution in Russia promised an end to anti-Semitism in that Allied nation, and a German defeat might lead to demands that its Turkish ally cede Palestine and create a national homeland for Jews.[69]

The last of Wilson's Fourteen Points, the one calling for establishment of a postwar league of nations, helped win the support of most of the prewar peace societies. Led by nationalists who believed in peace through order, the peace movement had shunned narrow pacifism even before the American declaration of war. Many of its members consequently supported preparedness, which in 1916 was defensive in orientation, and had joined new bodies like the League to Enforce Peace, which advocated an international organization to settle disputes and keep the peace—if necessary, by force! A "peace without victory," they believed, could remake the world and create the conditions in which a collective security agency could maintain a lasting peace. With that hope, the peace movement's most prestigious societies and their most influential members abandoned earlier opposition to American intervention.[70]

Wilson's promise to "make the world safe for democracy" also appealed to the liberal clergymen who led the large Protestant denominations, the

Federal Council of Churches (FCC), and the Church Peace Union. American intervention, they believed, constituted a "war against war," and the proposed league of nations represented, said the FCC, "the political expression of the Kingdom of God on earth." Believing such lofty goals justified a resort to violence, the churches for the most part threw themselves wholeheartedly into war work. A few individuals, however, lost track of the vision sustaining liberal Protestantism. They joined evangelist Billy Sunday who prayed that God, acting through the US Army, would bare His "mighty arm and beat back that great pack of hungry, wolfish Huns, whose fangs drip with blood and gore."[71]

A few churchmen, often those with a social-gospel background, and some of the social reformers drawn into the peace movement in 1914 nevertheless continued to support antiwar activities. They considered all war dehumanizing and therefore a direct challenge to the individual human fulfillment they considered the goal of life. For them no international body could keep the peace. Pacifists, instead, must work transnationally to eliminate the social injustices that bred war. Although not always party members, those radical pacifists tended to accept a Socialist analysis of the shortcomings of the world order. Along with nonresistants and Quakers, the radicals continued to oppose American intervention. To work for the early return of peace, they became active in such antiwar groups as the secular and leftist People's Council of America for Democracy and Peace or the religious Fellowship of Reconciliation—which together barely kept alive the much diminished antiwar movement.[72]

Most of the reform movement, though initially fearful that intervention would crush progressivism, nevertheless gave its support to the Wilson administration. The prewar reformers had believed they could use institutions to redesign society scientifically and eliminate its evils. Anticipating that war would expand the power of government, they therefore hoped to use that new power "not merely to defend our house," wrote Walter Lippmann, "but to put it in order." While fighting German despotism, he added, Americans could "turn with fresh interests to our own tyrannies—to our Colorado mines, our autocratic steel industries, our sweatshops, and our slums." Convinced that Wilson's liberal war aims and a war-strengthened government would both expand the scope and enhance the prospect of reform, American progressives for the most part enlisted in the war effort.[73]

Insofar as reform quite directly assisted the war effort, the progressives did score a few successes. The war, for example, proved decisive in the movement for national prohibition. Arguing that alcoholism, the saloon, and the liquor trade corrupted politics and caused crime, juvenile deliquency, poverty, prostitution, and disease, prohibition's advocates had by 1918 passed dry laws of varying extent in more than half the states. The wartime need to conserve grain and transportation, to protect the morals of soldiers, and to keep civilian heads clear for war production helped convert that simple majority into the 36 ratifications needed for a national prohibition amendment.[74]

The previously described agencies with which the government sought to regulate the wartime economy also represented a step toward the type of Federal economic regulation that the reformers desired, as did wartime support for the rights of labor. Those programs, moreover, became models for New Deal agencies created to meet a later economic and social rather than military crisis.[75]

But the reformers also achieved a number of minor wartime successes. Though applicable only to members of the armed forces, the war brought acceptance of family allowances and insurance as part of an employment contract. Servicemen's families received a monthly allowance until their discharge, disability, or death. In the event of death, the government paid the widow a monthly income, and permanent disability produced similar payments to the service member. The government also offered servicemen a voluntary life insurance program that wrote 4.5 million policies by 1919. The housing shortages created by the expansion of war plants drew the Federal Government into a new area when Congress authorized $60 million for a Federal housing program. Thousands of social reformers received an opportunity to practice the kind of welfare work they wished to extend to society generally when they took wartime jobs with the Red Cross, YMCA, and government bodies that aided soldiers' families or sought to protect the morals and sustain the morale of America's fighting men. At the state level, changed attitudes produced more enduring programs for aid to dependent children, voluntary workmen's compensation programs, and private pension schemes.[76]

In a somewhat different way, the wartime activities of women justified and assisted passage of the women's suffrage amendment. Women not only aided the war by entering the industrial work force, they also engaged in a wide range of volunteer work. They established canteens at military posts, helped war plants find qualified workers, aided soldiers' families, contributed to the success of the Food Administration's conservation program and the Treasury's Liberty Bond drives, provided trained volunteer drivers for government agencies, and prepared clothing and food kits for men overseas. Serving in the Women's Land Army, they eased the labor shortage by helping farmers harvest crops. And when the Navy and Marines recruited almost 24,000 women for usually clerical noncombatant work, women for the first time legally entered the armed services as enlisted persons. "The services of women during the supreme crisis," Woodrow Wilson told suffrage leader Carrie Chapman Catt, "have been of the most signal usefulness and distinction. It is high time that part of our debt should be acknowledged and paid." The Nineteenth Amendment became the first installment.[77]

The war aims formulated by President Wilson and the hopes of businessmen, union leaders, reformers, and women's groups to use the war to further some purpose besides victory had thus won to the war effort many Americans previously hostile to intervention. But the government remained unwilling to rely solely on indirect means to mobilize public opinion behind the war, and Wilson therefore created America's first wartime propaganda agency—the Committee on Public Information. Led by George Creel and many prominent muckrakers of the progressive era, and using their seemingly objective but actually quite emotional methods, the committee mobilized artists, writers, volunteer public orators, and the infant motion picture and advertising industries to promote the war. It enforced voluntary press censorship, and its daily and weekly summaries of military news shaped newspaper coverage of the war. Its millions of pamphlets and posters and thousands of speakers helped sell both the war and war bonds and instill in Americans a love of democracy, a hatred of German authoritarianism, and a crusading spirit determined to destroy America's enemies—at home or abroad.[78]

Should Americans fail to respond willingly to the appeal of patriotism, the government gained the services of American men by resorting to its first thoroughly modern military draft. Called Selective Service, the law raised over 70 percent of the nation's almost four million men in uniform, excluded states from the raising of troops (except for the units of the existing National Guard), and blocked the appointment of officers with little claim to a commission except their political connections. By eliminating commutation fees, the hiring of substitutes, and voluntary enlistments and selectively determining who would serve, the government also tried to keep men of draft age in those jobs where they might best contribute to the war effort.[79]

Although an immediate and extensive reliance on conscription reversed a national tradition, registration and induction proceeded with no significant opposition and none of the riots that had marked the Civil War draft. Almost 9.6 million of the 10.2 million men of draft age voluntarily registered. About 337,000 men dodged the draft, and local draft boards granted conscientious objector status to 56,830. Of the 20,873 conscientious objectors inducted, all but 3,989 mostly religious objectors decided during training to serve with their units. Of the latter number, one-third eventually accepted noncombatant service in the quartermaster, medical, or engineer corps, and another third accepted furloughs to work in civilian industry, agriculture, or overseas relief agencies. The rest were either tried and convicted for refusing to serve or were awaiting disposition at the time of the armistice. The conscientious objectors have subsequently received considerable attention, but they were truly a minor problem—especially in light of the large numbers of Americans opposed to intervention prior to 1917.[80]

For Americans of any age who would oppose the war effort, the government relied upon the 1917 Espionage Act, its later amendment—the Sedition Act—and selected provisions of certain older statutes to insure their silence and at least the appearance of cooperation. During the Civil War, Lincoln had used his war powers and military authorities to seize individuals who interfered with or directly threatened the war effort, and he promptly released them when assured of their future good behavior. Wilson, however, chose to act through Congress and the civil courts to punish with fines and prison terms any false statements designed to impede the war effort as well as any obstruction of military recruiting or attempts to cause disloyalty in the armed services. As amended by the Sedition Act, the law also prohibited obstruction of Liberty Bond sales, language likely to promote resistance to the war effort, and verbal attacks on the government, the Constitution, the armed forces, or the flag. The new laws also permitted the government to close the mails to publications whose contents constituted a violation of the Espionage Act. Passage of such legislation marked the revival of a threat to free speech such as had not occurred since the Alien and Sedition Acts of 1798.[81]

If carefully construed and enforced, the Espionage Act probably did not violate the Constitution, and the Supreme Court sustained it on review after the war. Indeed, the Act had grown out of legitimate attempts to prevent expected German sabotage and misinformation, and the Wilson administration may have initially applied it so vigorously out of a desire to preclude any widespread interference with conscription. The President, moreover, denied any intention to prevent legitimate discussion and comment on public affairs.[82]

In some 2,000 prosecutions under the Act, however, its application broke down at all levels—judges, juries, and prosecutors. Abuses became so gross, in fact, that late in 1918 the Attorney General forbade further prosecution by district attorneys without his specific approval. By that time, however, the quarter million members of 1,200 local branches of the American Protective League (APL), established to help the understaffed Bureau of Investigation uncover German spies, had produced widespread tyranny and oppression. Issued a 75-cent badge marked "Secret Service Division," APL members illegally impersonated Federal agents, conducted warrantless searches, intimidated fellow citizens, and even made arrests. A body created to counter an anticipated spy menace became instead the agent of local groups seeking to punish their enemies and enforce conformity of opinion and behavior under cover of law. Sustained by local prosecutors and courts, the action of the APL constituted a massive violation of civil liberties, for which the Wilson administration must share some of the responsibility.[83]

German-Americans became the most numerous victims of the APL and other self-appointed local bodies that claimed to define the meaning of "100 percent Americanism." Many German-Americans were tried and convicted for inconsequential statements that fevered minds saw as undermining the war effort. On the "testimony" of his five-year-old daughter, for example, one German in California received five years in prison for privately criticizing the President. Elsewhere local mobs attacked German-Americans for such "disloyalty" as failure to buy Liberty Bonds. Those attacks included being forced to publicly kiss the flag, tarring and feathering, threatened hangings, and the lynching of Robert Prager in Collinsville, Illinois. By November 1918, local groups had outlawed the teaching of German in schools, banned the playing of Beethoven's music, and boycotted performances by artists of German background. In a furor of misplaced and humorless patriotism, towns like Berlin, Iowa, changed their names (in that case to Lincoln), Cincinnati's German Street converted to English Street, and sauerkraut became "liberty cabbage." German family names like Ochs and Schwartz became Anglicized as Oaks and Black. In the end, such oppression demoralized a German-American community once proud of its heritage and forced it to seek safety by rapid assimilation into American life.[84]

The Federal Government joined with local interests in the persecution of two other unpopular groups that had taken positions critical of American intervention—the Socialists and the International Workers of the World (IWW). In the West, business-inspired local mobs attacked the latter with a vengeance—in Arizona, for example, kidnapping and expelling 1,300 IWW members and in Montana lynching a national IWW leader. In the Northwest, the Federal Government sent in army personnel to break an IWW strike in the lumber industry. Elsewhere, Justice Department agents acting under the Espionage Act raided IWW offices, arrested several hundred of the union's leaders, and wrongly convicted most of subversion—despite the union's careful avoidance of antiwar activities after April 1917. By the end of World War I, the government had effectively suppressed the IWW.[85]

The war's role in destroying the Socialist Party remains less clear. Internal personal, ethnic, and doctrinal disputes did play a role in the party's postwar decline. But so did wartime vigilante attacks on perhaps one-third of the party's local halls, the closure of the mails to Socialist publications, and the arrest and conviction of many party leaders, including Eugene V. Debs, its three-time Presidential nominee. During the war many native-born Socialists left the party in support of Wilson's liberal war aims and were often replaced by recently arrived immigrants. That development gave the postwar party a more alien character, just as its antiwar and pro-Bolshevik stance made it appear the agent of foreign governments. There can be little doubt that wartime events greatly—if not decisively—weakened the Socialist Party.[86]

President Wilson's efforts to create wartime unity by mobilizing public opinion behind a war to "make the world safe for democracy" thus ended in massive official and unofficial assaults on American civil liberties. Ironically, Wilson had predicted that result when in April 1917 he told *New York World* editor Frank Cobb:

> Once lead this people into war and they'll forget there ever was such a thing as tolerance. To fight you must be brutal and ruthless, and the spirit of ruthless brutality will enter into the very fibre of our national life, infecting Congress, the courts, the policeman on the beat, the man in the street. Conformity would be the only virtue, and every man who refused to conform would have to pay the penalty.[87]

The President nevertheless did little to prevent that result and much (perhaps unintentionally) to insure the accuracy of his prophecy. Moreover, the war in the end did little to achieve the sense of shared national unity and purpose he had sought, and the country emerged from its intervention in Europe more bitterly divided and frustrated—socially, economically, and politically—than in April 1917.

Roots of Social Tension

Unlike previous American wars, which tended to calm nativist feelings, World War I produced mixed results. After April 1917, anti-Catholicism became less significant, and ethnic hatreds previously directed at immigrants from southern and eastern Europe became intensely focused on German-Americans, perhaps because this was the first war with a country that had sent the United States a significant portion of its non-English, foreign-born population. With the end of the war and the German-Americans' conscious pursuit of complete Americanization, however, the purely ethnic strain of nativism, too, became less influential.[88]

The war, however, gave another aspect of nativism a new importance. Because radicals had opposed American intervention and had been the principal focus of wartime disunity, postwar nativism emphasized its antiradical strain. Because aliens unfortunately seemed to constitute a disproportionate share of the membership in radical organizations, nativists could overlook wartime sacrifices by Americans born in southern or eastern Europe and keep ethnic nativism alive, if in muted form, by associating allegedly un-American radicalism with the immigration of foreign ideas along with foreign peoples.

Wartime fear of radicalism thus led to varied forms of postwar hostility and social tension. It contributed, for example, to major legislative victories for those who would restrict the immigration of nationalities supposedly possessing undesirable ethnic or cultural traits and either deport or bar the entry of individuals professing radical political ideas.[89] Wartime hatred and the fear of radicalism also played a role in the Red Scare that convulsed the country and led to further massive civil liberties violations in 1919 and 1920.[90] Hostilities between radicals and reformers also impeded their cooperation in the postwar revival of the peace movement. Liberal internationalists, who worked for peace through governments and the promotion of international organizations, and liberal pacifists, who tended toward radicalism and suspicion of governmental bodies, generally formed separate organizations and remained wary of one another.[91]

Insofar as attitudes were concerned, the war also did little to improve race relations and, in fact, provoked racial tension. Despite the Wilson administration's systematic efforts to extend the modest, uneven segregation of the civil service that existed under the Republicans, and Wilson's failure to appoint blacks to midlevel governmental posts normally reserved to them, Afro-Americans had given their enthusiastic support to the war effort. An Allied victory in a war for democracy, claimed even the radical leader W.E.B. DuBois, would give black Americans "the right to vote and the right to work and the right to live without insult."[92]

As already described, the war attracted migration by blacks to the North, where they temporarily found better jobs and somewhat greater freedom. Racial discrimination thus became a national rather than a sectional issue. The war failed, however, to provide blacks an opportunity to enhance their social and political position through battlefield heroics. Only under considerable political pressure did the Wilson administration briefly open a single camp for training black officers and abandon its plans to confine black soldiers to menial noncombatant duty. Although the administration raised two black divisions, it prevented their regiments from training together in the United States—to insure that blacks remained a minority at every military post. When the black units reached France, General Pershing assigned the four regiments of the 93d Division to separate units of the French Army, where Americans easily ignored their wartime heroism. The 92nd Division, however, got more publicity than it desired. Filled with rural blacks who lacked the education, social cohesion, and self-esteem of the black National Guardsmen fighting so well with the French army, and led by poorly motivated noncommissioned officers and middle-class black junior officers who did not know their jobs and resented the supervision of more senior whites, the division predictably failed when committed to combat—a result that many white Americans eagerly accepted as further evidence of black racial inferiority. At home, blacks met extreme racism. As they crowded into Northern cities in search of jobs and housing and became more assertive of their rights, they met white hostility that on occasion burst forth in ugly race riots like those that killed several hundred black Americans in East St. Louis, Illinois.[93]

Unlike previous major wars, World War I thus heightened rather than quieted racism. In 1919, lynchings of Afro-Americans—ten of them ex-soldiers and several of them still in uniform—disgraced the United States at almost twice the 1917 rate. Blacks also faced job discrimination and labor violence, and a Chicago riot led to thirty-eight deaths and over five hundred serious injuries when a black swimmer unintentionally drifted onto a section of beach reserved for whites. Black soldiers had nevertheless returned from France with pride in their accomplishments, the experience of life in a white society that for the most part did not practice racial discrimination, and (along with increasing numbers of blacks who had remained at home) a determination to demand justice and win their rightful place in American society.[94]

For their contributions to the war effort—whether in the industrial work force, in the naval services, or in traditional and volunteer roles— American women received one tangible result: the right to vote. Public service may also have given women recognition, enhanced self-respect, and even a sense of sisterhood and feminist awareness. Nevertheless, few of the employment changes due solely to the war survived. Equal pay for equal work became a chimera, and possession of the vote brought no significant advance toward equal rights. Such wartime success as the women's movement achieved left its radical and conservative wings divided on the appropriate steps with which to follow the suffrage victory.[95]

Belying the wartime unity and religious enthusiasm with which American churches of all faiths joined in support of the war and Wilson's foreign policy, World War I marked the start of what Winthrop Hudson called the post-Protestant era in America and the appearance of a new division within the Protestant community. In part that new era stemmed from demographic change unrelated to the war—the arrival after 1880 of millions of immigrants of the Roman Catholic, Eastern Orthodox, or Jewish faiths. The new arrivals located in America's largest cities, whose power and influence in twentieth-century America magnified the significance of those minority faiths.[96]

In another sense, the new era stemmed from moral and cultural changes only partially related to the war, which seemed to speed the transition from the idealism and moral certainty of the nineteenth-century social order to the materialism, hedonism, and cynicism characteristic of many Americans in the 1920s.[97] As America's civil religion, Protestantism generally moved with that secular trend and increasingly focused on the problems of modern, urban, industrial America. Reflecting war experiences, the major denominations also became better organized, more bureaucratic, less preoccupied with doctrinal differences, and supportive of ecumenical cooperation and the creation of community churches that preached a generalized Protestantism.[98]

The war also made direct contributions to America's new religious developments. Although also somewhat more secularized, Roman Catholics, for example, found in the war a means of achieving social acceptability. Among Protestants, however, the war had a divisive effect. It seemed to challenge evolutionary belief in inevitable human social progress, and its attacks on everything German discredited the religious modernism and higher criticism (less literal interpretation) of the Bible associated with Germany. To some Protestants, the war also seemed to be the violent clash that would precede the Second Coming. While liberal Protestants overlooked those developments and embraced the modern order arising in America's urban areas, a rising Fundamentalist movement took them to heart. The Fundamentalists consequently challenged Darwin, scientific analysis of the Bible, and the social gospel. In so doing, they tried to return America to a religious orthodoxy already on the wane before World War I and succeeded only in opening a major new fissure in American religious life.[99]

Socially, the war had thus contributed to nativist antiradicalism, heightened race tension, unsettling moral changes, and divisions within American Protestantism. The war consequently helped shape several of the principal social issues of the 1920s—the Red Scare, the Scopes "monkey trial," and the birth of a new Ku Klux Klan devoted to 100 percent Americanism, which meant defense of the virtues of rural America, promotion of religious and political orthodoxy, and preference for Americans of Anglo-Saxon origin.

An Uncertain Economic Future

The war seemed to have brought great economic benefits to the United States by hastening its achievement of the world's industrial, commercial, and financial leadership. The speed of the war-induced changes, however, probably did the nation, and the world, a disservice by allowing it too little time to adapt its institutions and values for leadership in a world economic order suffering from revolution, reparations, war debts, excessive nationalism, and the human and material losses of four years of very bloody conflict.[100]

In addition to the previously described benefits to specific industries, businessmen drew general advantages from the war. It revived the turn-of-the-century push toward greater business concentration, encouraged standardization of products, and continued the trend toward greater mechanization and more efficient business organization. The war also spurred adoption of new production techniques—greater reliance on electricity, use of chemical processes, scientific management, and assembly-line methods. The wartime experience in industrial self-regulation under government control also improved attitudes toward businessmen and allowed such self-regulation to continue even as the government dismantled its wartime controls. The new trade associations, often formed at the government's suggestion, facilitated postwar self-regulation in fields with large numbers of highly competitive firms.[101]

In an effort to combat unions, businessmen built on wartime experiences by extending welfare capitalism—the use of fringe benefits, improved working conditions, and company-inspired labor organizations as alternatives to trade unionism.[102] Labor unions, however, expected to extend into the postwar period their wartime gains in membership and, with government support, their ability to coerce business into paying higher wages and granting a shorter work day. Labor's aggressiveness led to a new round of strikes (which contributed to fears of radicalism and the resultant Red Scare) but little government support. In frustration, union leaders realized that their close wartime relationship with government, unlike that of businessmen, had not survived the end of military hostilities.[103]

With the collapse of the wartime boost to agricultural prosperity, which extended into 1921, farmers received even greater disappointments. As a result of the war, overexpanded, overmechanized, and overmortgaged farmers faced two decades of declining prosperity caused by shrinking markets, falling prices, and rising costs. For farmers, the war left two positive legacies: a better appreciation of the government's ability to manage the agricultural economy for the benefit of farmers, and, in the farm extension service, the first of the new lobbying organizations with which they would seek to insure that the government used that ability.[104]

Political Upheaval

Wartime political conditions proved little more enduring than the war-induced economic cooperation or the sometimes coerced social harmony. Unlike Lincoln, Wilson avoided the unilateral assumption of wide powers and, as a legislative leader, worked with Congress in the determination of mobilization policy. Giving Congress a role sometimes delayed action (as with the Food and Fuel Control Act) and occasionally forced Wilson to offer compromises when he might have preferred inaction (as with the Overman Act to reorganize governmental departments). But Wilson also successfully opposed Congressional proposals for a Joint Committee on the Conduct of the War and similar efforts to oversee his supervision of the executive branch. Though he unquestionably preserved the tradition of wartime Presidential leadership, Wilson nevertheless successfully involved Congress in the making of overall mobilization policy—at the expense of a good deal of his energy and a full testing of his legislative skill in order to maintain the control over Congress he had established in 1913.[105]

The war, by disrupting the Democratic coalition, nevertheless ultimately led to the loss of both Wilson's control of Congress and the Democrats' control of the government. When Wilson and the Democrats won the 1912 elections, they clearly did so as a minority party whose triumph rested on a split in Republican ranks. By 1916, however, Wilson's progressive policies and skillful use of the peace issue enabled the Democrats to build a coalition just sufficient to defeat the reunited Republicans. Because of flaws in his wartime leadership, Wilson nevertheless failed to strengthen that coalition sufficiently to overturn the historic political dominance of the Republicans, which dated back to 1896, and to make the Democrats the new majority party. His wartime controls on wheat prices cost him the support of the Midwest, just as his government's violations of civil liberties and close cooperation with business drove many progressives out of Democratic ranks. The decision to intervene—plus wartime prohibition—may have offended German- and Irish-American Democrats, who later felt outrage at the results of the Versailles negotiations (German war guilt and no independent Ireland). To those war-related shocks to the Wilsonian coalition must be added the loss of labor votes due to the President's failure to support the unions in their postwar strikes.[106]

The Democrats' wartime loss became the Republicans' wartime gain. To avoid charges of disloyalty, the latter party took a strong prowar stance and publicly criticized the administration only for alleged inefficiency and lack of vigor in prosecuting the war. In an attempt to dominate the President while appearing to be superpatriots, the Republicans unsuccessfully advocated the creation of a wartime Joint Committee, tried to reorganize the military departments, proposed creation of supracabinet agencies that might bridle the President, and initiated several worrisome investigations of executive conduct. In no sense had the war adjourned politics. The Republicans fought Wilson at every step and used the defection of Democratic voters to win control of the Senate in 1918 and the government in 1920.[107]

Reformers in both parties found themselves in a weakened position, at least in part due to the war. As already described, when wartime reforms had been more than modest, they had been temporary—as with the government's operation of the railroads or general control of the economy. Moreover, the reformers' chief enemy—American businessmen—emerged from the war in a much strengthened position. The war had also dealt a blow to the progressives' idealism and faith in man's inherent goodness and rationality, just as war-inspired attacks on radicals destroyed the Socialists as an effective force and impeded their subsequent cooperation with the reform movement. Wartime sacrifices and disruptions may even have made the voters less eager to support a new era of political change. Progressivism, nevertheless, survived the war and the return to normalcy, as shown by Robert LaFollette's five million votes on a third-party Presidential ticket in 1924. More importantly, however, the progressives' approach to the wartime crisis became the model for many of the New Deal agencies and programs of the 1930s.[108]

That analogue also became the war-strengthened central government's principal legacy to the future. The war had, to be sure, given the Federal Government vast new powers in a whole range of areas. Contemporaries found the change so dramatic as to describe wartime America as more "thoroughly under centralized control" than any warring power and as having submitted to "autocracy in government." The government's control of business they described as "absolute" and making the United States "almost a socialist state."[109]

To the chagrin of the reformers, the controls did not survive the war, and from our perspective such descriptions considerably overstate the situation. Those who directed the wartime agencies, in fact, relied upon the voluntary cooperation of industry, and those who were controlled helped provide the supervisors; for the government lacked knowledgeable men with which to staff its agencies except as it drew them from business. Voluntarism, a piecemeal approach, and an early end to government supervision remained the guiding principles throughout the war, unless some crisis or obstructionism forced the government to take more drastic action.[110]

Fascinated with the temporary wartime relation between government and business, contemporaries overlooked two lasting changes. Although local boards operating under Federal supervision played a key part, World War I marked the final demise of the states' role in raising the armed forces (except for the National Guard) and of states-rights issues in determining mobilization policy. In addition, wartime limits on personal freedom sparked the rise of a civil liberties movement. Initially that took institutional form as the National Civil Liberties Bureau, renamed the American Civil Liberties Union after the war.[111]

Randolph Bourne had condemned the war as an opportunity for the upper classes to seize control of the government and enhance their power and social influence. They were hardly the only ones, however, to regard the war as an opportunity. Reformers hoped that an enlarged and more powerful central government would enable them to create a just social and economic order and that military victory would open the same possibilities on a global scale. Women, blacks, and workers tried to use the war's opportunities to improve their economic, social, and political position. The unions expected that cooperation with government and business might also enable them decisively to defeat the Socialists and the International Workers of the World, who challenged the unions for leadership of America's workers. Some businessmen and conservatives were happy to cooperate in using the war to destroy radicalism generally, while reserving to the postwar period their own efforts to weaken the unions. The campaign against radicals also enlisted the services of nativists, who saw the war as an opportunity to restrict immigration. Businessmen also hoped to use the war to recover their prestige and, through responsible cooperation with the government, win freedom from the threat of antitrust actions and demonstrate the advantages of industrial self-regulation. Farmers initially had fewer ambitions but nevertheless saw the war as an opportunity to enhance farm prosperity. In the continuing political struggle, Republicans hoped the war would return them to power just as the Democrats hoped victory would enable them to increase their hold on it.

More than the needs of modern war, then, shaped the way in which the United States government strove to mobilize its economy and its people for intervention in the European war. Called upon to serve many competing purposes, the newly created mobilization agencies consequently fell short of fully satisfying the war's needs. At the same time, the agencies often disappointed the hopes of those groups expecting to use them for other purposes. With the war's sudden end and the dismantling of the mobilization agencies, even groups satisfied by wartime policies often found their gains short lived. Frederick L. Paxson, the Great War's best contemporary historian, observed in a slightly more limited context that mobilizing the American people for war had been "a matter of continuous negotiation."[112]

4
WORLD WAR II

To American production, without which this war would have been lost.

Joseph Stalin's toast at the Teheran Conference[1]

The long-promised Anglo-American second front in Europe remained more than six months in the future as the Big Three met at Teheran in November 1943, and Marshal Stalin quite naturally reserved to the Red Army the leading role in the ultimate defeat of the Axis powers. In his toast he nevertheless praised the supporting part played by American industry, to which he diplomatically gave credit for preventing an early Axis triumph.

In so doing, Stalin acknowledged that victory in a protracted modern war required more than simply raising a large armed force. In such a contest, the belligerents must also maximize their productive capacity and divert from civilian uses whatever share of total output the armed forces require. Because those tasks "cannot be accomplished without controls," modern war required an expansion of the role of the state, a development already familiar to Stalin's planned economy but perhaps less welcome in the United States.[2]

Much of the history of the American home front during World War II is the story of those controls and their influences—economic, social, and political. For the degree and extent of wartime direction by the Federal Government had never been greater. Neither had such extensive controls ever been so protracted nor had they so influenced the shape of wartime developments.

Central control of war finance had, of course, begun with the Revolution, and during the Civil War the Confederates had, ineffectively, attempted to regulate industrial production and trade. World War I had brought rather extensive Federal involvement in all those areas, plus production controls in agriculture and food processing.

Despite such precedents, World War II Americans saw the Federal Government dominate "the American scene as never before in all the years of the Republic."[3] The government told businessmen what they could produce, the prices they would charge, and the profit they might make. Federal agencies not only drafted part of the labor force into the armed forces—an action never before commenced in peacetime—but helped, and sometimes coerced, workers to find essential wartime jobs and eventually limited the hourly wage they might earn. Federal authorities also controlled essential raw materials, rationed scarce consumer goods, and set the prices retailers might charge. As Washington acted to regulate prices, wages, hours, profits, rents, transportation, and communications, it moved into areas previously managed by the states—if at all—and reduced them virtually to the status of its agents, a position reinforced by Federal creation of draft boards, rationing agencies, civil defense groups, and a host of other local bodies.[4]

Although the trend toward Federal domination has nineteenth century roots, the exigencies of World War II accelerated the shift. The United States, for example, removed from the work force over three times as many men and women as were inducted into the armed services in World War I. American forces waged war along two fronts, across two vast oceans, for more than twice as long as the nation's involvement in the earlier world conflict. Although General Pershing eventually fought his battles with the help of both airplanes and tanks, they were relatively unsophisticated and few in number compared to World War II models. The fact that a typical division of World War II required the support of 400,000 mechanical horsepower to keep it moving (versus 3,500 for one of Pershing's units) well illustrates the more mechanized nature of the Second World War and its consequent demand on American industry.[5]

Reorganizing the nation's economy to meet such demands caused Federal civilian employment to more than triple between September 1939 and July 1943. As Table 4.1 indicates, 90 percent of that growth occurred in the two military departments and new agencies required by the emergency. As will be shown, the latter bodies took one of three forms: those concerned with a specific function or industry, such as increasing the output of rubber; those with broader authority over an economic area, such as regulating production or manpower; and those charged with coordinating the entire mobilization process. As emergency agencies expanded their control not only over all aspects of production but also over civil defense, transportation, foreign trade, scientific research, communications and information, and even housing, they pushed aside the old-line civilian departments, robbing them of authority and some of their best personnel.[6]

Table 4.1
Federal Civilian Employment, September 1939–July 1945
(Thousands)

Date	Total	War Department	Navy Department	Emergency War Agencies
Sep 1939	940	123	92	—
Jan 1942	1,703	530	328	30
Jul 1943	3,126	1,404	674	183
Jul 1945	2,900	1,138	698	160

Source: Gladys M. Kammerer, *Impact of War on Federal Personnel Administration, 1939–1945* (Lexington, KY: University of Kentucky Press, 1951), p. 17.

Controlling the Wartime Economy

Federal regulation of the economy began slowly, however. In an action unrelated to the looming military crisis, Congress, in April 1939, passed a Reorganization Act permitting the creation within the new Executive Office of the President of an Office of Emergency Management (OEM), which became the statutory home for many of the emergency agencies subsequently established by executive order.[7]

Also in 1939, President Franklin D. Roosevelt appointed a War Resources Board (WRB) of prominent businessmen to study and report on the armed forces' Industrial Mobilization Plan (IMP), which evolved from an unsophisticated 1923 plan prepared in response to a 1920 Congressional mandate. The IMP called for the establishment of Federal agencies to regulate industrial facilities, essential commodities, manpower, overseas trade, wholesale and retail prices, domestic and oceanic transportation, energy sources, war finance, public relations, and selective service. To coordinate the workings of those bodies, the IMP proposed creation of a War Resources Administration (WRA) comprising prominent industrialists and military leaders and reporting directly to the President—a system not unlike the one that eventually emerged, an agonizingly slow four years later.[8]

The WRB, led by Edward R. Stettinius, Jr., chairman of the board of US Steel, recommended against immediate establishment of the WRA, whose chairman would have become a virtual assistant President and whose creation would have placed supervision of mobilization entirely within military and industrial hands. Although Roosevelt ignored the WRB and its report, he seemingly agreed with its suggestion to delay naming a WRA. The President recognized that liberals and labor opposed any agency dominated by military and business leaders, and the powerful antiwar movement would surely have considered any implementation of the IMP as a Presidential effort to involve the United States in the European war that had broken out in September 1939. Because the United States had not become directly involved, Roosevelt saw no need to create a controversial war mobilization agency that might also inhibit his own freedom to act.[9]

During the period of "phony war," when Axis and Allied forces in Western Europe stared at one another while Germany and the Soviet Union completed the conquest of Poland, President Roosevelt took no further action on a mobilization agency. When the German blitzkrieg struck the Low Countries and France in May 1940, however, he reactivated the Advisory Commission (NDAC) of the 1916 Council of National Defense.

Although the NDAC had proved wanting in World War I, it nevertheless had certain advantages. Being already in the statute books, its resurrection did not require Congressional approval. An effort to obtain that approval seemed likely at the time to result in more restrictive legislation than the President wanted and to raise a political storm over American foreign policy that he wished to avoid in an election year. Its seven carefully chosen members represented industry, labor, farmers, railroaders, consumers, and New Dealers. Each headed a division concerned with a major aspect of war mobilization: industrial production, industrial materials, manpower, prices, civilian supply, agriculture, and transportation. To round out the NDAC, Roosevelt charged Donald Nelson, whom he had named to coordinate defense purchasing, to work closely with the Commission.[10]

On the other hand, the Advisory Commission also had some crippling weaknesses, including one that dated back to World War I. The NDAC had only advisory authority and consequently met bureaucratic resistance—especially from the military departments—when it attempted to assume executive functions. Each NDAC division also had its own staff and set of interests, which it tended to pursue even when that meant the Commission issued conflicting instructions. Unlike either the agencies proposed by the Industrial Mobilization Plan or the Commission's World War I predecessor, the NDAC had no head; this probably pleased Roosevelt, who wanted no mobilization czar that might weaken his authority. But the lack of effective leadership and corporate responsibility meant the agency could not coordinate its own policies, let alone the American mobilization effort![11] Moreover, with the United States not yet at war and many Americans vehemently opposed to involvement, the country lacked that sense of urgency and common danger essential to the functioning of an all-inclusive mobilization agency, especially one with only advisory powers.

Industrial Production. The Office of Production Management (OPM), Roosevelt's next creation in January 1941, had a far narrower focus. It sought primarily to stimulate industrial production and resolve related raw materials, manpower, and purchasing problems. Led jointly by William Knudsen of General Motors and Sidney Hillman, head of the Amalgamated Clothing Workers of America, it used a variety of devices to "increase, accelerate, and regulate" war production, coordinate related governmental activities, survey American and Allied defense requirements, and secure needed raw materials. Dividing the leadership between management and labor spelled trouble, as did the failure to give the OPM any direct authority over civilian production or any coercive power sufficient to accomplish that impressive list of duties.[12]

The OPM nevertheless moved industrial mobilization further along than had the NDAC. The new office's principal weapons, which lacked statutory authority, were the issuance of preference orders, which encouraged firms to push military work ahead of civil production, and priority ratings, which gave military contractors first claim on scarce raw materials. In the end such tools proved ineffective. The ability to order priority for defense work and to limit manufacturers' use of raw materials in nonessential products provided a weak incentive to convert civilian facilities to defense uses. With the economy still recovering from the Great Depression and the United States not yet at war, businessmen had strong reasons for delaying conversion: Revised civilian production might enable their firms once again to show healthy profits, but conversion to military production might once more, as after World War I, subject manufacturers to charges of war profiteering or being merchants of death. Worse, should the United States not enter the war, or should a quick settlement be achieved, conversion might saddle their firms with a lot of expensive, but useless equipment.[13]

The system of preferences and priorities broke down when the military demand for scarce raw materials and production facilities outran the supply. As the OPM had no power to coordinate and limit military procurement and the assignment of priorities, the system threatened to create the kind of bottlenecks that had almost led to a production breakdown in the winter of 1917–1918.[14]

The government therefore reinforced the priority system of the OPM—and the more effective War Production Board (WPB) which replaced OPM in January 1942—with several other programs designed to encourage industrial conversion. New tax laws authorized firms to depreciate the cost of conversion to war production over a five-year period and to recover wartime excess profits should they show a postwar loss. The military services suspended competitive bidding and offered cost-plus-fixed-fee contracts that guaranteed a profit. To help finance the cost of conversion, the services paid in advance up to 30 percent of the contract's value and wrote letters of intent guaranteeing to cover the cost of retooling for government work even while contracts remained under negotiation. Eventually, President Roosevelt also granted immunity from antitrust prosecution to firms that could show that collusion would increase the output of military goods.[15]

The Presidential war powers voted by Congress in early 1942 permitted Roosevelt to strengthen his new WPB. To hasten industrial conversion, the WPB could order curtailment of nonessential civilian construction and production, as it soon did in the case of automobiles, home appliances, metal office furniture, lawnmowers, residential oil burners, and a host of similar items that used scarce materials. Producers of such items could go out of business, seek war contracts, or enter new lines of civilian production. As tighter control of scarce metals often made the latter impossible, converting to defense production remained the logical and, after December 1941, the patriotic choice.[16]

With its new authority, the War Production Board also tried to make a success of the system of preference orders and priority ratings. Some $100 billion in military contracts let between January and June 1942, however, soon overwhelmed industry, which still lacked the facilities and raw materials to commence work on even those projects requiring immediate attention. The constant writing of new contracts carrying the highest priority also disrupted the scheduling of production.[17]

To avert the impending industrial chaos, the WPB implemented a Production Requirements Plan (PRP) that required each military contractor to submit his production schedule and raw materials requirements. The WPB then authorized the contractor's purchase of stated amounts of scarce materials. As the WPB failed to exercise its authority over military procurement, however, the armed services continued to disrupt production by letting contracts in excess of industry's capacity.[18]

That led to the development of the Controlled Materials Plan (CMP), which became fully operational only in mid-1943. Under that system, producers advised the War Production Board quarterly of their stocks of controlled materials and their production needs and schedules. Raw material suppliers similarly reported their expected output. The claimant agencies—such as the military departments—submitted their needs, identifying the supplies of materials required to build the desired quantities of ships, planes, tanks, and other military goods. The WPB compared supply and demand, issuing to each claimant an allocation that was often less than its request. The claimant had then to distribute its allocation among its contractors, limiting the number of items ordered to the available supply of raw materials. After almost four years of mobilization and over eighteen months of war, the United States had a fairly satisfactory system for controlling industrial production.[19]

Still, the War Production Board had serious shortcomings. It emphasized control of defense production when the entire economy—civilian and military—required direction. It left most procurement to the military services, which led to poor coordination with civilian and Allied needs and little advance planning. It took a voluntaristic approach to business, emphasizing profit incentives rather than coerced central direction. It allowed such important aspects of industrial mobilization as petroleum, rubber, prices, and manpower to escape its authority and fall under the direction of independent agencies. Its Production Requirements Plan and Controlled Materials Plan controlled only a few scarce materials and imposed an overwhelming paperwork burden on smaller manufacturers.[20] Behaving "as if there were no fund of [World War I] experience on which to draw," the United States engaged in a "similar pattern of trial and error groping" toward an efficient means to control production. In the end, "the control procedures established were always barely adequate to deal effectively with problems encountered in the period immediately preceding their adoption."[21]

Nevertheless, Stalin had been right. The miracle of American wartime production prevented an Allied defeat and opened the way to final victory. By mid-1945, the United States had produced—

> 5,600 merchant ships
> 79,125 landing craft
> 100,000 tanks and armored cars
> 300,000 airplanes
> 2,400,000 military trucks
> 2,600,000 machine guns
> 434,000,000 tons of steel
> 41,000,000,000 rounds of ammunition
> and 2 atomic bombs.[22]

Agriculture. Like industry, agriculture approached American involvement in World War II still reeling from the effects of the nation's worse depression, which had exacerbated the farm collapse of the late Twenties. Although increasingly extensive governmental control of agriculture began in the mid-Thirties, its purpose had then been to limit rather than encourage production and to boost rather than restrain prices. With the outbreak of war, and the resulting increase in agricultural demand, the government reversed its farm policy and adopted measures to expand output while restraining inflationary price increases.

Farmers, like industrialists, sometimes showed reluctance to follow the new course. After almost two decades of farm poverty, they felt entitled to enjoy higher prices, and with memories of World War I still fresh, they did not wish to find themselves again borne down by excess capacity in the wake of another war. Organized into a variety of cooperative marketing and purchasing associations and three large farm pressure groups and with allies in

Congress and the Department of Agriculture, farmers were in a position to insure that their mobilization for war developed along lines they found favorable.[23]

American farmers nevertheless quickly performed their own miracle of production. As Table 4.2 suggests, farm output and prices increased dramatically after 1941. The output of all livestock jumped by over 23 percent and of all crops by over 14 percent. Between 1940 and 1945, the number of persons supplied per farm worker rose from 10.7 to 14.6—a 36 percent increase in productivity within five years! With only 5 percent more acreage in crops and 10 percent fewer workers, American farmers had produced 50 percent more food than in World War I.[24]

Table 4.2
Output of Selected Farm Products, 1939–1945

	Grain Production (Millions of Bushels)				Liveweight Meat Production (Millions of Pounds)			
	Corn		Wheat		Hogs		Cattle	
Year	Output	Price	Output	Price	Output	Price	Output	Price
1939	2,581	$0.56	741	$0.69	17,079	$0.06	15,177	$0.07
1940	2,457	$0.62	815	$0.68	17,043	$0.05	15,702	$0.08
1941	2,652	$0.75	942	$0.94	17,489	$0.09	17,029	$0.09
1942	3,069	$0.92	969	$1.10	21,105	$0.13	18,568	$0.11
1943	2,966	$1.12	844	$1.36	25,375	$0.14	19,159	$0.12
1944	3,088	$1.03	1,060	$1.41	20,584	$0.13	19,708	$0.11
1945	2,869	$1.23	1,108	$1.49	18,843	$0.14	19,517	$0.12

Source: US, Department of Commerce, Bureau of the Census, *Historical Statistics of the United States, Colonial Times to 1970*, Bicentennial ed., 2 vols. (Washington, DC: US Government Printing Office, 1975), series K502–516, K564–582, 1:511, 519.

With large food stocks and unused farm capacity on hand in 1941, the government faced little immediate pressure to regulate agricultural production closely. Late in 1942, however, Roosevelt charged his Secretary of Agriculture to determine military and civilian food needs, carry out programs designed to meet those needs, assign priorities, allocate commodities in short supply, and insure "efficient and proper" distribution of available food. Those duties also required the Secretary to coordinate with the War Production Board regarding agricultural raw materials and industrial production essential to farm needs and with the emergency agencies that controlled both prices and transportation. Then, four months later, the President followed the World War I precedent and created a separate War Food Administration (WFA).[25]

The most controversial controls on wartime agriculture came not, however, from the WFA but as a result of governmental efforts to regulate money and prices. To see clearly why that was so requires an explanation of wartime fiscal and monetary policies and a description of the work of a new pricing agency.

Money and Prices. Even excluding veterans' benefits and payment of interest on the war debt, estimates of the cost of World War II to the United States vary considerably, depending upon the definition of defense outlays and what portion of the period between September 1939 and December 1941 and after August 1946 should be charged to the war. The numbers in Table 4.3, however, represent a conservative estimate.

Table 4.3
Gross National Product and
Federal Finances, 1939–1946
(Billions of Dollars)

Year	Total Federal Outlays	National Defense Outlays	Gross National Product	Gross Federal Debt
1939	$8.9	$1.1	$90.5	$48.2
1940	9.6	1.5	99.7	50.7
1941	14.0	6.0	124.5	57.5
1942	35.5	24.0	157.9	79.2
1943	78.9	63.2	191.6	142.7
1944	94.0	76.9	210.1	204.1
1945	95.2	81.6	211.9	260.1
1946	61.7	44.7	208.5	271.0

Source: US, Department of Commerce, Bureau of the Census, *Historical Statistics of the United States, Colonial Times to 1970*, Bicentennial ed., 2 vols. (Washington, DC: US Government Printing Office, 1975), series F1–5, Y466–471, Y488–492, 1:224, 2:1115–16.

A close examination of the table will reveal a unique aspect of World War II. The cumulative annual increases in the gross national product (GNP) ran ahead of the wartime growth in defense expenditures or, for that matter, total Federal outlays. As measured by current prices, Americans had a somewhat larger value of goods and services available for civilian use throughout the war than they had enjoyed in 1939. While the civilian population experienced some shortages and inconveniences, such measures of the general welfare as total consumer spending, per-capita calories in the daily diet, per-capita annual consumption of meat, clothing, and shoes, and residential use of energy all rose during the war years. Put another way, Americans fought their second world conflict out of increased production without a reduction in the value of goods and services available for civilian use, as occurred in World War I.[26]

Because the wartime increase in the GNP meant a roughly comparable growth in disposable income, however, the government had either to control the potential increase in civilian purchases or risk inflation as it bid against civilians for the products of American industry.

The previously described governmental restraints on civilian production and management of critical materials helped limit that potential competition by, in effect, removing certain goods and facilities from the market. Nevertheless, the government also used traditional methods to limit the inflationary consequences of increased civilian buying power. Between 1940 and 1944, for example, the government passed five revenue measures that lowered the minimum taxable individual income by at least 50 percent, and thus brought nearly all Americans within the Federal tax system and made income taxes the source of nearly three-quarters of all Federal revenues. The measures also raised the rates on individual and corporate incomes, a range of excise taxes, and levies from inheritances and gifts. While making the tax system more progressive, the wartime revenue acts also introduced the withholding principle, which made Americans pay their annual income taxes as they earned rather than in four quarterly installments during the following year. In addition to financing nearly half the war from taxes (versus one-third during World War I), the wartime fiscal controls thus laid the basis for the modern income tax system.[27]

In another effort to control consumer spending, the Federal Government conducted eight war-loan drives. Although it limited the purchases by banks (which World War I had demonstrated to have an inflationary effect) and used Madison Avenue sales techniques to reach individual investors, all but $43.3 billion of the $146.7 billion not sold to commercial banks went to insurance companies, savings banks, savings and loan associations, other corporations, brokers, and state and local governments. Resales later put one-third of the total into the banking system, which reinforced the inflationary influence of redemptions by individual purchasers. Nevertheless, higher wartime savings rates did curtail civilian buying power and help the government finance the war.[28]

As Table 4.3 indicates, however, gross Federal debt rose from $48.2 billion to $260.1 billion, much of it in the form of Federal securities handled by the nation's banking system. As a result, the government—in addition to controlling the use of individual and corporate income through taxes and loans—followed the precedent of World War I as the Treasury Department reasserted informal control of the Federal Reserve System. Sometimes against its better judgment, the Federal Reserve kept the rediscount rate low and made certain that banks had sufficient reserves to purchase Federal securities as they came onto the market. To hold down the cost of borrowing, the Federal Reserve System kept interest rates low and money easy. The supply of Federal Reserve Notes and other forms of money rose from $48.6 billion to $106 billion, or from $560 to $1,200 per capita. Government financial controls thus left within the economy a tremendous inflationary potential— the large gap between the wartime increase in national income and the money returned to the government in larger collections from taxes and loans.[29]

To limit the inflationary potential of that gap, the Federal Government introduced on a wide scale two kinds of regulation only hinted at in previous conflicts: price controls and rationing. Federal "price fixing" in World War I had focused primarily on industrial commodities and goods manufactured for use by the government, and the War Industries Board (WIB) and later Price-Fixing Committee had relied largely on voluntary agreements negotiated with industries and trade associations. To limit the price of food, the War Food Administration had used licensing agreements to limit the profits of processors, intervened in commodity markets to stabilize prices, and launched publicity campaigns that relied on voluntarism and social pressure to promote conservation and restrain retail prices.

Prior to December 1941, however, Roosevelt, unlike Wilson, could not rely upon a President's war powers to assert the right to control prices. The Price Stabilization Division of NDAC and the later (April 1941) Office of Price Administration and Civilian Supply (OPACS) had, therefore, to count on voluntaristic, commodity-oriented approaches like those of World War I. Both bodies announced ceilings on the prices of certain manufactured goods, limits the government could "enforce" only with publicity and the threatened loss of future contracts, and the OPACS-made agreements with industry groups that held selected prices at negotiated levels. Such selective price controls eventually covered almost half the wholesale markets and worked quite well until American industry began to use most of the resources and facilities formerly idled by the Great Depression.[30]

With the outbreak of war and the resulting surge in economic activity, the government abandoned the voluntaristic, selective approach. The January 1942 Emergency Price Control Act, stalled in Congress since mid-1941, gave the new Office of Price Administration (OPA) (Civilian Supply having been removed from its jurisdiction) statutory power to freeze many retail prices and to control rents in areas near major defense plants. The OPA's April 1942 General Maximum Price Regulation (GMPR) restricted sellers—whether retailers, wholesalers, manufacturers, or renters—to their highest price during March 1942. The act, however, limited the OPA's authority over food prices, at least until they rose to 110 percent of parity.[31]

Despite its virtually unprecedented assertion of governmental control over the marketplace, the act and resulting GMPR had still other shortcomings. The act failed to give the OPA control of wages, a major determinant of manufacturing costs and one sure to rise with the cost of food. The vagueness of the GMPR gave businessmen some room to boost prices if, for example, they had not produced or stocked a particular item in March 1942. They might make an item available in that month look "new" by changes in style, design, or packaging that would justify assigning a higher price. They might disguise a price increase by reductions in quality that boosted their profits while appearing to honor the March 1942 ceiling. Because the GMPR failed to require posting of retail price ceilings, consumers could not aid enforcement through their complaints, and even honest businessmen could reach different decisions as they struggled wth the GMPR's vague provisions.[32]

When prices continued to rise, President Roosevelt successfully pressed Congress to pass the October 1942 Economic Stabilization Act, which enabled the Office of Price Administration to hold agricultural prices at parity or the highest price paid between January and September 1942. By the following April, the OPA had posted local retail price ceilings, frozen rents nationwide, and—despite the inflationary growth of the money supply—achieved effective governmental control of the cost of living.[33]

A second, and truly unprecedented, Federal intrusion into the market place helped make that OPA price freeze effective. By using rationing to limit the consumption of the scarcest commodities, the government in effect demonetized their purchase. Without recourse to black markets, no amount of money would give a consumer more than his allotted share of such items as tires, gasoline, sugar, coffee, meats, butter, and many processed foods. While directly limiting consumption (and effective demand) of scarce items, rationing also had indirect effects: Cutting back on coffee imports saved shipping, limiting gasoline use conserved rubber, and eating fewer canned foods released tin for defense production. The books of red and blue stamps, the coupons for petroleum and shoes, and the special certificates for purchase of a typewriter or bicycle, all issued by local rationing boards, became common, if irritating, features of life during World War II, and they brought home to all Americans the extent to which the government had undertaken to manage the economy.[34]

Wartime control of wages, which like rationing helped sustain the price freeze, had a similar effect. The limit on wages, however, was but one part of the government's wartime control of the work force.

Manpower. The Selective Training and Service Act of September 1940, whose one-year military obligation the Congress (by a 203-202 vote) had extended by eighteen months in August 1941, represented the Federal Government's most dramatic assertion of control over manpower. Never before had the United States resorted to a peacetime draft. But the government also broke new ground as it attempted to stabilize wages, promote productivity, and recruit competent workers for essential industry.[35]

With more than eight million workers still looking for jobs in 1940 (and perhaps two million farm laborers underemployed), the government initially saw little need to intervene in labor markets. With the unions growing in membership and militancy, the prolabor Roosevelt administration had less reason to impose possibly irritating restrictions. It did, however, wish to achieve prompt settlement of any labor-management dispute that threatened war production.[36]

The result was the March 1941 National Defense Mediation Board (NDMB), which sought to avert labor shortages. (Some four thousand strikes had cost the nation twenty-three million man-days of work during 1941.) The board had no authority to impose settlements, however. It could only investigate and publish its findings. With a tripartite membership composed in equal parts of the representatives of labor, management, and government, the board tended to settle disputes by wage increases that pleased workers and war contractors, who passed the costs along to the government. Even so, the Mediation Board lost its effectiveness after November 1941, when the United Mine Workers successfully defied its authority in a ruling against the union shop in the mines.[37]

Pearl Harbor, however, prompted Roosevelt to renew his efforts to prevent stoppages within defense industries. One month after extracting a no-strike pledge from labor and management leaders in December 1941, the President appointed the tripartite National War Labor Board (NWLB). The board successfully negotiated a maintenance-of-membership agreement that protected the unions against a wartime loss of members. It also compromised both their demand that all war contractors accept the union shop and management's opposition to making union membership a condition of continued employment. To serve as a guide for future wage settlements, the NWLB developed a formula limiting growth of hourly wage rates to the 15 percent cost-of-living increase that had occurred between January 1941 and May 1942—the month after the OPA attempted to freeze prices with the General Maximum Price Regulation.[38]

In April 1942, President Roosevelt also created the War Manpower Commission (WMC), in part to give the unions a voice in determining manpower policy they believed they had been denied by the old NDAC and OPM as well as the new WPB. The WMC sought to restrain federal contracting methods that increased the competition for skilled workers and to overcome the reluctance of workers to move into essential jobs. As a coordinating body with little control over the policies of the agencies it worked with, however, the WMC had little early influence, and its battles with the War Department over the size of the army, which took skilled men from the work force, became particularly heated.[39]

While that struggle raged, the Economic Stabilization Act and the Presidents' April 1943 order to hold the line on prices converted the National War Labor Board from a mediation agency to a wage stabilization board, extending its authority to all wage settlements—not just disputes within essential industry—and directing it to reinforce the Office of Price Administration's attack on rising prices. Attempting to freeze wages at their level of September 1942 did little to contain strikes, which, as Table 4.4 shows, rose as prices and the competition for labor increased.

Table 4.4
Wartime Work Stoppages, 1940–1946

Year	Stoppages	Workers Involved (Millions)	Man-days Idle (Millions)
1940	2,508	0.6	6.7
1941	4,288	2.4	23.0
1942	2,968	0.8	4.2
1943	3,752	2.0	13.5
1944	4,956	2.1	8.7
1945	4,750	3.5	38.0
1946	4,985	4.6	116.0

Source: US, Department of Commerce, Bureau of the Census, *Historical Statistics of the United States, Colonial Times to 1970*, Bicentennial ed., 2 vols. (Washington, DC: US Government Printing Office, 1975), series D970–985, 1:179.

Except for certain NWLB policies, the situation might have grown worse. Committed only to maintaining hourly wage rates, the NWLB permitted workers to earn more by working longer hours at higher than normal, overtime rates. The NWLB also permitted unions and employers to disguise wage increases with payments for travel time and such fringe benefits as health insurance plans, shift differentials, incentive pays, and longer vacations and lunch breaks. Even without new contracts, employers often boosted wages by reclassifying jobs—giving workers a new title and a higher wage for performing the same work.[40]

By war's end the NWLB had approved 415,000 wage agreements covering 20 million workers. It had also imposed settlements in nearly 20,000 disputes affecting almost as many. To enforce its recommendations, the President had ordered the seizure of some forty plants. Wartime labor controls had thus virtually removed wages from the realm of collective bargaining.[41]

Before the war ended, organized labor had to face two more threats to its hard-won gains. The first arose because of the increase of strikes in 1943, especially the coal walkout that idled over a half million miners and led to a temporary Federal seizure of the Eastern coal mines. Congress responded with the War Labor Disputes Act, which imposed a thirty-day cooling-off period on any threatened strike, authorized Federal supervision of the workers' vote that must approve any strike, provided criminal penalties for anyone promoting an illegal strike, extended the President's authority to seize struck plants doing war-related work, and prohibited union contributions to political campaigns.[42]

The second threat failed to receive legislative sanction. Because of the unwillingness of some workers to move to essential industry, the War Manpower Commission in January 1943 issued its first work-or-fight order. It made occupation and not dependency the basis of draft deferment and thus threatened draft-age fathers with military duty if they failed to take essential jobs. When Congress overturned that order late in the year, the WMC explored other options before making a second effort in December 1944. It then threatened to draft any man under thirty-eight who had left an essential job or who changed jobs without the approval of his draft board. In the meantime the WMC also withdrew deferments from strikers, and Congress considered War Department proposals for broadening the work-or-fight concept with a true national-service law that would permit the Federal Government to tell each male citizen not already in the armed forces where he must work. Great Britain had already adopted such legislation, which became a central part of that nation's management of its wartime economy. Because the end of the war was in sight by 1944, and both labor and management opposed the national service concept, Congress let the legislation die despite its rather lukewarm support from the President.[43] National service nevertheless represented the logical culmination of the Federal Government's increasing wartime control over manpower.

Transportation and Trade. In contrast to the trend in industry, agriculture, prices, and manpower, wartime Federal controls over transportation and foreign trade went little further than the regulatory pattern established by World War I.

Prior to Pearl Harbor, the Federal Government used the Interstate Commerce Commission and then the NDAC Transportation Division (later moved to the Office of Emergency Management) to exercise its modest authority over transportation. Though the latter had no coercive power, it could investigate and coordinate industries that were prepared to cooperate. In December 1941, however, the President used his war powers to establish the Office of Defense Transportation (ODT), which he charged to coordinate the transportation policies of all government agencies, investigate essential requirements, determine the capacity of all carriers, advise on allocation of scarce resources, and avoid traffic congestion like that of World War I. The carriers formed advisory committees, and the government achieved its goals without seizures like that affecting the railroads in 1918.[44]

This time the voluntary approach achieved great success, as suggested by the wartime increase in intercity ton-miles indicated in Table 4.5. Despite the fact that the railroads in 1940 had fewer locomotives, fewer freight and passenger cars, and fewer employees than in 1918, they moved three-quarters of the wartime freight traffic and about one-third of the passengers. They did this with an improved system of centralized traffic control, efficient use of rolling stock, and better port operations. Someone had learned the lessons of 1917–1918.[45]

Table 4.5
Volume of Intercity Freight Traffic, 1939–1945
(Millions of Ton-Miles)

Year	Railroads	Highways	Waterways	Pipelines	Airlines	Total
1939	338,850	43,931	88,897	55,602	12	527,292
1940	379,201	50,047	110,005	59,277	14	598,544
1941	481,756	63,258	130,916	68,428	19	744,377
1942	645,422	48,626	138,791	75,087	34	907,960
1943	734,829	46,394	130,309	97,867	53	1,009,452
1944	746,912	47,395	136,963	132,864	71	1,064,205
1945	690,809	53,442	131,801	126,530	91	1,002,673

Source: Joseph R. Rose, *American Wartime Transportation* (New York: T. Y. Crowell, Co., 1953), p. 283.

Although contributing quantitatively less than the railroads, other transportation systems also rose to meet wartime demand—except as rubber shortages limited the use of highways. And the dramatic increase in the capacity of pipelines and air transport, as set out by Table 4.5, clearly forecast the future.

Overseas trade and transport also built on the lessons of World War I. After Pearl Harbor, Congress reinstated the 1917 Trading-With-the-Enemy Act, which gave the President control of communications and foreign trade, which he exercised through the Board of War Communications and the Board of Economic Warfare.[46] By supplying the Allies with Lend-Lease rather than loans, the United States also financed the four-fold increase in American exports without any significant increase in governmental loans or private investment.[47]

The government also followed earlier precedents for the control of the merchant marine. The 1936 Maritime Commission (which replaced the World War I Shipping Board and old Emergency Fleet Corporation) managed ship construction, and by using standard designs and mass-production techniques, turned out almost six thousand ships between 1942 and 1945. To operate that new fleet, the government also followed the earlier pattern and established a War Shipping Administration. By efficient central management and, by shattering the 1917–1918 construction record, the United States sent most (about 80 percent) of its war supplies abroad in its own ships—reversing the World War I dependency on foreign shipping.[48]

Superagencies. By mid-1942 the United States had created a number of Federal agencies designed to control specific industries or to manage an entire sector of economic activity. To that extent it had followed, and in some cases gone beyond, the models suggested by World War I and the interwar Industrial Mobilization Plan. One seemingly intractable problem remained: how to harmonize and focus the activities of those agencies and resolve the inevitable conflicts whenever their functions impinged on one another.

Roosevelt, assisted by the Office of Emergency Management, might have played that role. Although he lacked the time and staff to do it effectively, he seemed sometimes to relish the resulting chaos, which inevitably brought problems to his attention and preserved his authority. Apparently in part for that reason, he had rejected the War Resources Administration in 1939 and denied the NDAC a chairman in 1940.

By 1941, however, he could no longer manage or ignore the increasing clashes among the military departments, the Office of Price Administration (OPA), and the Office of Production Management (OPM). The first two wished to divert more of the economy to military production—even though the United States was not yet at war—and the overuse of preference orders and priority ratings had already begun to cause bottlenecks that plagued industry and the OPM. In an effort to restore order, Roosevelt in August 1941 established the Supply Priorities and Allocations Board (SPAB) and named Vice President Henry A. Wallace to its chairmanship. Real power over the civilian economy still lay beyond the SPAB's reach, however, and the rush of military orders after Pearl Harbor soon overwhelmed the system it had been created to supervise.[49]

The clashes therefore continued—between the OPA and the War Food Administration (WFA) and the Petroleum Administration for War over food and gasoline rationing and between the OPA and the War Production Board

(WPB) over prices. The dissension ultimately led to creation of the Office of Economic Stabilization (OES) in October 1942. Under the chairmanship of former Supreme Court Associate Justice James F. Byrnes, the OES directed the National War Labor Board (NWLB) to stabilize wages and supervised the OPA's fight against inflation. The OES also worked with the old-line Departments of Treasury, Labor, Commerce, and Agriculture to develop a comprehensive national policy on civilian purchasing, prices, rents, wages, profits, and rationing.[50]

Those efforts could succeed only to the extent that Byrnes also influenced war mobilization, and Roosevelt finally institutionalized Byrnes' growing authority by creating the Office of War Mobilization (OWM) in May 1943. From that post, Byrnes refereed the fight between the WPB and the military departments over the latters' share of national production. When in 1944 the focus of that fight shifted from conversion to reconversion—preparing the wartime economy for the postwar return to civilian production—the President expanded Byrnes' mandate to include that task.[51]

The United States had therefore taken until mid-1943 to develop a "coherent system of economic controls," which caused Bernard Baruch, chief of the 1918 War Industries Board, to "marvel at the regularity with which errors are repeated"—particularly the "failure to study and understand the records of past experience. . . . Faltering step by faltering step we moved toward controls, but those controls were never sufficient or far-reaching enough."[52]

The Economic Consequences of Total War

At least in the short run, the war's most popular economic consequence was the return of prosperity. Between 1939 and 1945, gross national product more than doubled, unemployment fell from over nine million to about one million, and the size of the civilian labor force held steady while the government created twelve million new "jobs" in the armed forces. A closer look at various sectors of the economy will reveal some perhaps equally important developments.

The wartime return of prosperity and the mechanized nature of World War II had a major impact on industry. America's young aircraft builders, who produced fewer than six thousand planes in 1939, came of age and grew to industrial gianthood when their annual output exceeded ninety-five thousand in 1944. The burgeoning aircraft industry also nourished expansion in related areas, such as the more than fourfold growth in national aluminum output between 1939 and 1943. As Table 4.6 shows, old-line industries also achieved outstanding wartime growth. Steel and pig-iron output rose by 16 and 19

Table 4.6
Output of Selected Industries, 1939–1945

Year	Pig Iron (Millions of Short Tons)	Steel Ingots (Millions of Short Tons)	Bituminous Coal (Trillions of BTUs)	Crude Petroleum (Trillions of BTUs)
1939	56.3	81.8	10,345	7,337
1940	55.7	81.6	12,072	7,849
1941	57.8	85.2	13,471	8,133
1942	60.6	88.9	15,267	8,043
1943	64.2	90.6	15,463	8,733
1944	67.9	93.9	16,233	9,732
1945	67.3	95.5	15,134	9,939

Source: US, Department of Commerce, Bureau of the Census, *Historical Statistics of the United States, Colonial Times to 1970*, Bicentennial ed., 2 vols. (Washington, DC: US Government Printing Office, 1975), series M76–92, P301–317, 1:588, 2:698.

percent, respectively, and petroleum and bituminous coal recovery leapt ahead between 35 and 46 percent. Even the automobile industry, precluded by government order from making cars, prospered. At the peak, it employed a million workers and produced $1 billion of armaments each month. By war's end, it had built one-third the wartime output of machine guns, two-fifths of the aircraft, and half the diesel engines. Overall it produced $29 billion worth of war goods.[53]

For smaller firms the war produced mixed results. With two-thirds of the government's $240 billion in military spending going to 100 of the 18,000 corporations that got a defense contract, small businesses had little direct access to the source of prosperity. Denied scarce materials and skilled workers, they often could not continue their prewar production of civilian goods. As a result, some half million small businessmen who failed to convert their facilities and snare a subcontract from some large arms manufacturer shut down during the war.[54]

Sympathetic to the wartime plight of small firms, Congress, in May 1942, created a Smaller War Plants Corporation to help finance their conversion. Congressional pressure on the President and the military departments led to the establishment within the War Production Board of a Smaller War Plants Division to aid small businesses in their pursuit of defense contracts. By 1944, efforts were also being made to allow small businesses to reconvert to civilian production ahead of the giant defense contractors, so as to gain a head start in the postwar pursuit of profits.[55]

Although that support for economic democracy led to the postwar Small Business Administration, it produced few results during the war. As a matter of efficiency and the maintenance of maximum capacity, the military services preferred to deal with large corporations. They had the plant, machinery, skilled workmen, managerial talent, finances, and suppliers to carry a large order through to completion. Using smaller firms required the services either to divide an order among several suppliers or to manage the work of the many subcontractors that produced a small part of the desired end item. Either approach complicated the services' work and might cut output. Saving small businesses by granting them an early return to civilian work, the services believed, would draw workers and materials from essential tasks, risk military shortages, and perhaps make civilians less willing to continue wartime sacrifices. Although the close wartime relation between the armed services and large defense contractors therefore represented no conspiracy, it established the precedent for the Cold War ties now known as the military-industrial complex.[56]

Not only did larger corporations draw the major direct benefits from wartime spending, they also experienced, according to business historian Alfred Chandler, wartime organizational changes that placed the "capstone" on prewar trends, "set the stage for the impressive growth of the modern business enterprise," and became the basis for the enormous postwar expansion of the entire economy.[57]

Prior to the Twenties, American corporations had generally remained within the same line of work and grown by integrating vertically or expanding their share of a specific market. In the interwar period, however, metals, chemicals, petroleum, electrical machinery, electronics, transportation-equipment manufacturers, and certain food processors began to expand horizontally by diversifying into new lines of work where their previously acquired technical, manufacturing, distributive, or managerial capacity gave them an edge. Corporations continued to grow even larger and production within specific fields remained highly oligopolistic. Competition, however, became more intense as the giant firms began to diversify and as their product lines broadened. World War II stimulated that tendency when it required large firms to enter new lines of work as they converted for defense production. Those firms gained expertise that they applied to new civilian products in the postwar period. In that sense, the war assisted the development of the new corporate organizations that have transformed both the economy and society since 1945.[58]

Those economic developments and wartime military requirements also altered the relation of science to American life. Prior to World War II, the Federal Government had given only limited and narrowly focused assistance to scientific research, such as the 1807 Coast Survey to aid shipping; the post-1865 Coast and Geodetic Survey to map the Far West; or Patent Office, and later Department of Agriculture, assistance to scientific farming. For its part, business virtually ignored scientific research in the nineteenth century. During both the Civil War and World War I, scientists had tried to reverse those attitudes, but the resulting National Academy of Sciences and a variety of military consulting boards proved weak vehicles for large, continuing industrial or governmental aid to research.[59]

Albert Einstein's August 1939 letter to President Roosevelt, which led to production of the atomic bomb, perhaps symbolized the new relation of science with both government and industry that emerged in World War II. Federal spending for scientific research, which had risen only from $3 million to $88 million between 1900 and 1940, increased to $1.5 billion in the next five years, as the new Office of Scientific Research and Development (OSRD) began to manage the programs and assure scientists access to the White House. The fastest growing and most diverse business corporations similarly grasped the importance of science as the wartime search for substitutes and new technology impressed upon them the need to create large, permanent research and development staffs.[60]

American medicine similarly benefited from the war, as it built upon advances in medical science derived from World War I. The earlier conflict had fostered a close tie between the original NDAC and the American Medical Association and American College of Surgeons in order to control the diseases that had decimated the army during the 1898 war with Spain. A better understanding of camp sanitation brought vast improvement—despite the susceptibility of Americans from isolated rural areas to the whole range of diseases that afflicted urban children. Even there, fewer American soldiers would have died from wounds than disease except for the worldwide influenza epidemic that began in the war's last year. That war also witnessed the development of better surgical procedures and the wide use of improved antisepsis, x-rays, tetanus antitoxin, blood transfusions, and motor evacuation to reduce battle deaths. A new vaccine virtually eliminated typhoid fever, and the government began to sponsor research to conquer venereal disease.[61]

World War II medicine built on that success. Vaccines developed earlier for smallpox, tetanus, typhoid, yellow fever, cholera, and typhus had eliminated many of the soldier's deadliest enemies. During World War II, OSRD research led to breakthroughs in antimalarial drugs and the large-scale production of penicillin, which had previously been regarded as a "biological curiosity of doubtful value." The wide availability of whole blood and blood plasma, penicillin and sulfa drugs, air and motor transport of the wounded, and field hospitals tested during World War I also dramatically reduced the death rate from battle wounds, making World War II America's most medically successful war to that date.[62]

The scientific and technological advances that sustained the sharp wartime increase in farm output were not a product of World War II. Nevertheless, the war deserves credit for making them more widespread. One recent effort to account for higher wartime yields traced some 14 percent of the increase to greater use of commercial fertilizer and lime, both of whose application more than doubled between 1939 and 1945. Soil and crop improvements, such as prewar soil conservation programs and the introduction of hybrid seeds, added another 14 percent, and more scientific disease control and better feeding, breeding, and management of livestock accounted for 31 percent of the wartime increase in food production. Technology also played a role. Between 1939 and 1945 farmers increased their stock of mechanical equipment by almost a million tractors, a half-million trucks, two hundred thousand grain combines, as many milking machines, and fifty thousand corn pickers. With more tractors, farmers required fewer horses, and the acreage and effort formerly used to grow their fodder provided some 7 percent of the wartime growth in food production. The additional machines also allowed farmers to expand their crop acreage (14 percent of the wartime gain) despite the wartime decline in farm population (six million) and the loss of farm labor to the armed forces. Greater wartime demand for food, in other words, prompted greater use of available scientific knowledge and technological advances, which accounted for perhaps 70 percent of the wartime increase in food production.[63]

Agricultural historians have referred to those developments as the "second American agricultural revolution" and the farmers' "mechanical revolution."[64] The change consisted of more, however, than the increased output traceable to science and technology. The war also meant higher farm prices and larger farm income. As shown by the indices in Table 4.7, farm prices more than doubled during the war years. Because the prices that farmers paid for the goods they bought grew much less rapidly, their overall terms of trade improved by about 40 percent. Farmers also expanded their share of the consumer's food dollar to 54 percent, a one-third increase between 1940 and 1944.[65]

Higher prices and better terms of trade translated into other benefits. Net farm income rose from $5.3 billion to $13.6 billion between 1939 and 1944. As per-capita farm income tripled during the war years (versus the doubling of per-capita income for industrial workers), farmers also advanced relative to other Americans. With more money, farmers reduced their indebtedness by one-quarter, and farm prosperity as usual led to a decline in tenancy. All those factors, plus the increase in output and decline in the farm population, constituted the revolution in American agriculture—a new rural order prompted and accelerated by World War II.[66]

The wartime gains made by American unions lacked the drama of the revolution on the farm or the transformation of big business, but as they did a quarter of a century before, the representatives of workingmen and women

Table 4.7
Index of Selected Farm Prices, 1939–1945
(1910–1914 = 100)

Year	All Farm Products	All Crops	Livestock & Products
1939	95	82	107
1940	100	90	109
1941	124	108	138
1942	159	145	171
1943	193	187	198
1944	197	199	196
1945	207	202	211

Source: Harold D. Guither, *Heritage of Plenty: A Guide to the Economic History and Development of US Agriculture* (Danville, IL: Interstate Printers and Publishers, Inc., 1972), p. 174.

seized the opportunity offered by a second prolabor administration and another world war to advance their position in American life. In addition to achieving full employment, the unions sought specifically to secure and then build upon their recent increase in membership, gain representation and influence within the wartime mobilization agencies, and insure that wage increases outpaced any advances in the cost of living.[67]

To a considerable degree, they succeeded. As indicated in Figure 4.1 the wartime increase in the cost of living consistently ran behind the rise in hourly earnings in manufacturing. The worst of the inflation, moreover, occurred either before the United States entered the war or after the return of peace, and wartime controls helped working people protect the buying power of their hourly wages, which in real terms rose from 64 cents (1939) to 81 cents (1944). Because wartime wage earners worked full time—often including overtime at even higher rates—and at superior jobs, they did even better on a weekly or annual basis, where they registered real gains in excess of 50 percent in the same years.[68]

As the national work force grew from fifty-five to sixty-six million, of whom about twelve million were in the armed forces, union membership rose steadily from 8.9 million (1940) to 14.8 million (1945). The newer Congress of Industrial Organizations (CIO), which became firmly established in steel, rubber, automobiles, and other mass-production industries, made the greatest gains and by 1945 almost equalled the size of the older American Federation of Labor (AFL). The wartime gain in union membership also increased the portion of workers protected by collective bargaining arrangements from 30 to 45 percent.[69]

Figure 4.1
Price and Wage Trends, 1939-1949
(August 1939=100)

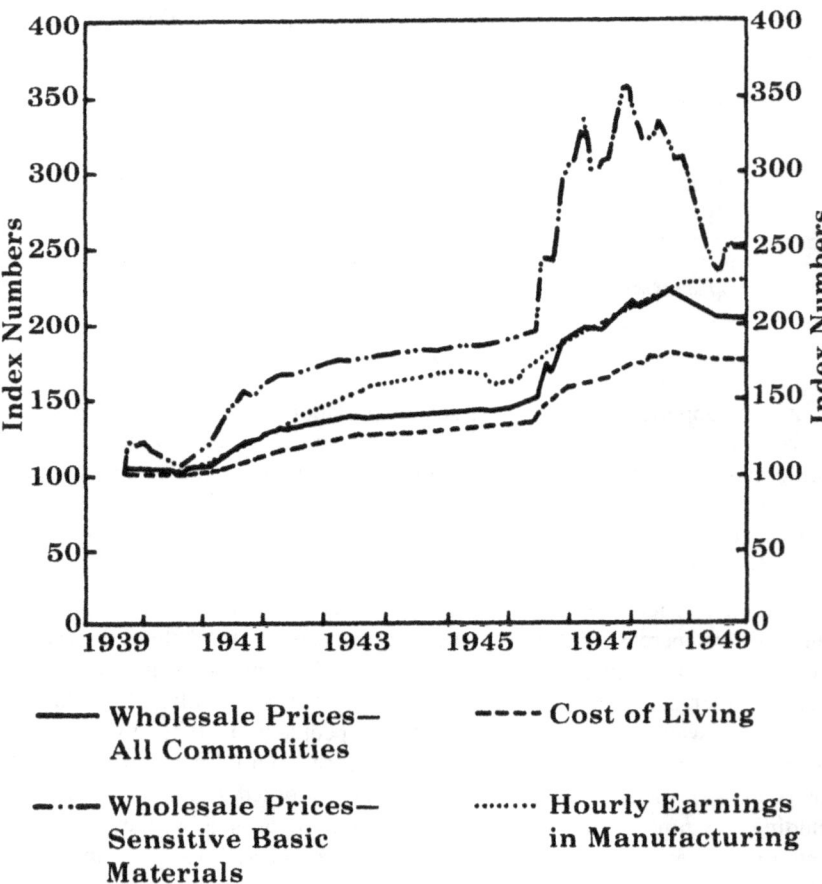

Source: Harold G. Moulton, *Can Inflation Be Controlled?* (Washington, DC: Anderson Kramer Associates, Inc., 1958), p. 126. Reprinted by permission of the publisher.

Despite the gains in union membership and advances in wartime wage rates, labor achieved only a qualified success in its relations with the government. On the one hand, unions did succeed in placing their leaders on important wartime boards. Sidney Hillman led a division of the Advisory Commission (NDAC) and jointly directed the Office of Production Management (OPM). Until forced out by ill health, he also headed the Labor Division of the War Production Board, on which both the AFL and CIO had an associate director. The War Production Board (WPB), War Manpower Commission (WMC), and Office of Price Administration (OPA) also established labor advisory bodies with union representation. On the other hand, unions never achieved a full partnership with business and government. Business-led agencies often circumvented their labor divisions or ignored labor advisory bodies. Unions for their part often named unqualified men to governmental positions, which they used to carry on the AFL-CIO "civil war" that divided the labor movement. Nevertheless, such service enhanced union prestige, and the government-sponsored labor-management collaboration set a precedent for postwar accommodation and collective bargaining.[70]

Especially as compared to their condition in the prewar depression, the three broad sectors of the American economy—industry, agriculture, and labor—drew immense benefit from World War II.

Liberal Reform and Total War

To the extent that economic recovery had been the New Deal's principal aim, World War II merits description as an agent of liberal reform—especially as it also validated the Keynesian economic theories that liberal governments would subsequently use to maintain full employment and justify welfare programs. American historians have nevertheless preferred to stress both the wartime controls imposed by the central government and the growth of big business, which have led them to characterize World War II—indeed all war—as an illiberal force.

Certain features of the war seemingly sustain that conclusion. After 1942 Congress terminated such New Deal programs as the Works Progress Administration (WPA), the Civilian Conservation Corps (CCC), the National Youth Administration (NYA), and the National Resources Planning Board (NRPB). Furthermore it starved for funds both the Rural Electrification Administration (REA) and Farm Security Administration (FSA). Except for veterans, the war years saw no further advances toward a higher minimum wage, broader social security coverage, or an extensive national health program. During the war, the administration also overlooked violations of the antitrust and child-labor laws.[71]

That evidence of liberal defeat deserves qualification, however. Wartime prosperity eliminated the need for the WPA, CCC, and NYA, just as the requirement to increase defense spending and conserve scarce materials explains cutbacks for the REA and FSA. Efforts to maximize industrial production account for the tendency to overlook antitrust violations and accept child workers. More relevant to the role of war in any of those liberal "defeats" is the fact that until passage of the GI Bill the New Deal had achieved no major reform legislation since 1937–1938. The conservative counterattack predated World War II, however much international conflict may have led to liberal setbacks.[72]

The best case for wartime illiberalism perhaps rests on civil-liberties issues, particularly the treatment of those Japanese-Americans who lived on the Pacific Coast. Some three months after the attack on Pearl Harbor, the United States Army rounded up 112,000 men, women, and children of Japanese ancestry, two-thirds of them native-born citizens, and shipped them to remote relocation centers that had the look of concentration camps. There, with certain exceptions, the Japanese-Americans remained until near the end of the war, meanwhile losing homes, land, businesses, and faith in American justice.[73]

While unquestionably the most discreditable act on the American home front during World War II, the relocation of the Japanese-Americans less represents wartime conservatism than a victory for racism, greed, hysteria, indifference, and moral cowardice. By 1942, West Coast prejudice against those of Japanese ancestry was a half-century old, having originated in working-class hostility to industrious immigrants willing to work for low wages. After 1910, when Japanese-Americans began to achieve modest success as small businessmen and farmers, the benefits of their exclusion also became apparent to two other West Coast economic groups. Japan's victory in its 1905 war with Russia and subsequent imperialistic bent then added a strategic dimension to racial prejudice and gradually spread it to all classes.[74]

There things might have rested but for the surprise attack on Pearl Harbor, which reinforced the stereotypical sneakiness long attributed to the Japanese by West Coast racists and led to false rumors that a Japanese-American fifth column had aided the assault on the Hawaiian Islands. When a government investigation "confirmed" those rumors and the Western Defense Command weakly abandoned its earlier good judgment that only a few critical areas needed to be closed to aliens, the tolerance initially shown the Japanese-Americans evaporated, and baser elements of greed and racism surfaced. Referring to a military necessity that was ultimately denied by the Washington military command, and under pressure from West Coast politicians and various labor, agricultural, business, and "patriotic" groups, President Roosevelt signed the order authorizing the relocation of aliens living in the three Pacific

Coast states. In the grip of racism and fear, the Congress, the courts, and Americans generally then acquiesced in a massive violation of the civil liberties of not only alien Japanese but their native-born children as well.[75]

If World War II showed a repressive face to Japanese immigrants and their children, it also demonstrated that the nation could avoid some of its earlier errors. Although the Federal Bureau of Investigation (FBI) arrested a few German aliens as potential spies or saboteurs and the government tried a handful of protofascists, the well-assimilated German-American community had little sympathy for Hitler, played no identifiable role in the effort to keep the United States out of the war, and thus avoided the suspicion, hostility, and suffering it had known in the earlier world conflict.[76]

The prewar behavior of the newer Italian immigrants, however, risked a repeat of the German-Americans' World War I experience. Until Italy's invasion of Ethiopia and subsequent alliance with Hitler, Italian-Americans had expressed great admiration for Mussolini, and as late as 1940, Italian-language newspapers still expressed fascist sympathies and urged American neutrality. Pearl Harbor, however, reversed Italian-American views, and the FBI detained only a few suspected spies after the President, in October 1942, lifted the last of the restrictions on aliens of Italian ancestry.[77]

Again with the exception of the Japanese, the war reduced nativist hostility generally and hastened the assimilation of quite diverse groups of immigrants. The interwar anti-Semitism of the Ku Klux Klan and the various American protofascist groups represented only the more extreme forms of hostility to Jewish Americans, who suffered considerable social discrimination in clubs, education, housing, and jobs even while avoiding outright persecution. American officials ignored mounting evidence of Nazi genocide and did little to assist the escape of European Jews. By the end of the war, however, Americans had come to value the scientific contributions of the Jewish refugees from Nazism and to perceive that the horror of genocide expressed a logical outcome of the false doctrine of racial superiority.[78]

Mexican-Americans, too, used the war to improve their position in American life—despite the well-publicized battles between young Mexican-American "zoot suiters" and sailors on leave in Los Angeles. The wartime demand for agricultural labor lifted the grinding poverty known by Mexican-Americans during the depression, and the intergovernmental bracero agreement of 1942 guaranteed the transportation, food, shelter, medical care, and wages of newly arrived agricultural workers. Many older residents stepped up to better jobs in the West Coast's rapidly expanding defense industries, and 350,000 Mexican-American draftees returned with new experiences, changed attitudes, and higher aspirations. For them, as well as other Americans of Mexican ancestry, World War II became a "watershed."[79]

Like the defeat of New Deal programs and the abuse of immigrant minorities, wartime civil-liberties violations also provide evidence for the allegedly illiberal character of war. The June 1940 Alien Registration (Smith) Act, for example, not only established a requirement for alien registration but added a prohibition against sedition that resurrected the widely abused legislation of World War I. But Roosevelt and his attorney general, well aware of earlier injustices, kept sedition cases and law enforcement agencies under close control. Only in 1943 did they respond to pressure and indict thirty members of several profascist, anti-Semitic groups that opposed American involvement in the war. When the judge died midway in the trial, moreover, the government dropped the case.[80]

Though not prompted by the war, the August 1939 Hatch Act has usually been offered as an example of wartime illiberalism because it made membership in an organization advocating overthrow of the government a bar to Federal employment and led to the loyalty program that investigated the backgrounds of all civil servants. Clear abuse of the act, however, came only at the end of the war, when revelations of Russian spying and Cold War tensions created a climate of fear and mistrust.[81]

As Roosevelt kept the Office of War Information (OWI), successor of the World War I Committee on Public Information, under close control (and Congress kept it short of funds), no governmental propaganda agency created the kind of hysteria that had led to extensive private assaults on the liberties of unpopular groups during 1917–1918.[82]

Even the opponents of American involvement in international conflict received much milder treatment during World War II—a surprising result in light of the strength and vigor of the prewar peace movement but an outcome demonstrating that war need not significantly curtail the civil liberties of its opponents. The internationalist wing of that movement had sought United States support for various international organizations, which it hoped would prevent war by economic reform and the threat of collective action. A group of liberal peace advocates had worked for disarmament, the outlawry of war, a war-referendum amendment to the Constitution, and better international socioeconomic conditions. The pacifists shared much of that program but joined to it an absolute prohibition on the use of force and, occasionally, political radicalism. A group of isolationists, whose views eventually found expression in the America First Committee, reinforced the peace movement at certain points—particularly in its determination to keep the United States out of another European war.[83]

The Italian invasion of Ethiopia, German rearmament, the collapse of the League of Nations, and Hitler's aggressions in Europe gradually undermined the peace movement, however. The internationalists willingly backed the military dimension of collective security and supported American aid to the Allies. Even many peace liberals and pacifists began to doubt their principles, which seemed to offer no counter to the evil of Nazism. Then, after December 1941, the "tottering American peace movement collapsed." Once the United States had been attacked, the isolationists, their policy discredited, quickly gave their support to the war, and only a few pacifists carried on a quiet opposition.[84]

Even the remaining pacifists received relatively gentle treatment. The Selective Service System recognized the conscientious objections both of members of the historic peace churches and of those with general religious opposition to war. It also offered conscientious objectors either noncombatant assignments in the armed forces or unpaid civilian service in work camps established by the peace churches. Potential large-scale pacifist opposition collapsed further when three-quarters of the Quakers set religious scruples aside and fought, and most of the remainder along with the Mennonites and Brethren accepted noncombatant service in the Medical Corps or joined a work camp. In the end, the government imprisoned only 5,500 individuals for failing to register, refusal to serve in any capacity, or resistance on some unrecognized religious or political grounds. Jehovah's Witnesses, for example, comprised three-quarters of those imprisoned because the government refused to exempt all male members as ministers and because some of the Witnesses expressed a willingness to fight in what they regarded as the final battle between good and evil at Armageddon. Seduced by governmental leniency and demoralized by the undeniable evil of Nazism, pacifists remained relatively quiet during the war, and the Federal authorities generally left them in peace.[85]

Comparing the civil liberties records of the two world wars, the American Civil Liberties Union in mid-1943 concluded that the war offered "strong evidence to support the thesis that our democracy can fight even the greatest of all wars and still maintain the essentials of liberty." The government's wise policies had also avoided "mob violence against dissenters . . . ; creation of a universal volunteer vigilante system; hysterical hatred of everything German . . . ; savage sentences for private expressions of criticism . . . ; and . . . suppression of public debate."[86] Not only was the World War II record on civil liberties and the treatment of immigrants relatively liberal, several wartime developments point, in fact, to the conclusion that the war advanced certain reforms.

The return of prosperity, for instance, allowed the government—to the extent that the war permitted—to turn its attention to more fundamental reform. Having, for instance, committed his administration to the international pursuit of the Four Freedoms in 1941, President Roosevelt three years later announced an Economic Bill of Rights entitling every citizen to a useful job at a living wage, decent housing, a good education, and protection against the economic consequences of old age, illness, accident, and unemployment. Although the war years permitted no general progress on that list, Roosevelt had written the agenda for the postwar decades.[87]

For veterans the war provided more than an agenda. The Servicemen's Readjustment Act (GI Bill), possibly Roosevelt's first step in reviving the New Deal, gave returning veterans generous unemployment benefits while they sought work, job preferences to help them get it, loans to start a business, buy a farm, or purchase a home, medical care for the disabled, and tuition and allowances for those receiving occupational training or a college education. Three times the anticipated number of veterans seized the latter opportunity, and many members of society's lower socioeconomic groups consequently moved into the middle and professional classes—a development of enormous significance for postwar America. Generous treatment of veterans broke an American pattern in which returning soldiers met frustration and flocked to a new veterans' organization that would pursue their interests through political action.[88]

In a sense, the GI Bill also provided postwar aid to higher education, but in fact the Federal Government had begun to grant assistance much earlier. Despite deferments for engineers, scientists, and doctors, and government use of the larger universities for instruction in Japanese and Russian, American colleges faced a crippling loss of enrollment after 1942. Prompted by the American Council on Education, the Federal Government came to the rescue as the military departments used colleges to prepare men already in the services for certain military specialties and opened their installations so that colleges could offer correspondence and extension courses to soldiers and sailors wishing to continue their education when not on duty.[89]

The perhaps most liberating and lasting reforms of World War II, however, required little special legislation and only modest Federal involvement. Those reforms occurred as women and black Americans seized the war's opportunities to overcome restrictions that had impeded their full personal development.

Almost a century after the Civil War and over two decades after W.E.B. DuBois had urged Afro-Americans to give their full support to World War I in exchange for total equality, American blacks still suffered intense discrimination.[90] In the capital city of the United States no black citizen could attend a theater (except local Jim Crow movie houses), eat in a public restaurant used by whites, sit next to a white passenger on a public bus, ride in a taxi driven by a white, or register in a hotel. To their eternal shame the Daughters of the American Revolution had closed Constitution Hall to black contralto Marian Anderson, with the result that Eleanor Roosevelt arranged the singer's triumphal 1939 Easter concert on the steps of the Lincoln Memorial. Elsewhere in the nation, only twelve states forbade segregated schools, and but seventeen white colleges admitted even one black. After an auto accident in Tennessee, black jazz singer Bessie Smith bled to death when a white hospital refused her admission.[91]

Despite so much cause for despair, by the eve of World War II blacks had at last achieved a position from which they might effectively protest such treatment. The migration of blacks to Northern cities, initiated by World War I, had enabled them to develop their own communities relatively free of white supervision and oppression. With the black middle class, the black press, and civil-rights organizations all growing larger and stronger in that environment, blacks at last had the leadership and the means to make their influence felt. When black voters switched to the Democrats in 1936, they also signaled their intention to cast their ballots for whichever party best served their interests. Those interests increasingly included demands for "Democracy in Our Time!" from younger blacks raised in the relatively free North without indoctrination in the gradualist, accommodationist philosophy of Booker T. Washington and by older blacks resentful of the way the 1917–18 war had frustrated their hopes.[92]

In such a situation, World War II became decisive. With its demand for the near-total mobilization of society, white Americans had at least to begin to do justice to blacks in order to obtain their willing support. Observant blacks realized the opportunity and warned: "If we don't fight for our rights during this war, while the government needs us, it will be too late after the war."[93]

A. Philip Randolph, head of the Brotherhood of Sleeping Car Porters, organized the March on Washington Movement (MOWM)—the first highly effective, and most significant, effort to implement that idea. In order to stave off the march, Roosevelt in June 1941 ordered creation of the Fair Employment Practice Committee (FEPC), which through investigations, exposure, and the threatened loss of Federal business, sought to implement new Federal orders barring discrimination by firms with government contracts. The executive order creating the FEPC, or at least the decision to bar discrimination in government contracts, may have been the most significant Presidential act between the Emancipation Proclamation and World War II. But the committee never fully achieved all its goals.[94]

The March on Washington Movement, which never held its march, was the beginning of the modern civil-rights movement in this country; it may also have been more significant than the FEPC. To keep out communists, stimulate black pride and self-confidence, and attract mass support from the lower class, Randolph excluded whites from his organization. He also threatened direct, though nonviolent, action rather than work through the courts or pursue behind-the-scenes negotiations. And he set a goal (jobs) as much sought by Northern urban blacks as those in the rural South.[95]

Whether due to black protest, to the work of the FEPC, or, more likely, to the wartime shortage of labor and sheer stupidity of a racially based failure to make full use of the nation's human resources, black employment improved sharply during World War II. The number of blacks in the industrial work force grew by almost a million, and the proportion in defense work increased from 3 to 8.3 percent. As black unemployment fell from just under a million to only 151,000, Afro-American workers increasingly moved from menial, unskilled jobs into semiskilled work and positions as craftsmen and foremen. The average urban black's annual wage jumped from $400 to $1,000. Black union membership almost doubled—most of it within the CIO, which, unlike the AFL, barred segregation and discrimination within its component organizations.[96]

As shown by Table 4.8, World War II also quickened the pace of net black interregional migration, which reinforced those previously described areas of black strength within American society.

Table 4.8
Net Black Interregional Migration, 1920–1950
(Thousands)

Region	1920–30	1930–40	1940–50
Northeast	+435	+273	+ 599
South	−903	−480	−1,581
North Central	+426	+152	+ 626
West	+ 42	+ 55	+ 356

Source: Simon S. Kuznets and Dorothy S. Thomas, *Population Redistribution and Economic Growth: United States, 1870–1950* (Philadelphia, PA: American Philosophical Society, 1957), 3:90. Reprinted by permission of the publisher.

Increased migration and better jobs unfortunately also led to rising racial tension. With whites becoming resentful of blacks' militancy and improving job prospects, the growing pressure on inadequate urban housing, transportation, and recreational facilities soon resulted in violent racial confrontation. In 1943 alone, 47 American cities experienced over 200 violent racial incidents. The United States also suffered 18 race riots in the war years—the worst being the June 1943 eruption in Detroit that resulted in 34 deaths (25 of them black), 700 injuries, and $2 million in property damage.[97]

Some of the racial violence also occurred on or near military installations, as black protest and the need to boost the morale of black soldiers led the armed services to moderate some of their discriminatory policies.[98] In 1940, the army had only 12 black officers and but 5,000 black soldiers—all assigned to one of a dozen segregated units. Convinced that blacks made poor fighting men, the army intended to assign all new black recruits to service and support units. Too small in 1940 to establish segregated units, the army's air corps barred all blacks—as did the marines—and the navy accepted them only as messmen.[99]

The administration at first responded to black protest with a few token gestures—promotion of the army's first black general, appointment of black advisors to the Secretary of War and the Director of Selective Service, and creation of a few new black Reserve Officers' Training Corps units. Blacks, however, demanded more, hoping that by fighting as equals they would be rewarded and treated as equals.[100]

After an often bitter struggle, and aided by a growing awareness within the services that segregation impeded efficiency and lowered the effectiveness of black soldiers, Afro-Americans began to achieve some of their goals. The draft started to take blacks in approximately proportionate numbers, and the army began to assign them to all branches—though it dropped segregation only for a brief but successful experiment following the Battle of the Bulge in 1944. In the interest of efficiency, however, it also integrated most of its officer training. In 1944, the army ordered—but often failed to enforce—an end to segregation in post theaters, exchanges, buses, and recreational facilities. In June 1942, the navy began to recruit blacks for jobs other than messmen. Segregation was continued, however, until late in the war when the navy successfully experimented with mixed crews on twenty-five ships. Moreover, 90 percent of the navy's blacks still remained messmen in 1945. Although the marines also began to accept blacks, that service formed only one segregated infantry battalion, which never saw combat. Black pressure, manpower shortages, and the inefficiencies of segregation also opened up the air forces, and the army eventually created several black fighter and bomber groups. By the war's end, the services had learned that segregation hurt the war effort because it wasted black manpower, lowered unit effectiveness, and created unnecessary racial tension. It also subjected the services' civilian leadership to pressure from civil-rights groups. In the end, the war prompted the first small steps toward integrated units and laid the foundation for the armed forces' postwar desegregation.[101]

Developments both in the services and on the home front caused one historian to claim that World War II had "propelled . . . blacks into the mainstream of American life," whetted their "appetite for further reforms," and "made it possible for many Negroes to conceive of first-class citizenship for the first time."[102] Blacks had clearly planted the seeds that would produce integrated military services within a decade, and wartime protest provided precedents for the civil-rights movement of the 1950s and beyond. Migration and better jobs had also raised blacks' expectations and produced a willingness to demand their rights. Blacks had undoubtedly reached the best position they had yet held in American life; whether they located that spot in the mainstream seems questionable. Still, the war had facilitated a massive move in that direction.[103]

World War II also opened comparable opportunities to American women, who used them to cast off some traditional restraints. At the end of the previous world conflict, women had won the vote and felt increasingly free to engage in sports, wear more comfortable clothes, expect personal fulfillment in marriage, and live independently while single working girls. The public nevertheless expected women to pursue marriage, home, and family—and abandon paid employment upon achieving those goals. To insure that they did, some states passed laws closing many jobs to married women, an attitude toward a woman's proper role that most unions supported. With the percentage of women who worked in 1940 still at 1910 levels, and the public hostile to further female employment, the prospects for women workers looked bad indeed on the eve of World War II.[104]

The war, however, quickly reversed that estimate. By July 1944 the work force included nineteen million women (47 percent more than in 1940), and the proportion of women who worked had jumped from 25 to 36 percent— a larger increase than during the previous four decades. Most of the 2.5 million new workers went into manufacturing, where the proportion of women employees rose by 110 percent. With the aid of government training programs, women soon took jobs alongside men in aircraft construction, shipbuilding, steelmaking, munitions, and the railroads. Moreover, the government and the public generally supported those changes—even if only as war measures.[105]

The director of the War Manpower Commission (WMC) had warned employers that they could not "afford to waste our labor resources . . . by unintelligent and unfair restrictions against women." Nevertheless, women found it harder to get places in even government training programs or to obtain professional work. Businessmen, with union support, often refused to hire women as foremen, supervisors, or managers. Women in factory jobs continued to earn only 65 percent of the average man's wage, in part because employers found loopholes in the WMC's equal pay order.[106]

More significant in the long run than those injustices, the war produced a change in the very character of women's employment. Not only had women in large numbers moved into war industry (and factory work generally), two million more women also found clerical work, most of it with the Federal

Government. At the other end of the scale women abandoned domestic work and other menial, service jobs in large numbers. Most important, however, married, widowed, or divorced women in the work force for the first time outnumbered those who were single, and the proportion of women workers over thirty-five rose to more than 60 percent—reversing another prewar pattern. By 1944, one-quarter of all married women in America had a paid job.[107]

Remembering how World War I women had quickly lost even more modest gains, many regarded the postwar period with grave concern. Apparently true to form, in the summer of 1945, three-quarters of the women in aircraft and shipbuilding lost their jobs, and manufacturers generally dismissed women workers at twice the rate of male employees. Between September 1945 and November 1946, over three million women left work or were laid off. Because women had not gone to work in 1942 solely out of patriotism, economic need and a desire for fulfillment soon caused almost that many women to reverse older patterns by finding new work. Within a few years women made up their postwar net loss of six hundred thousand jobs, while married women and those over thirty-five continued to dominate the female work force.[108] Much of the gain and the most significant changes survived World War II and would, in time, force Americans to reconsider the roles of both men and women in family, work, and national life.

World War II thus produced quite diverse social consequences. While helping destroy nativism and bring greater freedom to women and blacks, it became the occasion to rob Japanese-Americans of the most basic liberties. The government treated the opponents of war in a more enlightened fashion and guarded against the public hysteria that had previously led to local violations. The Smith and Hatch acts, however, marred an otherwise satisfactory civil-liberties record. If the Congress undermined certain New Deal programs and rejected Roosevelt's Economic Bill of Rights for all Americans, it also approved a GI Bill that gave most of those benefits to the returning veterans. To understand that decision requires an examination of the evolving wartime relationship among the branches of government and between the two political parties.

The Politics of Total War

Arthur Schlesinger, Jr., has quite accurately observed that World War II, like its predecessors, "nourished the Presidency." That seems particularly true in regard to foreign affairs. As a reaction to Wilsonianism, the interwar Congress had dominated American foreign policy, blocking United States membership in various international organizations, delaying rearmament, using neutrality legislation to impede Presidential efforts to aid Hitler's opponents, and creating in the public the suspicion that Roosevelt secretly sought to maneuver the nation into another useless European conflict. By discrediting those Congressional policies, Pearl Harbor restored Presidential direction of foreign policy. Further, it created in the public mind a new belief that Congress was institutionally unfit to play a leading role in foreign affairs. When late in the war the Republican party elected to support a bipartisan foreign policy, it further undermined Congressional influence and produced quite different results than at the end of World War I.[109]

Those special circumstances merely reinforced the foreign affairs advantages the President would normally have derived from his control of military strategy, just as the wartime need to mobilize society to fight the war initially enhanced his domestic authority. Whereas Roosevelt had relied upon specific legislative grants in dealing with the Great Depression, his prewar mobilization agencies had rested on voluntary compliance, emergency powers derived from old statutes, or questionable assertions of authority. After Pearl Harbor, however, Congress gave him two sweeping grants of war powers based on the legacy of the Wilson administration. In the manner of Lincoln, however, Roosevelt also defended creation of many of his wartime agencies by claiming war powers allegedly inherent in his office.[110] And in September 1942, when Congress seemed unwilling to give him the price-control legislation he desired, Roosevelt, in a crude assertion of Presidential war power, threatened that if "the Congress should fail to act, and act inadequately, I shall accept responsibility, and I will act."[111]

Congress yielded on that occasion, and, by voting funds indirectly, it gave its approval of the emergency agencies created by executive order. It began to reassert itself, however, after the initial shock administered by Pearl Harbor. Congress exercised particular influence over price controls and farm policy—farm prices being the occasion for the September 1942 clash. And, following the 1943 strikes, it forced unwanted labor legislation on the President. Throughout the war, Congress also sought to insure the survival of small businessmen, and it frequently overruled or reduced taxes the administration requested. Once the crisis passed, Congress also refused to rubber-stamp all Presidential appeals. It demanded that he justify each new request for authority, and favored only specific rather than general grants of power.[112]

Although Congress created no Civil War-style Joint Committee on the Conduct of the War, Truman's Senate Special Committee to investigate the National Defense Program and a lesser known House body performed some of its functions. The committees, however, stayed out of strategic and operational matters while accomplishing a very useful supervision of defense contracting. They also prodded the President to reform the mobilization agencies and attacked the military services, rather than Roosevelt, whenever discovering evidence of waste or corruption. In that sense, Congress used its investigatory power in harmony rather than in conflict with the President.[113]

Despite the confrontation of 1937, the Supreme Court generally adapted itself to the President's wartime actions when supported by Congress. It refused, for example, to address Constitutional issues when it rejected cases stemming from Roosevelt's seizure of war plants on the grounds that their owners again controlled them by the time the cases reached the Court in 1945. The Court also upheld wartime price controls. Although it discouraged prosecution or deportation for antiwar statements, which represented an improvement over World War I, the Court sustained the relocation of Japanese-Americans. Not until December 1944, when the government had already begun their release, did the court in *ex parte Endo* declare that, although the evacuation had been Constitutional, the government had no grounds for the continued detention of a loyal citizen.[114]

In one respect, the Court's decision in the Japanese-American cases seems "out of character" with a trend underway since the 1937 "court-packing" controversy. Thereafter, the Supreme Court abandoned its long struggle to block Federal regulation of the economy and instead turned toward asserting its control over the states' criminal procedures and the protection of civil rights.[115] In another sense, however, World War II confirmed the pattern that relied on Presidential self-restraint for the wartime protection of civil liberties, though the Court might reassert its prerogatives once the emergency had passed.

Like World War I, World War II heightened partisan competition and affected the relative strengths of the two parties. It did not, however, overturn the fifth national party system that had emerged between 1928 and 1936 and that had replaced its Republican-dominated predecessor with a new Democratic coalition uniting the South, the prairie states of the Midwest, and the labor, ethnic, and black vote of the nation's larger cities. Indeed, at the rhetorical level the voters might have believed that bipartisan harmony reigned in Washington as Republicans abandoned their prewar foreign policies and pledged their full support to the war and its principal aims.[116]

On the contrary, because Pearl Harbor enabled the Republicans to heal their principal divisions—those concerning foreign policy—and to adopt a bipartisan internationalist stance, the war allowed them to intensify opposition to the Democrats' domestic programs. While remaining genuinely committed to victory, the Republicans could criticize the harm war mobilization did to farmers or small businesses, point to examples of inefficiency or exorbitant profits, or condemn actions that might seem to infringe civil liberties. As "Mr. Republican," Senator Robert A. Taft, explained: While "Congress cannot assume to run the war," it "does have the job of reasonable criticism." The Republicans tried to insure that it did that job.[117]

Some weakening of the Democratic coalition helped the Republicans in their efforts. Southern Democrats, unhappy with the administration's support for black Americans and suspicious of its liberalism, often split ranks and joined with Republicans to abolish New Deal agencies, limit the legislative advance of liberal reform, adopt antilabor but profarm legislation, and moderate wartime price controls and tax increases. That coalition, which began to emerge in the late 1930s, is the true source of the wartime attack on liberal reform.[118]

Although the Democrats could still rely on the South to help them elect a President and retain at least nominal control of Congress, other developments affected both voting and representation. As farmers, for example, withheld their support out of irritation over price controls, the Democrats became more clearly an urban party, and place of residence became more important than socioeconomic class in shaping voter preference. Labor unions, on the other hand, abandoned their former approach to politics and cemented their alliance with the Democrats. The CIO's new Political Action Committee played a decisive electoral role after 1943, for example, and helped Democratic platforms and programs become more liberal.[119]

By the end of the war, then, partisan competition had revived and assumed a more nearly equal basis. Congress had begun to reassert itself, particularly on domestic issues, and the Supreme Court, despite its wartime compromises, prepared to move boldly into new areas.

The industrial production that Stalin so lavishly praised in November 1943 had only begun to hit its stride. With governmental controls only then beginning to take hold, the greatest triumphs of American industry still lay in the future. Indeed, only in 1943 had the government finally established a reasonably effective, though still largely voluntaristic and indirect, system of mobilization agencies. In the May 1943 Office of War Mobilization the United States at last had a body capable of coordinating the work of the various boards and commissions responsible for industrial production, manpower, agriculture, prices, and civilian supply, and harmonizing their efforts with the demands that the US military departments and the Allies placed on the American economy.

Industry clearly felt the heavy hand of government, which closed certain lines of civil production and provided labor and scarce raw materials only in exchange for doing essential work. But it also enjoyed the wartime return of prosperity. War-enforced diversification also hastened a developing trend to new corporate forms in those industries that would dominate the postwar economy. On the one hand, labor felt governmental pressure to limit wage increases and faced the threat of work-or-fight orders and national-service legislation as Federal authorities sought to move workers to essential jobs. On the other hand, unions experienced unprecedented growth in membership and exceeded their World War I participation in government, while workingmen and women gained a larger share of the rapidly growing national income. Farmers, with the return of agricultural prosperity, enjoyed larger incomes, though they chafed under wartime price controls while responding to the war in ways that produced America's second revolution in agriculture and laid the ground for postwar developments. To all major sectors of the economy, the war had brought both the restraint of central controls and the liberation of wartime prosperity.

The war's liberating influences also extended beyond the economy. With the glaring exception of the treatment accorded Japanese-Americans, the government resorted to few controls on civil liberties, and various previously disadvantaged groups won increased social acceptance and access to better jobs. The latter particularly applied to women and black Americans, for whom economic advance laid the ground for progress on broader fronts.

Politically, World War II moved the United States away from the isolationist tradition in foreign policy and the Republican party from a near-total opposition to the fundamental elements of the New Deal welfare state. Though the Republicans and their southern Democratic allies eliminated some peripheral programs, the war provided no opportunity to dismantle social security or to challenge governmental responsibility for maintaining economic prosperity through legislation affecting industry, banking, agriculture, and labor. For the war's veterans, even conservatives supported programs that liberals wished to extend to all Americans. As usual, the war partially freed the Presidency from normal legislative and judicial restraints, roused Congress to guard its prerogatives as best it could, and caused the Supreme Court to step aside until the emergency had passed.

World War II, therefore, not only freed Americans from the military threat of the Axis but liberated many of them, despite wartime controls, from crippling social, political, and economic restraints. The war had also readied the nation for what John Brooks described as the "great leap" it would take in the following quarter century.[120]

WAR AND SOCIETY IN AMERICA: A FEW ANSWERS

> *All thought which leads to decisions of public policy is in essence historical. Public decision in rational politics necessarily implies a guess about the future derived from the experience of the past. It implies an expectation, or at the very least a hope, that certain actions will produce tomorrow the same sort of results they produced yesterday. This guess about the future . . . involves, explicitly or implicitly, an historical judgment.*
>
> Arthur M. Schlesinger, Jr.[1]

Arthur Schlesinger's observations on the essentially historical nature of intelligent policymaking suggest that military and civilian officials who must plan against the possibility of war can profitably draw upon the historical record described in the preceding pages. Because each historical event is unique, however, that record is best understood when examined in detail. Only such study will reveal each war's special context and account for the often divergent results produced by particular circumstances that either neutralize or enhance the action of tendencies the wars have in common.

One other warning seems in order. The generalizations that follow derive from the study of four major wars, conflicts that required the American people to mobilize a significant portion of their human and material resources. Wars that have demanded a lesser effort have often produced important results—the stimulus to manufacturing given by the Jeffersonian embargoes preceding the War of 1812, the destructive dispute over the territorial extent of slavery resurrected by the Mexican War, or the debate over America's proper role in world affairs that emerged during the 1898 war with Spain and revived with special virulence during the conflict in Vietnam. However significant in those respects, such smaller wars seem less comprehensive in their total effects. They do not, that is, set in motion all the forces described in the following pages.

One of the clearest conclusions to emerge from this study is the ability of war to stimulate the economy. The reasons seem equally obvious. In the first instance, the armed forces have increased their purchases of supplies and equipment, which in turn raised civilian incomes and business profits and boosted the demand for both consumer and capital goods. That result has been much the same, whether the American armed forces created that new demand or, as during the period of American neutrality in the two twentieth-century wars, the new buying initially came from abroad.

When the war found the economy operating below capacity, that stimulation produced healthy economic results. Between 1939 and 1941, for example, the economic stimulation of war led to the return of prosperity, sufficient new capacity to supply the armed forces while maintaining civilian standards of living, and creation of a foundation of wealth and industrial capacity that sustained growth into the postwar period.

The wartime growth in demand has, of course, eventually overstimulated the economy—usually in the form of inflation. As the wars put marginal capacity to use, some wartime inflation would inevitably occur. The major economic difficulties stemmed, however, from more varied causes: In 1917 the declaration of war found the economy already operating near full capacity and unable to accommodate the sudden increase in American military demand. In the South during the Civil War, the total economy remained unequal to the burdens placed upon it. In all four wars, the United States paid for but a fraction of war costs out of current income and its war loans insufficiently reduced consumer buying power. The effort to divert civilian production to military use thus led to inflation, though American governments have shown an increasing ability to control its wartime extent.

Even as inflation has debilitated the economy, industry and agriculture have drawn profit from the war. Although the Revolution hurt rice- and indigo-producing areas of the deep South and the Civil War set back Southern agriculture generally, grain and livestock producers found profit from sales to the armed forces, profit sufficient to compensate for the occasional disruption of military operations on American soil. In the two world wars, no such developments qualified agricultural prosperity. As farmers fed soldiers and allied populations and entered markets newly opened by the war, farm prices and incomes grew. To meet the demand and overcome labor shortages, farmers turned to the use of more machinery and the latest discoveries of agricultural science. They also sometimes invested in more land—an action that led to a harmful indebtedness and overexpansion after the Civil War and World War I.

War has benefited industry in several ways. The Revolutionary boycotts, the Civil War tariffs, and the twentieth-century wartime disruption of the

European economy have all protected American producers from foreign competition, just as wartime demand provided an additional incentive for investment in new plant and equipment. Supplying the wartime market has also encouraged large-scale machine production among both established firms and new industries directly related to the war, such as meat packing, canning, ready-made clothing, chemicals, electronics, aircraft, metals, and, of course, munitions. The Civil War also encouraged business expansion to supply a national market while World War II speeded the diversification characteristic of the nation's industrial giants since 1945.

In addition to stimulating the economy and promoting industry and agriculture, war has provided the occasion for the government to increase its controls over American society generally. Such direction developed first in finance and banking. Initially little but a council of ambassadors, the Continental Congress eschewed total reliance on the state governments and elected to raise an army and finance the War for Independence, which caused it to begin issuing its own currency. The most nationalistic among the Revolutionaries unsuccessfully sought to extend those financial controls by creating a bank and proposing to give Congress the power to tax. The Civil War enhanced the taxing powers of the government when it implemented a wartime income tax and began to charter national banks, to which it issued America's first true national currency. During the two world wars, the government expanded its reliance upon income taxes and used the Federal Reserve System to insure that the nation's banks financially supported the war effort.

The Federal Government did not cease relying upon the states and developed its own controls only in matters that concerned finance. That same trend prompted wartime governments to extend their controls over other aspects of American life. Although state governments still raised most of the troops that fought the Civil War, by midway in that contest the central governments of both the Union and Confederacy had resorted to a centralized draft and asserted their right to supply even state forces when in national service. By the twentieth century, state militia forces had become a less significant part of the national army. The Federal Government eventually precluded volunteering in favor of systems for selecting the best place of service for each male citizen. Though not consummated, that trend approached its logical outcome with World War II proposals for national service.

Although somewhat later to develop, the same trend toward centralization affected the market economy. With twentieth-century warfare, the Federal Government lessened its reliance upon the marketplace for diverting production to military use. The government rarely resorted to seizure or other direct controls, but sought to influence the behavior of farmers and businessmen through such voluntaristic and indirect methods as appeals to patriotism, negotiated agreements, financial incentives, licensing, public corporations, its ability to deny labor, transport, or resources to recalcitrant firms, and, in the background, the threat of seizure. Use of even voluntaristic methods nevertheless required the creation of new wartime agencies and an expansion of the Federal bureaucracy.

The wartime growth of Federal power has also affected the relations among the government's three branches. In the face of grave emergency, the Supreme Court has generally supported the sometimes extra-Constitutional authority claimed by the President and Congress, or at least postponed any challenge until passage of the crisis.

The relation between the executive and legislative branches has been more complex. The Continental Congress had run the Revolution but found that it increasingly had to rely upon ever more independent executive bodies of its own creation. Lincoln blocked any early attempt by the Civil War Congress to direct the war when he delayed calling it into special session for several months. By that time he had established firm control based largely on the authority of his asserted war powers. Succeeding Congresses have also generally yielded to Presidential demands in the early phases of war. As the emergencies have moderated, however, they have universally sought to reassert their prerogatives.

The manner in which wartime Presidents have dealt with Congress has generally reflected the long-term trend in the developing relationship between the two branches of government. Lincoln often acted unilaterally in matters that concerned the war but offered Congress little legislative leadership in other areas—as was then the custom. Wilson, who had sought to lead Congress during peacetime, extended that effort into the war years. Roosevelt borrowed from both predecessors, sometimes asserting his office's inherent war powers and other times seeking statutory authority for his actions. War has nevertheless reinforced the general trend toward executive leadership, expansion, and domination of the Federal Government.

With the exception of the Civil War Confederacy—and probably to its disadvantage—warfare has not stilled partisan competition. Ever since the Radical-Nationalist split within the Continental Congress, major wars have prompted party formation and revitalized and intensified partisan competition. Except for the Civil War peace Democrats, that division has not been over support for the war itself, but has instead concerned either which party might most quickly and efficiently achieve victory or involved the form of war measures that would affect the postwar era.

If a major war's general economic and political influences seem rather clear, a good deal of ambiguity surrounds its social consequences. While wars undoubtedly open social opportunities, they do not determine which groups will use them and for what purposes.

On the darker side, wars have provided the occasion for restricting the civil liberties of the government's opponents and massive, sometimes unofficial, assaults on unpopular ethnic, racial, religious, or political minorities. American Revolutionaries persecuted Loyalists and pacifists, and Lincoln suspended the writ of habeas corpus and resorted to military tribunals to silence the extreme peace Democrats. World War I became the occasion for a governmental effort to crush radicalism and for widespread private persecution of German-Americans. The hatreds thus aroused reached their peak in the postwar Red Scare and the campaign to restrict immigration. Although the Roosevelt administration in most respects established the best civil liberties record to that date, its relocation of the Japanese-Americans represented race hatred at its worst.

Were that the whole story, it would establish a case for the repressive, illiberal character of war. A complete picture, however, emerges only when note is taken of those ethnic and religious minorities who forged ahead socially when the government's wartime need of their services forced destruction of old social barriers.

Such advance is particularly apparent for black Americans and women. The Revolution brought freedom to many individual blacks and led to gradual emancipation north of Maryland. The Civil War destroyed slavery, even if racism survived to defeat hopes for civil and political liberties and economic opportunity. Although World War I left similar hopes unfulfilled, the migration it prompted laid the base for later black protest, and a second world conflict led to considerable progress. To women, the Revolution gave a supporting role in education and politics. During that struggle and later in the Civil War, women also assumed many of their husbands' responsibilities on the farm and in business. In addition, the Civil War further opened the door to careers in nursing and teaching, and women assumed a supporting political role in the campaign for the Thirteenth Amendment. World War I contributions by women facilitated passage of the Nineteenth Amendment, but wartime improvement in women's employment opportunities did not endure. That was not the case, however, in the Second World War, which produced lasting improvement and a change in the typical woman worker from young and single to over thirty-five and married, usually with children.

Laboring people in general also made good use of the two world wars. Unions increased their membership and their voice in policymaking, and the government assumed new responsibilities to improve hours and working conditions and keep the increase in wages ahead of inflation.

This history of life on the American home front is consequently a record of change, a story not unlike the chronicle of most serious armed conflict. Major wars nearly always pose a test of a nation's traditions and institutions.

To counter the external enemy, the society must adapt in order to create a large, well-armed military force. To contain the internal unrest prompted either by the war itself or by that very adaptation, it must further evolve, usually by suppressing traditions and activities that impede the war effort and reinforcing those that lead to success. To do otherwise is to risk defeat and a victor's externally directed reorganization of society. In either manner, war becomes an engine of social, economic, and political change.

NOTES

Notes. War and Society in America: Some Questions

1. Adams, 12 December 1768 article, signed "Vindex," reprinted in *The Writings of Samuel Adams*, ed. Harry A. Cushing, 4 vols. (New York: G. P. Putnam's Sons, 1904–8), 1:264–65.

2. Arthur A. Ekirch, *The Civilian and the Military: A History of the American Antimilitarist Tradition* (New York: Oxford University Press, 1956). This history of American antimilitary thought from its English origins through the end of World War II describes these views of war's dangers and has guided my references to antimilitary thought in the following paragraphs.

3. See Robert Nisbet, "The Military Community," *Virginia Quarterly Review* 49 (Winter 1973):1-28; Stanislav Andreski, *Military Organization and Society* (Berkeley: University of California Press, 1971); Arthur Marwick, *War and Social Change in the Twentieth Century: A Comparative Study of Britain, France, Germany, Russia and the United States* (New York: St. Martin's Press, 1974); Pendleton Herring, *The Impact of War: Our American Democracy Under Arms* (New York: Farrar & Rinehart, 1941).

Notes. Chapter 1: The War for Independence

1. "Address by B. Rush to the People of the United States, Philadelphia, 1787," reprinted in Alden T. Vaughan, ed., *Chronicles of the American Revolution*, originally compiled by Hezekiah Niles (New York: Grosset & Dunlop, 1965), p. 334.

2. Ibid.

3. Ibid.

4. Don Higginbotham, *The War of American Independence: Military Attitudes, Policies, and Practice, 1763–1789* (New York: Macmillan, 1971), p. 389.

5. John W. Shy, "The Legacy of the American Revolutionary War," in *Legacies of the American Revolution*, eds. Larry R. Gerlach, James A. Dolph, and Michael L. Nicholls (Logan: Utah State University Press, 1978), pp. 45–46.

6. Charles Royster, *A Revolutionary People at War: The Continental Army and American Character, 1775–1783* (Chapel Hill: University of North Carolina Press for Institute of Early American History and Culture, 1980), pp. 295–304.

7. Quoted by Elizabeth Cometti, "Women in the American Revolution," *New England Quarterly* 20 (September 1947):330.

8. Elmer J. Ferguson, *The Power of the Purse: A History of American Public Finance, 1776–1790* (Chapel Hill: University of North Carolina Press for Institute of Early American History and Culture, 1961), p. 333; Emory R. Johnson, *History of Domestic and Foreign Commerce of the United States*, 2 vols. (Washington: Carnegie Institution of Washington, 1915), 1:158; Robert R. Palmer, *The Age of the Democratic Revolution: A Political History of Europe and America, 1760–1800*, 2 vols. (Princeton: Princeton University Press, 1959–65), 1:188.

9. Merle E. Curti, *The Growth of American Thought*, 3d ed. (New York: Harper and Row, 1964), pp. 125–26; Dixon R. Fox, *Ideas in Motion* (New York: D. Appleton-Century, 1935), pp. 39–40.

10. Philip S. Foner, *Blacks in the American Revolution* (Westport: Greenwood Press, 1976), pp. 41–44; Benjamin Quarles, *The Negro in the American Revolution* (Chapel Hill: University of North Carolina Press for Institute of Early American History and Culture, 1961), pp. 8–11.

11. Quarles, *Negro in the Revolution*, pp. 13–18.

12. Quarles, *Negro in the Revolution*, pp. 18–19, 52–67, 102–3; Jack D. Foner, *Blacks and the Military in American History: A New Perspective* (New York: Praeger, 1974), pp. 10–14.

13. Foner, *Blacks and the Military*, pp. 17–18; John Hope Franklin, *From Slavery to Freedom: A History of American Negroes*, 5th ed. (New York: Knopf, 1980),

p. 88; Willie Lee Rose, "The Impact of the American Revolution on the Black Population," in *Legacies of the Revolution*, p. 186.

14. Adams quoted in Franklin, *Slavery to Freedom*, p. 83.

15. Arthur Zilversmit, *The First Emancipation: The Abolition of Slavery in the North* (Chicago: University of Chicago Press, 1967), pp. 114–93, 227–29; Foner, *Blacks in the Revolution*, pp. 75–104.

16. Gary Nash, "The Forgotten Experience: Indians, Blacks, and the American Revolution," in *The American Revolution: Changing Perspectives*, eds. William M. Fowler, Jr., and Wallace Coyle (Boston: Northeastern University Press, 1979), p. 36.

17. Eleanor Flexnor, *Century of Struggle: The Woman's Rights Movement in the United States*, rev. ed. (Cambridge: Belknap Press of Harvard University Press, 1975), pp. 13–14; Mary P. Ryan, *Womanhood in America: From Colonial Times to the Present* (New York: New Viewpoints, 1975), pp. 90–91.

18. Cometti, "Women in the Revolution," *New England Quarterly*, p. 329; Higginbotham, *War of Independence*, pp. 397–98; Linda G. DePauw, "Women in Combat: The Revolutionary War Experience," *Armed Forces and Society* 7 (Winter 1980):209–26.

19. Mary B. Norton, *Liberty's Daughters* (Boston: Little, Brown, 1980), pp. xiv–xv, 191–93, 295; Marylynn Salmon, "'Life, Liberty and Dower': The Legal Status of Women after the American Revolution," in *Women, War, and Revolution*, eds. Carol R. Berkin and Clara M. Lovett (New York: Holmes & Meier, 1980), pp. 86–100.

20. Norton, *Liberty's Daughters*, pp. 155–56, 177, 188, 195–96, 225–42; Linda Kerber, *Women of the Republic: Intellect and Ideology in Revolutionary America* (Chapel Hill: University of North Carolina Press for Institute of Early American History and Culture, 1980), pp. 8–10.

21. Kerber, *Women of the Republic*, pp. 284–85.

22. Ibid., p. 235.

23. Norton, *Liberty's Daughters*, pp. 256, 273–78; Ryan, *Womanhood in America*, p. 124.

24. John Teaford, "The Transformation of Massachusetts Education, 1670-1780," *History of Education Quarterly* 10 (Fall 1970):297–99; Frederick Rudolph, *The American College and University: A History* (New York: Knopf, 1962), pp. 34–43; Jackson T. Main, "The Results of the American Revolution Reconsidered," *Historian* 31 (August 1969):545; Robert Middlekauff, *Ancients and Axioms: Secondary Education in Eighteenth-Century New England* (New Haven: Yale University Press, 1963), pp. 116–22; Allan Nevins, *The American States during and after the Revolution, 1775-1789* (New York: Macmillan, 1924; reprint ed., New York: A. M. Kelley, 1969), pp. 466–68; Meyer Reinhold, "Opponents of Classical Learning in America during the Revolutionary Period," *Proceedings of the American Philosophical Society* 112 (15 August 1968):223.

25. Fielding H. Garrison, *An Introduction to the History of Medicine*, 4th ed. (Philadelphia: W. B. Saunders, 1929), p. 376; Fox, *Ideas in Motion*, pp. 45–46, 65–66; Silvio A. Bedini, *Thinkers and Tinkers: Early American Men of Science* (New York: Charles Scribner's, 1975), pp. 237–73.

26. James S. Olson, *The Ethnic Dimension in American History* (New York: St. Martin's Press, 1979), pp. 32–33, 46.

27. Olson, *Ethnic Dimension*, p. 46; Leonard Dinnerstein, Roger L. Nichols, and David M. Reimers, *Natives and Strangers: Ethnic Groups and the Building of America* (New York: Oxford University Press, 1979), pp. 24–26; Carl F. Wittke, *We Who Built America: The Saga of the Immigrant*, rev. ed. (Cleveland: Press of Western Reserve University, 1967), p. 41; Oscar Handlin, *Adventure in Freedom: Three Hundred Years of Jewish Life in America* (New York: McGraw-Hill, 1954), pp. 22–23; Jacob R. Marcus, "Jews and the American Revolution: A Bicentennial Documentary," *American Jewish Archives* 27 (November 1975): 103, 113–15.

28. Ian C. C. Graham, *Colonists from Scotland: Emigration to North America, 1707-1783* (Ithaca: Cornell University Press, 1956), pp. 20–21, 129–50, 177, 183; *Harvard Encyclopedia of American Ethnic Groups*, ed. Stephan Thernstrom, s.v. "Scots," by Gordon Donaldson.

29. Olson, *Ethnic Dimension*, pp. 24–25.

30. John C. Miller, *The Triumph of Freedom, 1775–1783* (Boston: Little, Brown, 1948), p. 15; Rodney Atwood, *The Hessians: Mercenaries from Hessen-Kassel in the American Revolution* (Cambridge: Cambridge University Press, 1980), pp. 184–205; LaVern J. Rippley, *The German-Americans* (Boston: Twayne Publishers, 1976), p. 38.

31. Olson, *Ethnic Dimension*, pp. 24–25; Rippley, *The German-Americans*, pp. 30, 32–37, 39–40; Theodore Huebner, *The Germans in America* (Philadelphia: Chilton, 1962), pp. 42–43.

32. James G. Leyburn, *The Scotch-Irish: A Social History* (Chapel Hill: University of North Carolina Press, 1962), pp. 297–308, 317; *Harvard Encyclopedia*, s.v. "Scotch-Irish," by Meldwyn A. Jones; Olson, *Ethnic Dimension*, pp. 27–31.

33. Charles Murphy, *The Irish in the American Revolution* (Groveland: Charles Murphy Publications, 1975), pp. 35–37, 43–52, 99, 103; *Harvard Encyclopedia*, s.v. "Irish," by Patrick J. Blessing; Wittke, *We Who Built America*, pp. 47–49; Wittke, *The Irish in America* (Baton Rouge: Louisiana State University Press, 1956), pp. vi-viii; Joe R. Feagin, *Racial and Ethnic Relations* (Englewood Cliffs: Prentice-Hall, 1978), pp. 82–85; John T. Ellis, *American Catholicism* (Chicago: University of Chicago Press, 1956), pp. 35–37.

34. William W. Sweet, *Religion in the Development of American Culture, 1765–1840* (Boston: Scribner's, 1952; reprint ed., Gloucester: Peter Smith, 1963), pp. 45–46.

35. Carroll quoted in Martin I. J. Griffin, *Catholics and the American Revolution*, 3 vols. (Ridley Park: Author, 1907–11), 1:352; Sweet, *Religion in American Culture*,

p. 49; Ellis, *American Catholicism*, pp. 18–34; Anthony I. Marino, *The Catholics in America* (New York: Vantage Press, 1960), p. 39.

36. Mark A. Noll, *Christians in the American Revolution* (Grand Rapids: Christian University Press, 1977), pp. 51–59, 79–84; Sweet, *Religion in American Culture*, pp. 33–36; Edward F. Humphrey, *Nationalism and Religion in America* (Boston: Chipman Law, 1924), pp. 490–502; Miller, *Triumph of Freedom*, pp. 355–56.

37. Noll, *Christians in the Revolution*, pp. 51–59, 80–84; Miller, *Triumph of Freedom*, p. 355.

38. Dwight quoted by James A. Henretta, *The Evolution of American Society, 1700–1815: An Interdisciplinary Analysis* (Lexington: D. C. Heath, 1973), p. 169; Trumbull quoted by Winthrop S. Hudson, *American Protestantism* (Chicago: University of Chicago Press, 1961), p. 50; Jack R. Pole, *Foundations of American Independence, 1763–1815* (Indianapolis: Bobbs-Merrill, 1972), pp. 126–27; Sweet, *Religion in American Culture*, p. 53.

39. This and the following paragraph are based upon: Catherine L. Albanese, *Sons of the Fathers: The Civil Religion of the American Revolution* (Philadelphia: Temple University Press, 1976), pp. 46–111; Noll, *Christians in the Revolution*, pp. 158–60, 163–69; Edmund S. Morgan, "The American Revolution Considered as an Intellectual Movement," in *Paths of American Thought*, eds. Arthur M. Schlesinger, Jr., and Morton White (Boston: Houghton Mifflin, 1963), p. 11.

40. Sweet, *Religion in American Culture*, p. 14; Noll, *Christians in the Revolution*, pp. 104–7; Hudson, *American Protestantism*, pp. 55–56.

41. Wittke, *We Who Built America*, p. 90; Arthur J. Mekeel, "The Relation of Quakers to the American Revolution," *Quaker History* 65 (Spring 1976): 15–16; Peter Brock, *Pacifism in the United States: From the Colonial Period to the First World War* (Princeton: Princeton University Press, 1968), p. 183.

42. Mekeel, "Quakers in the Revolution," *Quaker History*, pp. 14–17; Miriam L. Luke, "The Fighting Quakers of the American Revolution," *Daughters of the American Revolution Magazine* 110 (February 1976): 183.

43. Arthur J. Mekeel, *The Relation of Quakers to the American Revolution* (Washington: University Press of America, 1979), pp. 325–29; Brock, *Pacifism in the United States*, pp. 193–95; Rufus M. Jones, *The Quakers in the American Colonies* (London: Macmillan, 1911), pp. 556–80.

44. Resolution quoted by James W. Thompson, "Anti-Loyalist Legislation during the American Revolution," *Illinois Law Review* 3 (June–October 1908):86.

45. Wallace Brown, *The Good Americans: The Loyalists in the American Revolution* (New York: Morrow, 1969), pp. 127–29; Miller, *Triumph of Freedom*, pp. 39–40, 58.

46. William H. Nelson, *The American Tory* (Oxford: Clarendon Press, 1961), p. 146.

47. Brown, *Good Americans*, pp. 136ff.

48. Don Higginbotham, "The American Militia: A Traditional Institution with Revolutionary Responsibilities," in *Reconsiderations on the Revolutionary War: Selected Essays*, ed. Don Higginbotham (Westport: Greenwood Press, 1978), pp. 93, 95; John W. Shy, "The Military Conflict Considered as a Revolutionary War," in his *A People Numerous and Armed* (New York: Oxford University Press, 1976), pp. 217-20.

49. Nelson, *American Tory*, p. 115; Brown, *Good Americans*, p. 227.

50. Jack M. Sosin, *The Revolutionary Frontier, 1763-1783* (New York: Holt, Rinehart and Winston, 1967), pp. 82, 93-94, 99, 102-3, 161-64, 171.

51. Proclamation of 1763 reprinted in Wayne D. Rasmussen, ed., *Agriculture in the United States: A Documentary History*, 4 vols. (New York: Random House, 1975), 1:235.

52. Sosin, *Revolutionary Frontier*, pp. 10-19; John T. Schlebecker, *Whereby We Thrive: A History of American Farming, 1607-1972* (Ames: Iowa State University Press, 1975), pp. 16-18; Robert V. Wells, "Population and the American Revolution," in *American Revolution*, p. 114.

53. Higginbotham, *War of Independence*, pp. 322-25; John R. Alden, *The South in the Revolution, 1763-1789* (Baton Rouge: Louisiana State University Press, 1957), pp. 281-89; Miller, *Triumph of Freedom*, p. 655.

54. Shy, "Legacy of the Revolutionary War," in *Legacies of the Revolution*, pp. 48-49; Pole, *Foundations*, p. 152; Miller, *Triumph of Freedom*, p. 653; Walter K. Nugent, *Structures of American Social History* (Bloomington: Indiana University Press, 1981), pp. 72-73.

55. Nash, "Forgotten Experience," in *American Revolution*, pp. 38-40.

56. David C. Skaggs, "The American Revolution as a Quest for Equality," *Old Northwest* 2 (March 1976): 7-10; Linda G. DePauw, "Land of the Unfree: Legal Limitations on Liberty in Pre-Revolutionary America," *Maryland Historical Magazine* 68 (Winter 1973): 356-66; Jackson T. Main, *The Social Structure of Revolutionary America* (Princeton: Princeton University Press, 1965), p. 286.

57. Cecelia M. Kenyon, "Republicanism and Radicalism in the American Revolution: An Old Fashioned Interpretation," *William and Mary Quarterly*, 3d ser., 19 (April 1962): 181; Richard B. Morris, "Class Struggle and the American Revolution," *William and Mary Quarterly*, 3d ser., 19 (January 1962): 22; Main, *Social Structure*, p. 287. In *The American Revolution as a Social Movement*, J. Franklin Jameson made the classic statement of the argument that a social revolution accompanied political independence from England.

58. Shy, "Military Conflict," in *People*, pp. 216-23; Skaggs, "American Revolution," *Old Northwest*, p. 13.

59. Merrill Jensen, "The American People and the American Revolution," *Journal of American History* 57 (June 1970): 24; Skaggs, "American Revolution," *Old Northwest*, pp. 11-12, 15-16.

60. Miller, *Triumph of Freedom*, p. 650.

61. Robert A. East, *Business Enterprise in the American Revolutionary Era* (New York: Columbia University Press, 1938; reprint ed., New York: AMS Press, 1969), pp. 30–48, 213–38.

62. Joseph A. Ernst, "Economic Change and the Political Economy of the American Revolution," in *Legacies of the Revolution*, p. 124.

63. Gordon C. Bjork, "The Weaning of the American Economy: Independence, Market Changes, and Economic Development," *Journal of Economic History* 24 (December 1964): 543, 556–58; Rasmussen, *Agriculture in the United States*, 1:232; Lewis C. Gray, *Agriculture in the Southern United States to 1860*, 2 vols. (Washington: Carnegie Institution of Washington, 1933), 2:585, 593–97; Pole, *Foundations*, p. 101; Merrill Jensen, "The American Revolution and American Agriculture," *Agricultural History* 43 (January 1969): 112–14.

64. Harold D. Guither, *Heritage of Plenty: A Guide to the Economic History and Development of U.S. Agriculture* (Danville: Interstate Printers & Publishers, 1972), pp. 33–34; Evarts B. Greene, "The War's Economic Effects," in his *The Revolutionary Generation, 1763–1790* (New York: Macmillan, 1943), pp. 278–81; Main, "Results of Revolution," *Historian*, pp. 540–41.

65. Emory R. Johnson, et al., *History of Domestic and Foreign Commerce of the United States*, 2 vols. (Washington: Carnegie Institution of Washington, 1915), 1:128; Schlebecker, *Whereby We Thrive*, pp. 54–55, 162; Rasmussen, *Agriculture in the United States*, 1:231–32.

66. Rasmussen, *Agriculture in the U.S.*, 1:231; Schlebecker, *Whereby We Thrive*, p. 162.

67. Victor S. Clark, *History of Manufactures in the United States*, 3 vols. (New York: McGraw-Hill for the Carnegie Institution of Washington, 1929), 1:226; James A. Mulholland, *A History of Metals in Colonial America* (University: University of Alabama Press, 1981), pp. 118–42.

68. Clark, *History of Manufactures*, 1:215–27.

69. Clark, *History of Manufactures*, 1:219–25; Curtis P. Nettles, *The Emergence of a National Economy, 1775–1815* (New York: Harper and Row, Harper Torchbook, 1962), pp. 44–45.

70. Robert L. Heilbroner, in collaboration with Aaron Singer, *The Economic Transformation of America* (New York: Harcourt Brace Jovanovich, 1977), pp. 17–19; Nettles, *National Economy*, p. 45.

71. Nettles, *National Economy*, pp. 2–3, 13.

72. Nettles, *National Economy*, pp. 4, 6–8, 13–21; Miller, *Triumph of Freedom*, pp. 590–91; Johnson, *History of Commerce*, 1:122, 127; James M. Morris, *Our Maritime Heritage: Maritime Developments and Their Impact on American Life* (Washington: University Press of America, 1979), p. 61; Greene, "War's Economic Effects," in *Revolutionary Generation*, pp. 259–73; James F. Shepherd and Gary M. Walton, "Economic Change after the American Revolution: Pre- and Post-War Comparisons of Maritime Shipping and Trade," *Explorations in Economic History* 13 (October 1976): 397–99.

NOTES. CHAPTER 1   185

73. Nettles, *National Economy*, pp. 8–13; Miller, *Triumph of Freedom*, p. 111; Greene, "War's Economic Effects," in *Revolutionary Generation*, pp. 266–72, 276.

74. Thomas C. Cochran, *Basic History of American Business* (Princeton: Van Nostrand, 1959), pp. 28, 35–36; Nettles, *National Economy*, pp. 21–22.

75. Elizabeth Cometti, "The Labor Front during the Revolution," in *The American Revolution: The Home Front*, West Georgia College Studies in the Social Sciences no. 15 (Carrollton: West Georgia College, 1976), pp. 80–85; Joseph G. Rayback, *A History of American Labor*, rev. ed. (New York: Free Press, 1966), pp. 41–42; Richard B. Morris, *Government and Labor in Early America* (New York: Columbia University Press, 1946), pp. 280–81.

76. Rayback, *History of Labor*, pp. 38–39; William Miller, "The Effects of the Revolution on Indentured Servitude," *Pennsylvania History* 7 (July 1940): 133–34, 140; Richard B. Morris, "Class Struggle," *William and Mary Quarterly*, p. 17.

77. East, *Business Enterprise*, pp. 30–48, 213–38, 285–306, 322–25; Simeon E. Baldwin, "American Business Corporations before 1789," *American Historical Review* 8 (April 1903): 450–65; Cochran, *Basic History*, pp. 35–40.

78. Franklin quoted in William G. Sumner, *The Financier and the Finances of the American Revolution*, 2 vols. (New York: Dodd Mead, 1891; reprint ed., New York: A. M. Kelley, 1968), 2:136.

79. DeKalb quoted in Higginbotham, *War of Independence*, p. 399.

80. Pickering quoted in James T. Adams, *New England in the Republic, 1766–1850* (Boston: Little, Brown, 1926), p. 28; Washington quoted in Sumner, *Financier*, 2:148.

81. Shy, "Legacy of War," in *Legacies of the Revolution*, pp. 48–51; Miller, *Triumph of Freedom*, pp. 478–86, 526–45; Marvin A. Kreidberg and Merton G. Henry, *History of Military Mobilization in the United States Army, 1775–1945* (Washington: Department of the Army, 1955), pp. 17–19.

82. Ferguson, *Power of the Purse*, the best description of Revolutionary War finance, is the basis of this section.

83. Ibid., p. 10; Richard Buel, Jr., "Time: Friend or Foe of the Revolution?" in *Reconsiderations*, pp. 128–31.

84. Arthur Nussbaum, *A History of the Dollar* (New York: Columbia University Press, 1957), pp. 3–26; Ferguson, *Power of the Purse*, pp. 26–27.

85. Ferguson, *Power of the Purse*, pp. 66–67; Nussbaum, *Dollar*, p. 39; Nettles, *National Economy*, pp. 23–25; Paul Studenski and Herman E. Krooss, *Financial History of the United States: Fiscal, Monetary, Banking, and Tariff, Including Financial Administration and State and Local Finances* (New York: McGraw-Hill, 1952), p. 30.

86. Ferguson, *Power of the Purse*, pp. 29–44; Nettles, *National Economy*, pp. 29–30, 32; Studenski, *Financial History*, pp. 29–30.

87. Ferguson, *Power of the Purse*, pp. 48–51.

88. Jack N. Rakove, *The Beginnings of National Politics: An Interpretative History of the Continental Congress* (New York: Knopf, 1979), pp. 212–15; Ferguson, *Power of the Purse*, pp. 46–53, 275–87.

89. Jack P. Greene, "The Role of the Lower Houses of Assembly in Eighteenth-Century Politics," in *The Growth of American Politics: A Modern Reader*, eds. Frank O. Gatell, Paul Goodman, and Allen Weinstein (New York: Oxford University Press, 1972), pp. 36–58; Nevins, *American States*, p. 119. Carl Ubbelonde, *The American Colonies and the British Empire, 1607–1763* (New York: Crowell, 1968), pp. 79–87, maintains that at least until 1763 skillful governors who respected local interests sometimes won the colonists' respect.

90. Margaret B. Macmillan, *War Governors in the American Revolution*, Studies in History, Economics and Public Law no. 503 (New York: Columbia University Press, 1943), pp. 57–63, 69–70; Gordon S. Wood, *Creation of the American Republic, 1776–1787* (Chapel Hill: University of North Carolina Press for Institute of Early American History and Culture, 1969), pp. 136–43.

91. Macmillan, *War Governors*, pp. 72–73; Wood, *Creation*, pp. 150–57, 161.

92. Wood, *Creation*, pp. 167–71.

93. Pole, *Foundations*, p. 90; Merrill Jensen, "Democracy and the American Revolution," in *Causes and Consequences of the American Revolution*, ed. Esmond Wright (Chicago: Quadrangle Books, 1966), pp. 268, 281–82, and *The American Revolution within America* (New York: New York University Press, 1974), pp. 56–58, 84–100, 106–8; Jackson T. Main, "Social Origins of a Political Elite: The Upper House in the Revolutionary Era," *Huntington Library Quarterly* 27 (February 1964): 147–54.

94. Pole, *Foundations*, p. 94; Jensen, "Democracy and Revolution," in *Causes and Consequences*, p. 268; Miller, *Triumph of Freedom*, pp. 346–50.

95. Macmillan, *War Governors*, p. 71; Nevins, *American States*, p. 171.

96. Macmillan, *War Governors*, pp. 275–77.

97. Nevins, *American States*, pp. 169, 171; Macmillan, *War Governors*, p. 71; Charles C. Thach, *The Creation of the Presidency, 1775–1789: A Study in Constitutional History*, Johns Hopkins University Studies in Historical and Political Science, ser. 40, no. 4 (Baltimore: Johns Hopkins University, 1922; reprint ed., New York: Da Capo Press, 1960), pp. 52–53.

98. Miller, *Triumph of Freedom*, pp. 349–50; Madison quoted in Nevins, *American States*, p. 168.

99. Jennings B. Sanders, *The Presidency of the Continental Congress, 1774–89: A Study in American Institutional History*, rev. ed. (Chicago: Author, 1930; reprint ed., Gloucester: Peter Smith, 1971), pp. 11–25, 39–42, 71.

100. Jennings B. Sanders, *Evolution of Executive Departments of the Continental Congress, 1774–1789* (Chapel Hill: University of North Carolina Press, 1935; reprint ed., Gloucester: Peter Smith, 1971), pp. 6–7.

101. Rakove, *National Politics*, pp. 198–201; Sanders, *Executive Departments*, pp. 4, 8–11.

102. Paul A. C. Koistinen, *The Military-Industrial Complex: A Historical Perspective* (New York: Praeger, 1980), pp. 6–7, 106–9, 113.

103. Elmer J. Ferguson, "Business, Government, and Congressional Investigation in the Revolution," *William and Mary Quarterly*, 3d ser., 16 (July 1959): 293–95.

104. Ibid., pp. 293–98, 308, 318.

105. Rakove, *National Politics*, pp. 198–201; Sanders, *Executive Departments*, pp. 5–92; Thach, *Presidency*, pp. 57–62; Louis Smith, *American Democracy and Military Power: A Study of Civil Control of the Military Power in the United States* (Chicago: University of Chicago Press, 1951), pp. 173–74; Jay C. Guggenheim, "The Development of the Executive Departments, 1775–1789," in *Essays in the Constitutional History of the United States in the Formative Period, 1775–1789*, ed. J. Franklin Jameson (Boston: Houghton Mifflin, 1889; reprint ed., Freeport: Books for Libraries Press, 1970), pp. 120, 148; Royster, *Revolutionary People*, p. 187.

106. Sanders, *Executive Departments*, pp. 98–152; Guggenheim, "Executive Departments," in *Constitutional History*, pp. 117–27, 185; Rakove, *National Politics*, p. 192.

107. Thach, *Presidency*, pp. 56–57; Edward C. Burnett, *The Continental Congress* (New York: Macmillan, 1941), p. 502.

108. Nevins, *American States*, p. 115. See also Merrill Jensen, *The New Nation: A History of the United States during the Confederation, 1781–1789* (New York: Knopf, Vintage Books, 1950), pp. 43–53, 83, and *The Articles of Confederation: An Interpretation of the Social-Constitutional History of the American Revolution, 1774–1781* (Madison: University of Wisconsin Press, 1940), p. 56; Miller, *Triumph of Freedom*, pp. 425–33; Wood, *Creation*, pp. 356, 390.

109. Rakove, *National Politics*, pp. 92–100, 192–97; Burnett, *Continential Congress*, p. 502.

110. Burnett, *Continental Congress*, pp. 504–10.

111. Ferguson, *Power of the Purse*, pp. xv, 111–24; Jensen, *American Revolution*, p. 167.

112. Miller, *Triumph of Freedom*, p. 678. See also Ferguson, *Power of the Purse*, pp. 109–10; Merrill Jensen, "The Idea of National Government during the American Revolution," *Political Science Quarterly* 58 (September 1943): 378–79; Rakove, *National Politics*, pp. 325–29; Richard D. Brown, *Modernization: The Transformation of American Life, 1600-1865* (New York: Hill and Wang, 1976), p. 74.

113. Stanley M. Elkins and Eric L. McKitrick, "The Founding Fathers: Young Men of the Revolution," *Political Science Quarterly* 76 (June 1961): 207. See also Linda K. Kerber, "The Federalist Party," in *History of U.S. Political Parties*, ed. Arthur M. Schlesinger, Jr., 4 vols. (New York: Chelsea House, 1973), 1:7–8.

114. Wood, *Creation*, pp. 20–21, 53–59, 62–71, 92–93, 108, and "Rhetoric and Reality in the American Revolution," *William and Mary Quarterly*, 3d ser., 23

(January 1966): 26; Gerald N. Grob, "The Political System and Social Policy in the Nineteenth Century: Legacy of the Revolution," *Mid-America* 58 (January 1976): 8, 19.

115. Miller, *Triumph of Freedom*, pp. 81–82, 96–100, 455–56, 471–77; Wood, *Creation*, pp. 415–19, 425–29.

116. Wood, *Creation*, pp. 259–60, 274–75, 281, 430–67, 608–12.

Notes. Chapter 2: The Civil War

1. Oliver Wendell Holmes, *Speeches* (Boston: Little, Brown, 1913), p. 11.

2. Ibid., p. 3.

3. Basil L. Gildersleeve quoted in Benjamin Quarles, *The Negro in the Civil War* (Boston: Little, Brown, 1953), p. 41.

4. Peter J. Parish, *The American Civil War* (New York: Holmes & Meier, 1975), pp. 339–40.

5. Ibid.

6. Irwin Unger, *The Greenback Era: A Social and Political History of American Finance, 1865–1879* (Princeton: Princeton University Press, 1964), pp. 13–15.

7. Paul W. Gates, *Agriculture and the Civil War* (New York: Knopf, 1965), p. 227; Parish, *Civil War*, pp. 340–43.

8. Fred A. Shannon, *American Farmers' Movements* (Princeton: Van Nostrand, 1957), p. 48; Murray R. Benedict, *Farm Policies of the United States, 1790–1950: A Study of Their Origins and Development* (New York: Twentieth Century Fund, 1953), p. 84; Allan Nevins, *War for the Union*, 4 vols. (New York: Scribner's, 1959–71), 3:234.

9. Clarence H. Danhof, *Change in Agriculture: The Northern United States, 1820–1870* (Cambridge: Harvard University Press, 1969), pp. 278–79, 289; Wayne D. Rasmussen, "The Civil War: A Catalyst of Agricultural Revolution," *Agricultural History* 39 (October 1965):193–95.

10. Carl B. Swisher, *American Constitutional Development* (Boston: Houghton Mifflin, 1943), pp. 311–82.

11. Benedict, *Farm Policies*, pp. 29, 84; Bray Hammond, *Sovereignty and an Empty Purse: Banks and Politics in the Civil War* (Princeton: Princeton University Press, 1970), p. 356.

12. James M. Morris, *Our Maritime Heritage: Maritime Developments and Their Impact on American Life* (Washington: University Press of America, 1979), pp. 190–97; John G. B. Hutchins, "The Effect of the Civil War and the Two World Wars on American Transportation," *American Economic Review* 42 (May 1952):629.

13. Victor S. Clark, *History of Manufactures in the United States*, 3 vols. (New York: McGraw-Hill for the Carnegie Institution of Washington, 1929), 2:23–25.

14. Robert Cruden, *The War That Never Ended: The American Civil War* (Englewood Cliffs: Prentice-Hall, 1973), p. 176.

15. Thomas Weber, *The Northern Railroads in the Civil War, 1861–1865* (New York: King's Crown Press, 1952; reprint ed., Westport: Greenwood Press, 1970), pp. 220–21; Emerson D. Fite, *Social and Industrial Conditions in the North during the Civil War* (New York: Macmillan, 1910; reprint ed., New York: Ungar, 1963), pp. 42–77; Thomas C. Cochran and William Miller, *The Age of Enterprise: A Social History of Industrial America*, rev. ed. (New York: Harper Torchbooks, 1961), p. 114.

16. Hutchins, "American Transportation," *AER*, pp.628–29; Emerson D. Fite, "The Canal and the Railroad from 1861 to 1865," *Yale Review* 15 (August 1906):195–213.

17. Clark, *History of Manufactures*, 2:26–31.

18. Ibid., 2:32–33.

19. Ibid., 2:33; Gates, *Agriculture and War*, p. 236.

20. Fite, *Social and Industrial Conditions*, p. 24; Cruden, *War That Never Ended*, p. 175.

21. Herman E. Krooss, *American Economic Development: The Progress of a Business Civilization*, 3rd ed. (Englewood Cliffs: Prentice-Hall, 1974), p. 507; Clark, *History of Manufactures*, 2:18–20.

22. Nevins, *War for Union*, 3:254.

23. Ibid., 2:472–73.

24. Clark, *History of Manufactures*, 2:12.

25. Stephen Salisbury, "The Effect of the Civil War on American Industrial Development," in *The Economic Impact of the American Civil War*, 2d ed., ed. Ralph Andreano (Cambridge: Schenkman, 1967), p. 184; Ross M. Robertson and Gary M. Walton, *History of the American Economy*, 4th ed. (New York: Harcourt Brace Jovanovich, 1979), p. 249.

26. Roger Ransom and Richard Surch, "The Impact of the Civil War and of Emancipation on Southern Agriculture," *Explorations in Economic History* 12 (January 1975):4–5; Gates, *Agriculture and War*, p. 108.

27. James L. Roark, "From Lords to Landlords," *Wilson Quarterly* 2 (Spring 1978): 124–32; Eugene M. Lerner, "Southern Output and Agricultural Income, 1860–1880," in *The Economic Impact of the American Civil War*, 2d ed., ed. Ralph Andreano (Cambridge: Schenkman, 1967), pp. 112–21.

28. John F. Stover, *The Railroads of the South, 1865-1900: A Study in Finance and Control* (Chapel Hill: University of North Carolina Press, 1955), pp. 13–22.

29. Louise B. Hill, *State Socialism in the Confederate States of America* (Charlottesville: Historical Publishing, 1936), pp. 3–4, 7–9, 14, 16–19.

30. Clark, *History of Manufactures*, 2:41–42; Cruden, *War That Never Ended*, p. 184.

31. Eugene M. Lerner, "Money, Prices, and Wages in the Confederacy, 1861-65," in *The Economic Impact of the American Civil War*, 2d ed., ed. Ralph Andreano (Cambridge: Schenkman, 1967), pp. 45-49, and "Southern Output," in *Economic Impact*, pp. 113-14; Cruden, *War That Never Ended*, pp. 184-85; Clark, *History of Manufactures*, 2:53.

32. David B. Sabine, "Resources Compared: North vs. South," *Civil War Times Illustrated* 6 (February 1968):5, 10.

33. Brown quoted in Parish, *Civil War*, p. 222.

34. John W. Chambers, II, ed., *Draftees or Volunteers: A Documentary History of the Debate over Military Conscription in the United States, 1787-1973* (New York: Garland, 1975), p. 123; Cruden, *War That Never Ended*, pp. 88, 125; William L. Shaw, "The Confederate Conscription and Exemption Acts," *American Journal of Legal History* 6 (October 1962):379-82.

35. Charles W. Ramsdell, "The Control of Manufacturing by the Confederate Government," *Mississippi Valley Historical Review* 8 (December 1921):232; Parish, *Civil War*, pp. 137-38, 148-50; Cruden, *War That Never Ended*, p. 88.

36. Paul P. Van Riper and Harry N. Scheiber, "The Confederate Civil Service," *Journal of Southern History* 25 (November 1959):450-51, 469-70; William L. Barney, *Failed Victory: A New Perspective on the Civil War* (New York: Praeger, 1975; reprint ed., Washington: University Press of America, 1980), pp. 21-22; Parish, *Civil War*, p. 155.

37. Marvin A. Kriedberg and Merton G. Henry, *History of Military Mobilization in the United States Army, 1775-1945* (Washington: Department of the Army, 1955), pp. 137-38; Raimondo Luraghi, "The Civil War and the Mobilization of American Society: Social Structure and Industrial Revolution in the Old South before and during the War," *Civil War History* 18 (September 1972):245; Clark, *History of Manufactures*, 2:42-45, 48-49; Richard N. Current, "God and the Strongest Battalions," in *Why the North Won the Civil War*, ed. David Donald (New York: Macmillian, Collier Books, 1960), pp. 24-25.

38. Eugene M. Lerner, "The Monetary and Fiscal Programs of the Confederate Government 1861-65," *Journal of Political Economy* 62 (December 1954):507-13.

39. Ibid., pp. 514-18.

40. Ibid., pp. 519-22; Bell I. Wiley, "Life in the South," *Civil War Times Illustrated* 8 (January 1970):45; Current, "God and Battalions," in *Why the North*, p. 22.

41. Johnson quoted in ibid., p. 29; Lerner, "Money," in *Economic Impact*, pp. 31, 34, 50-52; Parish, *Civil War*, pp. 314-21.

42. Emory M. Thomas, *The Confederacy as a Revolutionary Experience* (Englewood Cliffs: Prentice-Hall, 1971), pp. 58-73.

43. Eric L. McKitrick, "Party Politics and the Union and Confederate War Efforts," in *The Growth of American Politics: A Modern Reader*, 2 vols., eds. Frank O. Gatell, Paul Goodman, and Allen Weinstein (New York: Oxford University Press, 1972),

1:428; Van Riper and Scheiber, "Civil Service," *JSH*, p. 449; Cruden, *War That Never Ended*, pp. 87–88.

44. Parish, *Civil War*, pp. 215–20; Thomas, *Confederacy*, p. 75; David Donald, "Died of Democracy," in *Why the North Won the Civil War*, ed. David Donald (New York: Macmillan, Collier Books, 1960), pp. 84–88.

45. Ibid., pp. 88–90; Parish, *Civil War*, pp. 220–25; McKitrick, "Party Politics," in *American Politics*, 1:434–35; Wilfred B. Yearns, *T he Confederate Congress* (Athens: University of Georgia Press, 1960), pp. 218–34.

46. McKitrick, "Party Politics," in *American Politics*, 1:430–46; William B. Hesseltine, *Lincoln and the War Governors* (New York: Knopf, 1948), pp. 273, 311–15, 361–84; Harry J. Carman and Reinhard H. Luthin, *Lincoln and the Patronage* (New York: Columbia University Press, 1943), pp. 331–36.

47. Leon Friedman, "The Democratic Party, 1860–1884," in *History of U.S. Political Parties*, 4 vols., ed. Arthur M. Schlesinger, Jr. (New York: Chelsea House, 1973), 2:885–888; Parish, *Civil War*, pp. 642–44; E. H. Hall, "Civil War Pensions," *Proceedings of the Massachusetts Historical Society*, 3d ser., 2 (January 1909): 119–20, 127; Dixon Wecter, *When Johnny Comes Marching Home* (Boston: Houghton Mifflin, 1944), pp. 247–51.

48. Friedman, "Democratic Party," in *Political Parties*, 2:888; William G. Carleton, "Civil War Dissidence in the North: The Perspective of a Century," *South Atlantic Quarterly* 65 (Summer 1966):392–99; Leonard P. Curry, "Congressional Democrats, 1861–1863," *Civil War History* 12 (September 1966):213–29.

49. Christopher Dell, *Lincoln and the War Democrats: The Grand Erosion of Conservative Tradition* (Rutherford: Fairleigh Dickinson University Press, 1975), pp. 15–20; Eric J. Cardinal, "Disloyalty of Dissent: The Case of the Copperheads," *Midwest Quarterly* 19 (Autumn 1977):27–32; Edward C. Smith, *The Borderlands in the Civil War* (New York: Macmillian, 1927; reprint ed., Freeport: Books for Libraries Press, 1969), pp. 322–29; Cruden, *War That Never Ended*, p. 95; Carleton, "Civil War Dissidence," *SAQ*, pp.390–91; Wood Gray, *The Hidden Civil War: The Story of the Copperheads* (New York: Viking Press, 1942), pp. 211, 219.

50. Phillip E. Stebbins, "Lincoln's Dictatorship," *American History Illustrated* 6 (November 1971):34; Nevins, *War for Union*, 4:127–28.

51. Elbert J. Benton, *The Movement for Peace without a Victory during the Civil War*, Collections of the Western Reserve Historical Society no. 99 (Cleveland: Western Reserve Historical Society, 1918; reprint ed., New York: Da Capo Press, 1972), pp. 56–57, 62, 67–70.

52. James G. Randall, *Constitutional Problems under Lincoln*, rev. ed. (Urbana: University of Illinois Press, 1951), p. 513; Lincoln quoted in ibid., p. 2; Douglas quoted in Gray, *Hidden War*, p. 59.

53. Stebbins, "Dictatorship," *AHI*, pp. 36–37; James MacG. Burns, *Presidential Government: The Crucible of Leadership* (Boston: Houghton Mifflin, 1966), p. 35; Lincoln quoted in ibid., p. 36; Swisher, *Constitutional Development*, pp. 276–91.

54. Nevins, *War for Union*, 2:350–36, 4:83–88.

55. Louis Smith, *American Democracy and Military Power: A Study of Civil Control of the Military Power in the United States* (Chicago: University of Chicago Press, 1951), pp. 194–206; Hans L. Trefousse, "The Joint Committee on the Conduct of the War: A Reassessment," *Civil War History* 10 (March 1964):6–16.

56. Lawrence H. Chamberlain, *The President, Congress and Legislation* (New York: AMS Press, 1967), pp. 11–19; Parish, *Civil War*, pp. 231–37; Harold M. Hyman, *Union and Confidence: The 1860s* (New York: Crowell, 1976), pp. 185–89.

57. Clinton L. Rossiter, *The American Presidency*, rev. ed. (New York: Harcourt Brace Jovanovich, Harvest Book 1960), pp. 83–84, 99–101.

58. Swisher, *Constitutional Development*, pp. 278–81; Joseph G. Gambone, "Ex Parte Milligan: The Restoration of Judicial Prestige?" *Civil War History* 16 (Sep-

59. Ibid., pp.252–53; Clinton L. Rossiter, *The Supreme Court and the Commander in Chief* (Ithaca: Cornell University Press, 1951), pp. 65–77; Swisher, *Constitutional Development*, p. 287.

60. Robert G. McCloskey, *The American Supreme Court* (Chicago: University of Chicago Press, 1960), pp. 98–99; Gambone, "Milligan," *CWH*, pp. 246–47; Swisher, *Constitutional Development*, pp. 287–89.

61. Cochran and Miller, *Age of Enterprise*, p. 10.

62. Paul Studenski and Herman E. Krooss, *Financial History of the United States: Fiscal, Monetary, Banking, and Tariff, Including Financial Administration and State and Local Finance* (New York: McGraw-Hill, 1952), pp. 143–47; Arthur Nussbaum, *A History of the Dollar* (New York: Columbia University Press, 1957), pp. 100–1; Cruden, *War That Never Ended*, p. 177.

63. Current, "God and Battalions," in *Why the North*, p. 21.

64. Studenski and Krooss, *Financial History*, pp. 149–51; Parish, *Civil War*, pp. 357–59; Louis M. Hacker, *The Course of American Economic Growth and Development* (New York: Wiley, 1970), p. 181.

65. Studenski and Krooss, *Financial History*, p. 153; Marshall A. Robinson, "Federal Debt Management: Civil War, World War I, and World War II," *American Economic Review* 45 (May 1955):389; Parish, *Civil War*, pp. 359–60; Cruden, *War That Never Ended*, p. 177.

66. Studenski and Krooss, *Financial History*, pp. 154–55; Margaret G. Myers, *A Financial History of the United States* (New York: Columbia University Press, 1970), pp. 163–65.

67. Parish, *Civil War*, pp. 352–62; Studenski and Krooss, *Financial History*, p. 160; Unger, *Greenback Era*, p. 3.

68. Paul A. C. Koistinen, *The Military-Industrial Complex: A Historical Perspective* (New York: Praeger, 1980), p. 7, 109–10; Krooss, *American Economic Development*, p. 514.

69. Paul P. Van Riper and Keith A. Sutherland, "The Northern Civil Service: 1861–1865," *Civil War History* 11 (December 1965):353–57, 367–69.

70. Nevins, *War for Union*, 1:350–59; Parish, *Civil War*, pp. 135–37; Curden, *War That Never Ended*, pp. 117, 125–26.

71. Fred A. Shannon, *The Organization and Administration of the Union Army, 1861–1865*, 2 vols. (Cleveland: Arthur Clark, 1928), 1:265–67, 276–92; Krideberg and Henry, *Military Mobilization*, pp. 101–4.

72. Ibid., p. 108; Parish, *Civil War*, pp. 135–37.

73. Hesseltine, *War Governors*, pp. 273, 311–15, 361–86, 390–92; Shannon, *Army Administration*, 1:22–30; McKitrick, "Party Politics," in *American Politics*, 1:434–36.

74. Song quoted in Wecter, *When Johnny Comes Marching Home*, p. 170; Bell I. Wiley, "Women of the Lost Cause," *American History Illustrated* 8 (December 1973):11–20; Eleanor Flexnor, *Century of Struggle: The Woman's Rights Movement in the United States*, rev. ed. (Cambridge: Belknap Press of Harvard University Press, 1975), pp. 109–12.

75. Ibid., p. 107; Mary E. Massey, *Bonnet Brigades* (New York: Knopf, 1966), pp. 87–107.

76. Barton quoted in ibid., pp. 339–40; Ann D. Wood, "The War within a War: Women Nurses in the Union Army," *Civil War History* 18 (September 1972):198–201, 212.

77. Massey, *Bonnet Brigades*, pp. 131–51; Edith Abbott, *Women in Industry: A Study in American Economic History* (New York: D. Appleton, 1910; reprint ed., New York: Arno, 1969), p. 141; Bernice M. Deutrich, "Propriety and Pay," *Prologue* 3 (Fall 1971):67–72; W. Elliott Brownlee and Mary M. Brownlee, *Women in the American Economy: A Documentary History, 1675–1929* (New Haven: Yale University Press, 1976), pp. 21–22; Agatha Young, *The Women and the Crisis: Women of the North in the Civil War* (New York: McDowell, Obolensky, 1959), p. 351.

78. Thomas, *Confederacy*, p. 105; Bell I. Wiley, "Life in the South," *Civil War Times Illustrated* 8 (January 1970):44, and *Confederate Women* (Westport: Greenwood Press, 1975), pp. 178–79; Anne F. Scott, *The Southern Lady: From Pedestal to Politics, 1830–1930* (Chicago: University of Chicago Press, 1970), pp. 3–123.

79. Massey, *Bonnet Brigades*, p. 367.

80. Conrad Taeuber and Irene B. Taeuber, *The Changing Population of the United States* (New York: Wiley, 1958), p. 51.

81. Ibid., p. 56.

82. *Harvard Encyclopedia of American Ethnic Groups*, ed. Stephen Thernstrom, s.v. "Scots," by Gordon Donaldson; Carl F. Wittke, *We Who Built America: The Saga of the Immigrant*, rev. ed. (Cleveland: Press of Western Reserve University, 1967), pp. 257, 325–29; Ella Lonn, *Foreigners in the Union Army and Navy* (Baton Rouge: Louisiana State University Press, 1951; reprint ed., New York: Greenwood Press,

1969), pp. 58–65; Bertram W. Korn, *American Jewry in the Civil War* (Philadelphia: Jewish Publication Society of America, Meridian Books, 1961), pp. 1–5, 156, 218; Henry Feingold, *Zion in America: The Jewish Experience from Colonial Times to the Present* (New York: Twayne, 1974), pp. 34–51, 96.

83. Lonn, *Foreigners in Union Army*, p. 663; John Higham, *Strangers in the Land: Patterns of American Nativism, 1860-1925* (New York: Atheneum, 1963), pp. 4, 13.

84. Wittke, *We Who Built*, pp. 217, 232–37; LaVern J. Rippley, *The German-Americans* (Boston: Twayne Publishers, 1976), pp. 52–53.

85. *Harvard Encyclopedia*, s.v. "Germans," by Kathleen N. Conzen; Wittke, *We Who Built*, p. 238; Theodore Huebner, *The Germans in America* (Philadelphia: Chilton, 1962), pp. 112–13; Rippley, *German-Americans*, pp. 58–59.

86. *Harvard Encyclopedia*, s.v. "Irish," by Patrick J. Blessing, and "Scotch-Irish," by Maldwyn A. Jones; Wittke, *We Who Built*, pp. 132–35; Taeuber and Taeuber, *Changing Population*, p. 56; Lonn, *Foreigners in Union Army*, p. 41.

87. William V. Shannon, *The American Irish* (New York: Macmillan, 1963), p. 59; *Harvard Encyclopedia*, s.v. "Irish," by Patrick J. Blessing; Wittke, *We Who Built*, p. 163.

88. Williston H. Lofton, "Northern Labor and the Negro during the Civil War," *Journal of Negro History* 34 (July 1949):256–70; song quoted in Dudley T. Cornish, *The Sable Arm: Negro Troops in the Union Army, 1861–1865* (New York: W. W. Norton, 1966), p. 230.

89. Ella Lonn, *Foreigners in the Confederacy* (Chapel Hill: University of North Carolina Press, 1940; reprint ed., Gloucester: Peter Smith, 1965), pp. 29–35, 417–38; Rippley, *German-Americans*, pp. 66–68; Wittke, *We Who Built*, pp. 107, 239.

90. Higham, *Strangers in the Land*, p. 13; Taeuber and Taeuber, *Changing Population*, p. 53; Benjamin A. Gould, *Investigations in the Military and Anthropological Statistics of American Soldiers* (New York: Hurd and Houghton for U.S. Sanitary Commission, 1869; reprint ed., New York: Arno Press, 1979), pp. 27–29; Nevins, *War for Union*, 3:219–20.

91. Parish, *Civil War*, p. 227.

92. Douglass quoted in James M. McPherson, *Marching toward Freedom: The Negro in the Civil War, 1861–1865* (New York: Knopf, 1967), p. 68; see also ibid., pp. 8–9; Benjamin Quarles, *The Negro's Civil War* (Boston: Little, Brown, 1953), pp. 24–31, 40.

93. Ibid., pp. 109–20; James M. McPherson, *The Negro's Civil War: How American Negroes Felt and Acted during the War for the Union* (New York: Random House, Vintage Books, 1965), pp. 44–52.

94. Ibid., pp. 164–66, 170–80; McPherson, *Marching toward Freedom*, pp. 24–25, 117; Jack D. Foner, *Blacks and the Military in American History: A New Perspective* (New York: Praeger, 1974), pp. 38, 45–47; Cornish, *The Sable Arm*, p. 288.

95. Butler quoted in ibid., pp. 290–91; McPherson, *Negro's Civil War*, pp. 245–70, and *Marching toward Freedom*, pp. 133–47; Foner, *Blacks and Military*, p. 52;

Mary F. Berry, *Military Necessity and Civil Rights Policy: Black Citizenship and the Constitution, 1861–1865* (Port Washington: Kennikat, 1977), pp. x, 104–5.

96. McPherson, *Negro's Civil War*, pp. 111–32; John W. Blassingame, "The Union Army as an Educational Institution for Negroes, 1862-1865," *Journal of Negro Education* 34 (Spring 1965):155–57, 195.

97. Bell I. Wiley, *Southern Negroes, 1861–1865* (New Haven: Yale University Press, 1965), pp. 3–172; James H. Brewer, *The Confederate Negro: Virginia's Craftsmen and Military Laborers, 1861–1865* (Durham: Duke University Press, 1969), pp. 4–6, 9–11, 55–57, 165–67; Davis quoted in Quarles, *Negro in Civil War*, p. 272.

98. Jean McC. Currin, "Why Indian Territory Joined the Confederacy," *Lincoln Herald* 69 (Summer 1967):83–89; James W. Ware, "Indian Territory," *Journal of the West* 16 (April 1977):102–12.

99. LeRoy H. Fischer, "Introduction," *Journal of the West* 16 (April 1977):5–6, 8; Kenny L. Brown, "Dakota and Montana Territories," *Journal of the West* 16 (April 1977):10, 18; Thomas D. Isern, "Colorado Territory," *Journal of the West* 16 (April 1977):66, 67; James A. Howard II, "New Mexico and Arizona Territories," *Journal of the West* 16 (April 1977):93–95.

100. Nevins, *War for Union*, 3:239–40; Sara J. Richter, "Washington and Idaho Territories," *Journal of the West* 16 (April 1977):31–34; James Thomas, "Nevada Territory," *Journal of the West* 16 (April 1977):36, 40, 43; Gary L. Watters, "Utah Territory," *Journal of the West* 16 (April 1977):53–55; Larry D. Duke, "Nebraska Territory," *Journal of the West* 16 (April 1977):73–83; Brown, "Dakota & Montana," *JW*, p. 24; Isern, "Colorado," *JW*, pp. 59, 62–64; Howard, "New Mexico & Arizona," *JW*, pp. 90–94, 98.

101. Charles DeBenedetti, *The Peace Reform in American History* (Bloomington: Indiana University Press, 1980), pp. 30–34.

102. Ibid., pp. 55–57; Peter Brock, *Pacifism in the United States, From the Colonial Era to the First World War* (Princeton: Princeton University Press, 1968), pp. 689–91, 711–12.

103. Ibid., pp. 734–41, 744, 764, 782–85; R. R. Russell, "Development of Conscientious Objector Recognition in the United States," *George Washington Law Review* 20 (March 1952):417–19; Edward N. Wright, *Conscientious Objectors in the Civil War* (Philadelphia: University of Pennsylvania Press, 1931), pp. 39–40, 65.

104. Richard L. Zuber, "Conscientious Objectors in the Confederacy: The Quakers of North Carolina," *Quaker History* 67 (Spring 1978):1–7, 13–18; Brock, *Pacifism*, pp. 765–75, 805–21; Samuel Horst, *Mennonites in the Confederacy: A Study in Civil War Pacifism* (Scottdale: Herald Press, 1967), pp. 7, 50–61, 112–14.

105. Nevins, *War for Union*, 1:257; Chester F. Dunham, *The Attitude of Northern Clergy toward the South, 1860–1865* (Toledo: Gray, 1942; reprint ed., Philadelphia: Porcupine Press, 1974), pp.10–27; Charles R. Wilson, *Baptised in Blood: The Religion of the Lost Cause, 1865–1920* (Athens: University of Georgia Press, 1980), pp. 5–8; James H. Moorhead, *American Apocalypse: Yankee Protestants and the Civil War, 1860–1869* (New Haven: Yale University Press, 1978), p. x; W. Harrison Daniel,

"Protestantism and Patriotism in the Confederacy," *Mississippi Quarterly* 24 (Spring 1971):117-28.

106. Anson P. Stokes and Leo Pfeffer, *Church and State in the United States*, rev. ed. in one vol. (New York: Harper and Row, 1964), p. 300; Wilson, *Baptised in Blood*, pp. 7-10; Kenneth K. Bailey, "The Post-Civil War Racial Separations in Southern Protestantism: Another Look," *Church History* 46 (December 1977):456, 459.

107. John T. Ellis, *American Catholicism* (Chicago: University of Chicago Press, 1956), pp. 89-100; Benjamin J. Blied, *Catholics and the Civil War* (Milwaukee: Author, 1945), pp. 50, 69, 82; Walter G. Sharrow, "Northern Catholic Intellectuals and the Coming of the Civil War," *New York Historical Society Quarterly* 58 (January 1974):36-38, 43-56.

108. George Forgie, *Patricide in the House Divided: A Psychological Interpretation of Lincoln and His Age* (New York: Norton, 1979), pp. 283-93; Robert N. Bellah, "Civil Religion in America," in *American Civil Religion*, eds. Russell E. Richey and Donald G. Jones (New York: Harper and Row, 1974), pp. 30-33.

109. Davis quoted in Nevins, *War for Union*, 3:4.

Notes. Chapter 3: World War I

1. Randolph S. Bourne, "The State," *War and the Intellectuals: Essays by Randolph S. Bourne, 1915-1919*, ed. Carl Resek (New York: Harper & Row, Harper Torchbooks, 1964), p. 71.

2. Ibid., pp. 65-104.

3. Margaret G. Myers, *A Financial History of the United States* (New York: Columbia University Press, 1970), pp. 271-72; Charles Gilbert, *American Financing of World War I* (Westport: Greenwood Press, 1970), pp. 14-29; Aaron A. Godfrey, *Government Operation of the Railroads, 1918- 1920: Its Necessity, Success, and Consequences* (Austin: Jenkins Publishing, 1974), p. 16.

4. Gilbert, *American Financing*, p. 25.

5. W. Elliot Brownlee, *Dynamics of Ascent: A History of the American Economy*, 2d ed. (New York: Knopf, 1979), p. 366.

6. Ibid., pp. 366, 369.

7. Gilbert, *American Financing*, pp. 32-44.

8. Victor S. Clark, *History of Manufactures in the United States*, 3 vols. (New York: McGraw-Hill for the Carnegie Institution of Washington, 1929), 3:310-11, 315-18; Herman E. Krooss, *American Economic Development: The Progress of a Business Civilization*, 3d ed. (Englewood Cliffs: Prentice-Hall, 1974), p. 510; Gerd Hardach, *The First World War, 1914-1918* (Berkeley: University of California Press, 1977), pp. 98-99; Arthur Marwick, *War and Social Change in the Twentieth Century: A Comparative Study of Britain, France, Germany, Russia, and the United States* (New York: St. Martin's Press, 1974), p. 69.

9. Clark, *History of Manufactures*, 3:301, 306-8, 314, 318-22; James E. Fickle, "Defense Mobilization in the Southern Pine Industry: The Experience of World War I," *Journal of Forest History* 22 (October 1978): 206-9.

10. James H. Shideler, *Farm Crisis, 1919-1923* (Berkeley: University of California Press, 1957), pp. 4-8; Ross M. Robertson and Gary M. Walton, *History of the American Economy*, 4th ed. (New York: Harcourt Brace Jovanovich, 1979), p. 422; Willard W. Cochrane, *The Development of American Agriculture: A Historical Analysis* (Minneapolis: University of Minnesota Press, 1979), p. 111; John M. Clark, *The Costs of the World War to the American People* (New Haven: Yale University Press, 1931; reprint ed., New York: A. M. Kelley, 1970), p. 231.

11. Maxcy R. Dickson, *The Food Front in World War I* (Washington: Council on Public Affairs, 1944), pp. 11-12.

12. Hardach, *First World War*, pp. 256–57; Benjamin H. Hibbard, *Effects of the Great War Upon Agriculture in the United States and Great Britain* (New York: Oxford University Press, 1919), pp. 160–61.

13. Harold D. Guither, *Heritage of Plenty: A Guide to the Economic History and Development of U.S. Agriculture* (Danville: Interstate Printers & Publishers, 1972), p. 127; John T. Schlebecker, *Whereby We Thrive: A History of American Farming, 1607-1972* (Ames: Iowa State University Press, 1975), p. 207.

14. Chester W. Wright, "Economic Lessons from Previous Wars," in *Economic Problems of War and Its Aftermath*, ed. Chester W. Wright (Chicago: University of Chicago Press, 1942; reprint ed., Freeport: Books for Libraries Press, 1972), p. 56; Simon S. Kuznets, *National Product in Wartime* (New York: National Bureau of Economic Research, 1945; reprint ed., New York: Arno Press, 1975), p. 102.

15. Philip S. Foner, *Women and the American Labor Movement*, 2 vols. (New York: Free Press, 1979–80), 2:4–6.

16. Joseph A. Hill, *Women in Gainful Occupations, 1870 to 1920*, Census Monograph no. 9 (Washington: Government Printing Office, 1929), pp. 32–35; David M. Katzman, *Seven Days a Week: Women and Domestic Service in Industrializing America* (New York: Oxford University Press, 1978), pp. 47–48, 53, 284; Michaele Cohen, "Women: The Ambiguous Emancipation," *Mankind* 5 (February 1977): 26; US, Department of Labor, Women's Bureau, *The New Position of Women in American Industry*, Bulletin no. 12 (Washington: US Government Printing Office, 1920), pp. 21, 34–35; Maureen Greenwald, "Women Workers and World War I: The American Railroad Industry, A Case Study," *Journal of Social History* 9 (Winter 1975): 154–61; Nancy E. Malan, "How 'Ya Gonna Keep 'Em Down?: Women and World War I," *Prologue* 5 (Winter 1973): 209.

17. T. Lynn Smith, "The Redistribution of the Negro Population of the United States, 1910–1960," *Journal of Negro History* 51 (July 1966): 163; Dewey H. Palmer, "Moving North: Negro Migration During World War I," *Phylon* 28 (Spring 1967): 53, 53n; Karl E. Taeuber and Alma F. Taeuber, "The Negro Population in the United States," in *The American Negro Reference Book*, 2 vols., ed. John P. Davis (Yonkers: Educational Heritage, 1966), pp. 114–15, 118–19; Clark, *Costs of World War*, pp. 257–58.

18. Palmer, "Moving North," *Phylon*, pp. 53, 55; Robert Higgs, "The Boll Weevil, the Cotton Economy, and Black Migration, 1910-1930," *Agricultural History* 50 (April 1976): 337–43, 348.

19. Conrad Taeuber and Irene B. Taeuber, *The Changing Population of the United States* (New York: Wiley, 1958), p. 57; US, Bureau of the Census, *Historical Statistics of the United States, Colonial Times to 1970*, Bicentennial ed., 2 vols. (Washington: US Department of Commerce, 1975), series C89–101, 1:105.

20. Joseph G. Rayback, *A History of American Labor*, rev. ed. (New York: Free Press, 1966), pp. 260–72.

21. Foster R. Dulles, *Labor in America: A History* (New York: Crowell, 1949), p. 225; Simeon Larson, *Labor and Foreign Policy: Gompers, the AFL, and the First*

World War, 1914–1918 (Rutherford: Fairleigh Dickinson University Press, 1975), pp. 160–61.

22. Benjamin M. Anderson, *Economics and the Public Welfare: Financial and Economic History of the United States, 1914–1946* (New York: D. Van Nostrand, 1949), pp. 23–26.

23. Ibid., pp. 41–44; Milton Friedman and Anna J. Schwartz, *A Monetary History of the United States, 1867-1960* (Princeton: Princeton University Press, 1963), pp. 189–93, 196–98, 205, 212–17.

24. Brownlee, *Dynamics of Ascent*, p. 371.

25. US, War Industries Board, *A Report of the War Industries Board*, by Bernard M. Baruch (Washington: Government Printing Office, 1921), pp. 19–21. The best recent history of the Board is Robert D. Cuff, *The War Industries Board: Business-Government Relations during World War I* (Baltimore: Johns Hopkins University Press, 1973).

26. Dickson, *Food Front*, pp. 20–21.

27. Ibid., pp. 50–51, 138–53; William F. Willoughby, *Government Organization in War Time and After: A Survey of the Federal Civil Agencies Created for Prosecution of the War* (New York: Appleton, 1919), pp. 258–92.

28. Shideler, *Farm Crisis*, pp. 13–14, 19–20.

29. Willoughby, *Government Organization*, pp. 293–313.

30. James P. Johnson, "The Wilsonians as War Managers: Coal and the Winter Crisis," *Prologue* 9 (Winter 1977): 194–202, 207–8.

31. Godfrey, *Railroads*, pp. 6–7.

32. Ibid., pp. 17–26; John G. B. Hutchins, "The Effect of the Civil War and the Two World Wars on American Transportation," *American Economic Review* 42 (May 1952): 634.

33. Willoughby, *Government Organization*, pp. 173–74; Frank H. Dixon, "Federal Operation of Railroads during the War," *Quarterly Journal of Economics* 33 (August 1919): 587–98.

34. Godfrey, *Railroads*, pp. 167–68.

35. Willoughby, *Government Organization*, pp. 143–48; Hutchins, "Wars and Transportation," *AER*, pp. 631–32.

36. Willoughby, *Government Organization*, pp. 156–58; James M. Morris, *Our Maritime Heritage: Maritime Developments and Their Impact on American Life* (Washington: University Press of America, 1979), pp. 209–12.

37. Willoughby, *Government Organization*, pp. 154; Hutchins, "Wars and Transportation," *AER*, pp. 632–33; Clark, *War Costs*, pp. 250–53.

38. Louis B. Wehle, "Labor Problems in the United States during the War," *Quarterly Journal of Economics* 32 (February 1918): 334–35, and "War Labor Policies

and Their Outcome in Peace," *Quarterly Journal of Economics* 33 (February 1919): 321; Willoughby, *Government Organization*, pp. 202-204.

39. Ibid., pp. 200-201, 225-42, 249-53; Rayback, *History of Labor*, pp. 274-75.

40. Wehle, "War Labor Policies," *QJE*, p. 325; Marc Karson, *American Labor Unions and Politics, 1900-1918* (Carbondale: Southern Illinois University Press, 1958), pp. 94-96; William E. Leuchtenburg, "The New Deal and the Analogue of War," in *Change and Continuity in Twentieth Century America*, eds. John Braeman, Robert Bremner, and Everett Walters (Columbus: Ohio State University Press, 1964), pp. 86-87; John S. Smith, "Organized Labor and Government in the Wilson Era, 1913-1921: Some Conclusions," *Labor History* 3 (Fall 1962): 267-77.

41. Anderson, *Economics and Welfare*, pp. 23-26; Frederic L. Paxson, *American Democracy and the World War*, 3 vols. (Boston: Houghton Mifflin, 1936-48), 2:14-15.

42. Ibid., 2:155; Gilbert, *American Financing*, pp. 69-73, 233-34.

43. Ibid., pp. 82, 138-42, 163-68.

44. Ibid., pp. 177-98; Friedman and Schwartz, *Monetary History*, pp. 205, 212-13, 217, 220; David M. Kennedy, *Over Here: The First World War and American Society* (New York: Oxford University Press, 1980), p. 105; Harold Barger, *The Management of Money: A Survey of the American Experience* (Chicago: Rand McNally, 1964), pp. 54-56.

45. Willoughby, *Government Organization*, pp. 50-66.

46. Charles O. Hardy, *Wartime Control of Prices* (Washington: Brookings Institution, 1940), pp. 115-22, 143-93, 209-10; Krooss, *American Economic Development*, pp. 505-6.

47. Paxson, *Democracy and War*, 2:109-12; Wright, "Economic Lessons," in *Economic Problems*, pp. 64-65.

48. Kennedy, *Over Here*, pp. 141-43; Cuff, *WIB*, pp. 1, 265, 273-75.

49. Ibid., pp. 3-5; Robert D. Cuff, "Business, the State, and World War I: The American Experience," in *War and Society in North America*, eds. J. L. Granatstein and Robert D. Cuff (Toronto: Thomas Nelson, 1971), pp. 1-19.

50. David B. Danbom, "The Agricultural Extension System and the First World War," *Historian* 41 (February 1979): 323-24, 330-31.

51. Houston, *New York Times*, and Midwest editor quoted in Allen Churchill, *Over Here: An Informal Re-creation of the Home Front in World War I* (New York: Dodd, Mead, 1968), pp. 17-18.

52. Henry F. May, *The End of American Innocence: A Study of the First Year of Our Own Time, 1912-1917* (New York: Knopf, 1959), pp.9-51, 355-64.

53. Mark Sullivan, *Our Times: The United States, 1900-1925*, vol. 5: *Over Here, 1914-1918* (New York: Scribner's, 1933), pp. 47-59; Paxson, *Democracy and War*, 1:163-79; Edward R. Ellis, *Echoes of Distant Thunder: Life in the United States, 1914-1918* (New York: Coward, McCann & Geoghegan, 1975), pp. 164-216, 228-

34; Ross Gregory, *The Origins of American Intervention in the First World War* (New York: Norton, 1971), p. 10.

54. Clifton J. Child, *The German-Americans in Politics, 1914–1917* (Madison: University of Wisconsin Press, 1939; reprint ed., New York: Arno Press, 1970), pp. 12–13; Frederick C. Leubke, *Bonds of Loyalty: German-Americans and World War I* (DeKalb: Northern Illinois University Press, 1974), pp. 29–30, 50, 87–89, 201; *Harvard Encyclopedia of American Ethnic Groups*, ed. Stephen Thernstrom, s.v. "Germans," by Kathleen N. Conzen; Carl F. Wittke, *We Who Built America: The Saga of the Immigrant*, rev. ed. (Cleveland: Press of the Western Reserve University, 1967), pp. 206–10.

55. George M. Stephenson, "The Attitude of Swedish-Americans toward the World War," *Proceedings*, Mississippi Valley Historical Association, pt. 1 (1920): 79–81.

56. *Harvard Encyclopedia*, s.v. "Irish," by Patrick J. Blessing.

57. Edward Cuddy, "Pro-Germanism and American Catholicism, 1914–1917," *Catholic Historical Review* 54 (October 1968): 427–32, 442–46, 454; Frederick Nohl, "The Lutheran Church—Missouri Synod Reacts to United States Anti-Germanism during World War I," *Concordia Historical Institute Quarterly* 35 (July 1962): 55–58.

58. Oscar Handlin, *The American People in the Twentieth Century* (Boston: Beacon Press, 1963), pp. 117–18; *Harvard Encyclopedia*, s.v. "Jews," by Arthur A. Goren.

59. Taeuber and Taeuber, *Changing Population*, p. 57.

60. Edward G. Hartmann, *The Movement to Americanize the Immigrant* (New York: Columbia University Press, 1948), pp. 19–104; John Higham, *Strangers in the Land: Patterns of American Nativism, 1860–1925* (New York: Atheneum, 1965), pp. 158–86, 218–19; John F. McClymer, *War and Welfare: Social Engineering in America, 1890–1925* (Westport: Greenwood Press, 1980), pp. 84–100.

61. Hartmann, *Americanize the Immigrant*, pp. 105–7; Kennedy, *Over Here*, pp. 66–67; McClymer, *War and Welfare*, pp. 105–43.

62. Peter Brock, *Twentieth-Century Pacifism* (New York: Van Nostrand Reinhold, 1970), pp. 2–7.

63. Ibid., pp. 7–10; C. Roland Marchand, *The American Peace Movement and Social Reform, 1898–1918* (Princeton: Princeton University Press, 1972), pp. 381–82; Charles De Benedetti, *The Peace Reform in American History* (Bloomington: Indiana University Press, 1980), pp. 79–86.

64. On the preparedness movement, see John P. Finnegan, *Against the Spectre of a Dragon: The Campaign for American Military Preparedness, 1914–1917* (Westport: Greenwood Press, 1974).

65. Marchand, *Peace Movement*, p. 382; Charles Chatfield, *For Peace and Justice: Pacifism in America, 1914–1941* (Knoxville: University of Tennessee Press, 1971), pp. 11–13; De Benedetti, *Peace Reform*, pp. 91–92.

66. Mother quoted in Steven Jantzen, *Hooray for Peace, Hurrah for War: The United States during World War I* (New York: Knopf, 1972), p. 136; Luebke, *Bonds of*

Loyalty, pp. 226–33, 311; Child, *German-Americans*, p. 162; John B. Duff, "German-Americans and the Peace, 1918–1920," *American Jewish Historical Quarterly* 59 (June 1970): 424; Ralph L. Moellering, "Some Lutheran Reactions to War and Pacifism, 1917–1941," *Concordia Historical Institute Quarterly 41* (August 1968): 121, 123.

67. *Harvard Encyclopedia*, s.v. "Irish," by Patrick J. Blessing; Handlin, *American People*, p. 120; Carl F. Wittke, *The Irish in America* (Baton Rouge: Louisiana State University Press, 1956), pp. 283–85.

68. Cuddy, "Pro-Germanism," *CHR*, pp. 441–42.

69. Rufus Learsi, *The Jews in America: A History* (New York: World Publishing, 1954; reprint ed., New York: KTAV Publishing House, 1972), pp. 241–42.

70. De Benedetti, *Peace Reform*, pp. 90–92, 106.

71. David T. Morgan, "The Revivalist as Patriot: Billy Sunday and World War I," *Journal of Presbyterian History* 51 (Summer 1973): 202–3, 205; James L. Lancaster, "The Protestant Churches and the Fight for Ratification of the Versailles Treaty," *Public Opinion Quarterly* 31 (Winter 1967–1968): 598, 605.

72. Chatfield, *Peace and Justice*, pp. 30–41; Marchand, *Peace Movement*, pp. 382–83; De Benedetti, *Peace Reform*, p. 106.

73. Lippmann quoted in Charles Hirschfield, "Nationalist Progressivism and World War I," *Mid-America* 45 (July 1963): 145, 147. See also McClymer, *War and Welfare*, pp. xii–xiii, 3–5, 79, 82.

74. Norman H. Clark, *Deliver Us from Evil: An Interpretation of American Prohibition* (New York: W. W. Norton, 1976), pp. 9–13, 129; Carl B. Swisher, *American Constitutional Development* (Boston: Houghton Mifflin, 1943), pp. 621–23.

75. Leuchtenburg, "Analogue of War," in *Change and Continuity*, pp. 83–96.

76. Paxson, *Democracy and War*, 2:207–8; Willoughby, *Government Organization*, pp. 255–57; McClymer, *War and Reform*, pp. 153–72; Marwick, *War and Change*, pp. 89–90.

77. Wilson quoted in William H. Chafe, *The American Woman: Her Changing Social, Economic, and Political Roles, 1920–1970* (London: Oxford University Press, 1972), p. 20; Malan, "Women and WWI," *Prologue*, p. 209; Mrs. Coffin Van Rensselaer, "The National League for Women's Service," *Annals of the American Academy of Political and Social Science* 79 (September 1918): 275–82; Linda L. Hewitt, *Women Marines in World War I* (Washington: History and Museums Division, US Marine Corps, 1974), p. 3; Eunice C. Dessez, *The First Enlisted Women, 1917–1918* (Philadelphia: Dorrance, 1955), pp. 11–13, 24–25.

78. Stephen L. Vaughn, *Holding Fast the Inner Lines: Democracy, Nationalism, and the Committee on Public Information* (Chapel Hill: University of North Carolina Press, 1980), pp. 61–115; Willoughby, *Government Organization*, pp. 35–39; Paxson, *Democracy and War*, 2:45–47; Kennedy, *Over Here*, p. 59.

79. John W. Chambers II, *Draftees or Volunteers: A Documentary History of the Debate over Military Conscription in the United States, 1787–1973* (New York: Garland, 1975), pp. 203–4.

80. Brock, *Twentieth-Century Pacifism*, pp. 33–56; Chatfield, *Peace and Justice*, pp. 68–71; Paxson, *Democracy and War*, 2:101; Allen Churchill, *Over Here: An Informal Re-creation of the Home Front in World War I* (New York: Dodd, Mead, 1968), pp. 74–75.

81. Donald Johnson, *Challenge to Freedom: World War I and the Rise of the American Civil Liberties Union* (Lexington: University Press of Kentucky, 1963), p. viii; Paul L. Murphy, *The Meaning of Freedom of Speech: First Amendment Freedoms from Wilson to FDR* (Westport: Greenwood Press, 1972), p. 4; Zechariah Chafee, Jr., *Free Speech in the United States* (Cambridge: Harvard University Press, 1946), p. 105.

82. Johnson, *Challenge to Freedom*, pp. 55–63; Swisher, *Constitutional Development*, pp. 604, 607; Horace C. Peterson and Gilbert C. Fite, *Opponents of War, 1917–1918* (Madison: University of Wisconsin Press, 1957), p. 26; Chafee, *Free Speech*, p. 42.

83. Higham, *Strangers in the Land*, p. 211; Swisher, *Constitutional Development*, pp. 606–7; Chafee, *Free Speech*, pp. 67–69.

84. Leubke, *Bonds of Loyalty*, pp. xv, 3–24, 247–48, 282, 329.

85. Melvyn Dubofsky, *We Shall Be All: A History of the Industrial Workers of the World* (Chicago: Quadrangle Books, 1969), pp. 354–97, 405–7, 449, 480–84; Philip Taft, "The Federal Trials of the I.W.W.," *Labor History* 3 (Winter 1962): 57–61; Higham, *Strangers in the Land*, pp. 219–21.

86. James Weinstein, *The Decline of Socialism in America, 1912–1925* (New York: Monthly Review Press, 1967), pp. 160–63, 182–83, 192–205, 304–9, 322, provided most of the data for this section, though he does not share my conclusion and traces the collapse to the postwar dissension. See also Daniel Bell, *Marxian Socialism in the United States* (Princeton: Princeton University Press, 1967), especially pp. 96–116.

87. Cobb's report of Wilson's words in Ellis, *Echoes of Distant Thunder*, pp. 318–19.

88. Higham, *Strangers in the Land*, pp. 195–99, 215–16.

89. Ibid., pp. 218–19, 223–26, 240–41.

90. Robert K. Murray, *Red Scare: A Study in National Hysteria, 1919–1920* (Minneapolis: University of Minnesota Press 1955), pp. 3–17, 33–81, 105–89.

91. De Benedetti, *Peace Reform*, p. 106.

92. Du Bois quoted in Jack D. Foner, *Blacks and the Military in American History: A New Perspective* (New York: Praeger, 1974), p. 109; Jane L. Scheiber and Harry N. Scheiber, "The Wilson Administration and the Wartime Mobilization of Black Americans, 1917–1918," *Labor History* 10 (Summer 1969): 437–38; August Meier

and Elliott Rudwick, "The Rise of Segregation in the Federal Bureaucracy, 1900–1930," *Phylon* 28 (Summer 1967): 178–84.

93. Foner, *Blacks and Military*, pp. 110–25; Scheiber and Scheiber, "Wilson Administration," *Labor History*, pp. 442–46; Ellis, *Echoes of Distant Thunder*, pp. 416–17; Florette Henri, *Black Migration: Movement North, 1900–1920* (Garden City: Anchor Doubleday, 1975), pp. 265–68, 306; Allan R. Millet, *The General: Robert L. Bullard and Officership in the United States Army 1881–1925* (Westport: Greenwood Press, 1975), pp. 245ff.

94. Ibid., pp. 307–9; Foner, *Blacks and Military*, pp. 110–26; John Hope Franklin, *From Slavery to Freedom: A History of American Negroes*, 5th ed. (New York: Knopf, 1980), pp. 474–82; Arthur I. Waskow, *From Race Riot to Sit-In, 1919 and the 1960s: A Study in the Connection between Conflict and Violence* (Garden City: Doubleday, 1966), pp. 38–104.

95. William L. O'Neill, *Everyone Was Brave: A History of Feminism in America* (Chicago: Quadrangle, 1971), pp. 194–98, 222–23; Eleanor Flexnor, *Century of Struggle: The Woman's Rights Movement in the United States*, rev. ed. (Cambridge: Belknap Press of Harvard University Press, 1975), pp. 294, 298–301; Barbara J. Steinson, " 'The Mother Half of Humanity': American Women in the Peace and Preparedness Movements in World War I," in *Women, War, and Revolution*, eds. Carol R. Berkin and Clara M. Lovett (New York: Holmes & Meier, 1980), pp. 268–75.

96. Winthrop S. Hudson, *American Protestantism* (Chicago: University of Chicago Press, 1961), pp. 129–31.

97. May, *End of American Innocence*, pp. 387–98.

98. Hudson, *Protestantism*, pp. 131–53; Paul F. Piper, Jr., "The American Churches in World War I," *Journal of the American Academy of Religion* 38 (June 1970): 150–55.

99. Ibid., p. 149; Norman Furniss, *The Fundamentalist Controversy, 1918–1931* (New Haven: Yale University Press, 1954; reprint ed., Hamden: Archon Books, 1963), pp. 10–13, 22–29.

100. Brownlee, *Dynamics of Ascent*, pp. 365, 381.

101. Clark, *History of Manufactures*, 3:304, 358; Kennedy, *Over Here*, p. 271; Harry W. Laidler, *Concentration of Control in American Industry* (New York: Thomas Y. Crowell, 1931), p. 10; Thomas C. Cochran and William Miller, *The Age of Enterprise: A Social History of Industrial America*, rev. ed. (New York: Harper, 1961), pp. 298–304; Thomas C. Cochran, *American Business in the Twentieth Century* (Cambridge: Harvard University Press, 1972), p. 70.

102. Kennedy, *Over Here*, p. 262.

103. Rayback, *History of Labor*, pp. 273–79.

104. Shideler, *Farm Crisis*, pp. 10–41; Danbom, "Agriculture and WWI," *Historian*, pp. 323–31.

105. Kennedy, *Over Here*, pp. 125-26; Wilfred E. Binkley, *President and Congress* (New York: Knopf, 1947), pp. 202-15.

106. David Burner, *The Politics of Provincialism: The Democratic Party in Transition, 1918-1932* (New York: Knopf, 1968), pp. 28-41, and "The Democratic Party, 1910-1932," in *History of U.S. Political Parties*, 4 vols., ed. Arthur M. Schlesinger, Jr. (New York: Chelsea House, 1973), 3:1814-18; Keith I. Polakoff, *Political Parties in American History* (New York: Wiley, 1981), pp. 297-302.

107. Seward W. Livermore, *Politics Is Adjourned: Woodrow Wilson and the War Congress, 1916-1918* (Middletown: Wesleyan University Press, 1966), pp. 15-104; Kennedy, *Over Here*, pp. 233-44.

108. Leuchtenburg, "Analogue of War," in *Change and Continuity*, pp. 81-143; Kennedy, *Over Here*, pp. 244-83.

109. Quotations are from Sullivan, *Over Here*, p. 489, and Benedict Crowell and Robert F. Wilson, *The Giant Hand: Our Mobilization and Control of Industry and National Resources, 1917-1918* (New Haven: Yale University Press, 1921), p. 7.

110. Robert D. Cuff, "Herbert Hoover, the Ideology of Voluntarism and War Organization during the Great War," *Journal of American History* 64 (September 1977): 358-72.

111. Swisher, *Constitutional Development*, p. 660; Johnson, *Challenge to Freedom*, pp. 194-98.

112. Paxson, *Democracy and War*, 2: 260.

Notes. Chapter 4: World War II

1. Stalin quoted in Francis Walton, *Miracle of World War II: How American Industry Made Victory Possible* (New York: Macmillan, 1956), p. 3.
2. Harry B. Yoshpe, "Economic Mobilization Planning between the Two World Wars," *Military Affairs* 15 (Winter 1951): 119.
3. John R. Craf, *A Survey of the American Economy, 1940–1946* (New York: North River Press, 1947), p. vii.
4. Cabel Phillips, *The 1940's: Decade of Triumph and Trouble* (New York: Macmillan, 1955), p. 104; Robert E. Cushman, "The Impact of War on the Constitution," in *The Impact of War on America*, ed. Keith L. Nelson (Ithaca: Cornell University Press, 1942), pp. 3–5.
5. Herman E. Krooss, *American Economic Development: The Progress of a Business Civilization*, 3rd ed. (Englewood Cliffs: Prentice–Hall, 1974), pp. 511–12.
6. Luther H. Gulick, *Administrative Reflections from World War II* (University: University of Alabama Press, 1948), p. 23.
7. Louis Brownlow, "Reconversion of the Federal Administrative Machinery from War to Peace," *Public Administration Review* 4 (Autumn 1944): 311–12; Craf, *American Economy*, pp. 18–28. See also Richard Polenberg, *Reorganizing Roosevelt's Government: The Controversy over Executive Reorganization, 1936–1939* (Cambridge: Harvard University Press, 1966), and Barry D. Karl, *Executive Reorganization and Reform in the New Deal: The Genesis of Administrative Management, 1900–1939* (Cambridge: Harvard University Press, 1963).
8. James F. Heath, "Domestic America During World War II: Research Opportunities for Historians," *Journal of American History* 58 (September 1971): 393–94; Carl B. Swisher, *American Constitutional Development* (Boston: Houghton Mifflin, 1943), p. 1004; Yoshpe, "Economic Mobilization," *Military Affairs*, pp. 200–1.
9. Ibid., pp. 201–4; Philips, *1940's*, pp. 77–78; Albert A. Blum, "Roosevelt, the M–Day Plans, and the Military–Industrial Complex," *Military Affairs* 36 (April 1972): 44–46.
10. Craf, *American Economy*, p. 4; US, Bureau of the Budget, *The United States at War: Development and Administration of the War Program by the Federal Government* (Washington: Bureau of the Budget, 1946; reprint ed., New York: Da Capo Press, 1972), pp. 20–25.
11. Keith E. Eiler, "The Constant Service: A Biography of Robert P. Patterson" (book in preparation).
12. Ibid.

13. Richard Polenburg, *War and Society: The United States, 1941–1945* (Philadelphia: J. B. Lippincott, 1972), p. 10.

14. Craf, *American Economy*, pp. 52–56; David Novick, Melvin Anshen, and W. C. Truppner, *Wartime Production Controls* (New York: Columbia University Press, 1949; reprint ed., New York: Da Capo Press, 1976), pp. 36–43.

15. Polenberg, *War and Society*, pp. 12–13.

16. Craf, *American Economy*, pp. 31–35.

17. Novick et al., *Production Controls*, pp. 30–31; Paul A. C. Koistinen, *The Military-Industrial Complex: A Historical Perspective* (New York: Praeger, 1980), p. 72.

18. Polenberg, *War and Society*, pp. 13–14; Novick et al., *Production Controls*, pp. 39–40.

19. Ibid., pp. 31–32.

20. Polenberg, *War and Society*, pp. 9–11; Richard R. Lingeman, *Don't You Know There's a War On?: The American Home Front, 1941–1945* (New York: G.P. Putnam's, Capricorn Books, 1970), p. 114.

21. Novick et al., *Production Controls*, pp. 3, 35.

22. Walton, *Miracle of Production*, pp. 5, 521.

23. Murray R. Benedict, *Farm Policies of the United States, 1790–1950: A Study in Their Origins and Development* (New York: Twentieth Century Fund, 1953), pp. 402–3; Lowry Nelson, "Farms and Farming Communities," in *American Society in Wartime*, ed. William F. Ogburn (Chicago: University of Chicago Press, 1943; reprint ed., New York: Da Capo Press, 1972), pp. 83–85.

24. US, Department of Commerce, Bureau of the Census, *Historical Statistics of the United States, Colonial Times to 1970*, 2 vols. (Washington: Government Printing Office, 1975), series K407–413, 1:498; Walter W. Wilcox, *The Farmer in the Second World War* (Ames: Iowa State College Press, 1947), p. 3.

25. Wayne D. Rasmussen, ed., *Agriculture in the United States: A Documentary History*, 4 vols. (New York: Random House, 1975), 4:3188–94; US, Department of Agriculture, *Century of Service: The First 100 Years of the United States Department of Agriculture* (Washington: Department of Agriculture, 1963), pp. 273–323.

26. Paul Studenski and Herman E. Krooss, *Financial History of the United States: Fiscal, Monetary, Banking, and Tariff, Including Financial Administraton and State and Local Finance* (New York: McGraw-Hill, 1952), p. 436; Gulick, *Administrative Reflections*, pp. 67–68.

27. Ibid., pp. 488, 450; Polenberg, *War and Society*, pp. 27–29.

28. Ibid., pp. 29–30; Henry C. Murphy, *The National Debt in War and Transition* (New York: McGraw-Hill, 1950), p. 162.

29. Studenski and Krooss, *Financial History*, pp. 439–43, 455; Margaret G. Myers, *A Financial History of the United States* (New York: Columbia University Press,

1970), pp. 350, 352–53, 355; Krooss, *American Economic Development*, pp. 504–6.

30. Harvey C. Mansfield et al., *A Short History of the OPA* (Washington: Office of Price Administration, 1947), pp. 19–20, 23, 26–27, 41.

31. Ibid., pp. 21, 27; Benedict, *Farm Policies*, p. 413.

32. Polenberg, *War and Society*, pp. 31–32.

33. Ibid.; Benedict, *Farm Policies*, pp. 415–16; Phillips, *1940's*, p. 86.

34. Ibid., pp. 86–87; Polenberg, *War and Society*, p. 32; John K. Galbraith, "Reflections on Price Control," *Quarterly Journal of Economics* 60 (August 1946): 476–79.

35. Milton Derber, "Labor-Management in World War II," *Current History* 48 (June 1965): 340–45.

36. Ibid., p. 341; Polenberg, *War and Society*, pp. 155, 157.

37. Mansfield, *History of OPA*, pp. 28–29.

38. Dulles, Foster R., *Labor in America: A History*, 2nd rev. ed. (New York: Crowell, 1960), pp. 334–36.

39. Polenberg, *War and Society*, p. 20; Paul A. C. Koistinen, "Mobilizing the World War II Economy: Labor and the Industrial-Military Alliance," *Pacific Historical Review* 42 (November 1973): 451–52; Albert A. Blum, *Drafted or Deferred: Practices Past and Present* (Ann Arbor: University of Michigan, 1967), pp. 33–46. See also George Q. Flynn, *The Mess in Washington: Manpower Mobilization in World War II* (Westport: Greenwood Press, 1979).

40. Jane C. Record, "The War Labor Board: An Experiment in Wage Stabilization," *American Economic Review* 34 (March 1944): 98–101; Polenberg, *War and Society*, pp. 26–27; Dulles, *Labor in America*, pp. 345–46.

41. Ibid., pp. 346–47; Polenberg, *War and Society*, pp. 26–27.

42. Dulles, *Labor in America*, pp. 343–44; Roland A. Young, *Congressional Politics in the Second World War* (New York: Columbia University Press, 1956), pp. 63–65.

43. Albert A. Blum, "Work or Fight: The Use of the Draft as a Manpower Sanction during the Second World War," *Industrial and Labor Relations Review* 16 (April 1963): 366–80; Polenberg, *War and Society*, pp. 176, 179–82.

44. Joseph R. Rose, *American Wartime Transportation* (New York: Crowell, 1953), pp. 1–9, 14.

45. Ibid., pp. 37–83.

46. Craf, *American Economy*, pp. 25, 27–28.

47. US, Census, *Historical Statistics*, series U1–25, U26–31, 2:864, 869.

48. James M. Morris, *Our Maritime Heritage: Maritime Developments and Their Impact on American Life* (Washington: University Press of America, 1979), pp. 217–20.

49. Eiler, "Constant Service," n.p.; Phillips, *1940's*, pp. 83–84.

50. Craf, *American Economy*, p. 149; Polenberg, *War and Society*, p. 35.

51. Ibid., pp. 35–36, 220–35.

52. Ibid., p. 36; Baruch quoted in Mansfield, *History of OPA*, p. 27.

53. US, Census, *Historical Statistics*, series M256–267, 1:605; Walton, *Miracle of WW II*, pp. 237–38.

54. Lingeman, *There's a War On?*, p. 65.

55. James F. Heath, "American War Mobilization and the Use of Small Manufacturers, 1939–1943," *Business History Review* 46 (Autumn 1972): 316–17; John M. Blum, *V Was for Victory: Politics and American Culture during World War II* (New York: Harcourt Brace Jovanovich, 1976), pp. 124–31.

56. Lingeman, *There's a War On?*, p. 65; Heath, "War Mobilization," *BHR*, pp. 298–99.

57. Alfred D. Chandler, Jr., *The Visible Hand: The Managerial Revolution in American Business* (Cambridge: Belknap Press of Harvard University Press, 1977), p. 176.

58. Alfred D. Chandler, Jr., "The Structure of American Industry in the Twentieth Century: A Historical Overview," *Business History Review* 43 (Autumn 1969): 256–58, 270–79; Alfred D. Chandler, Jr., and Louis Galambos, "The Development of Large-Scale Economic Organizations in Modern America," *Journal of Economic History* 30 (March 1970): 201–17; W. Elliott Brownlee, *Dynamics of Ascent: A History of the American Economy*, 2nd ed. (New York: Knopf, 1979), pp. 445–46; John Brooks, *The Great Leap: The Past Twenty-Five Years in American History* (New York: Harper & Row, Colophon Books, 1966), pp. 12, 38–53.

59. Kent C. Redmond, "World War II, a Watershed in the Role of the National Government in the Advancement of Science and Technology," in *The Humanities in an Age of Science*, ed. Charles Angoff (Rutherford: Fairleigh Dickinson University Press, 1968), pp. 169–71.

60. Ibid., pp. 167–68, 178–80; Chandler, *Visible Hand*, pp. 476–95.

61. James Bordley and A. M. Harvey, *Two Centuries of American Medicine, 1776–1976* (Philadelphia: W. B. Saunders, 1976), pp. 111–14.

62. Ibid., pp. 126, 452–53.

63. US, Census, *Historical Statistics*, series K1–6, K184–191, K192–194, 1:457, 469; Wilcox, *Farmers in WW II*, pp. 287–88, 291; Rasmussen, *Agriculture in US*, 4:2917.

64. Ibid.; Willard W. Cochrane, *The Development of American Agriculture: A Historical Analysis* (Minneapolis: University of Minnesota Press, 1979), pp. 126–29, 137.

65. US, Census, *Historical Statistics*, series K344–353, 1:489; Wilcox, *Farmers in WW II*, p. 81.

66. Ibid., pp. 249, 251, 307; US, Census, *Historical Statistics*, series K361–375, 1:491.

67. Dulles, *Labor in America*, p. 332.

68. Thomas R. Brooks, *Toil and Trouble: A History of American Labor*, 2d rev. ed. (New York: Delacorte Press, 1971), p. 207; US, Census, *Historical Statistics*, series D722-72, 1:164.

69. Ibid., series D927-939, D940-945, 1:176-77; Colin D. Campbell, ed., *Wage-Price Controls in World War II, United States and Germany: Reports by Persons Who Observed and Participated in the Programs* (Washington: American Enterprise Institute for Public Policy Research, 1971), p. 47.

70. Bruno Stein, "Labor's Role in Government Agencies during World War II," *Journal of Economic History* 17 (September 1957): 396-97, 399-400, 403-4, 408.

71. Polenberg, *War and Society*, pp. 76-89.

72. Richard Polenberg, *One Nation Divisible: Class, Race, and Ethnicity in the United States since 1938* (New York: Viking Press, Penguin Books, 1980), pp. 21-22.

73. On the Japanese-Americans and the camps, see: Roger Daniels, *Concentration Camps: North America, Japanese in the United States and Canada during World War II*, rev. ed. (Malabar: Robert E. Krieger, 1981); Audrie Girdner and Ann Loftis, *The Great Betrayal: The Evacuation of the Japanese-Americans during World War II* (New York: Macmillan, 1969); and Jacobus ten Broek, Edward N. Barnhart, and Floyd W. Matson, *Prejudice, War and the Constitution: Cause and Consequences of the Evacuation of the Japanese-Americans in World War II* (Berkeley: University of California Press, 1954).

74. Ibid., pp. 62-67.

75. Ibid., pp. 70-86, 327-32.

76. Blum, *V Was for Victory*, p. 172; La Vern J. Rippley, *The German-Americans* (Boston: Twayne Publishers, 1976), pp. 206-10.

77. Polenberg, *One Nation*, p. 59; Lawrence F. Pisani, *The Italian in America: A Social Study and History* (New York: Exposition Press, 1957), pp. 204-9; Blum, *V Was for Victory*, pp. 149-55.

78. Ibid., pp. 172-74; Oscar Handlin, *Adventure in Freedom: Three Hundred Years of Jewish Life in America* (New York: McGraw-Hill, 1954), pp. 184-210.

79. *Harvard Encyclopedia of American Ethnic Groups*, ed. Stephan Thernstrom, s.v. "Mexicans," by Carlos E. Cortes; Stanley Steiner, *La Raza: The Mexican Americans* (New York: Harper, 1970), p. 196; Carey McWilliams, *North From Mexico: The Spanish-Speaking People of the United States* (Philadelphia: J. B. Lippincott, 1949), pp. 259-72.

80. Phillips, *1940's*, pp. 115-21; Polenberg, *War and Society*, pp. 47-48.

81. Ibid., pp. 49-51; Gladys M. Kammerer, *Impact of War on Federal Personnel Administration, 1939-1945* (Lexington: University of Kentucky Press, 1951), pp. 118-33.

82. Allan M. Winkler, *The Politics of Propaganda: The Office of War Information, 1942–1945* (New Haven: Yale University Press, 1978), pp. 1, 4–6, 49–50; Phillips, *1940's*, pp. 96, 99–101, 103.

83. Charles DeBenedetti, *The Peace Reform in American History* (Bloomington: Indiana University Press, 1980), pp. 109–29; Wayne S. Cole, *America First: The Battle Against Intervention, 1940–1941* (Madison: University of Wisconsin Press, 1953), pp. 8–10.

84. Laurence Wittner, *Rebels Against War: The American Peace Movement, 1941–1960* (New York: Columbia University Press, 1969), pp. 19–23, 30, 34, 51–55.

85. Polenberg, *War and Society*, pp. 54–60.

86. ACLU report quoted in Richard Polenberg, ed., *America at War: The Home Front, 1941–1945* (Englewood Cliffs: Prentice-Hall, 1968), p. 91

87. Blum, *V Was for Victory*, p. 249.

88. Ibid., p. 250; Keith W. Olson, *The G.I. Bill, the Veterans, and the Colleges* (Lexington: University Press of Kentucky, 1974), pp. 43, 109; David R. B. Ross, *Preparing for Ulysses: Politics and Veterans during World War II* (New York: Columbia University Press, 1969), pp. 1–3.

89. Isaac L. Kandal, *The Impact of the War on American Education* (Chapel Hill: University of North Carolina Press, 1948), pp. 123–61.

90. Jack D. Foner, *Blacks and the Military in American History: A New Perspective* (New York: Praeger, 1974), p. 109.

91. Brooks, *Great Leap*, pp. 275, 278, 280–83.

92. Lee Finkle, "The Conservative Aims of Militant Rhetoric: Black Protest during World War II," *Journal of American History* 60 (December 1973): 697; Phillip McGuire, "Judge Hastie, World War II, and Army Racism," *Journal of Negro History* 62 (October 1977): 351; Donald R. McCoy and Richard T. Ruetten, "The Civil Rights Movement, 1940–1954," *Midwest Quarterly* 11 (Autumn 1969): 11–16; Harvard Sitkoff, "Racial Militancy and Interracial Violence in the Second World War," *Journal of American History* 58 (December 1971): 661; Neil A. Wynn, *The Afro-American and the Second World War* (New York: Holmes and Meier, 1975), pp. 19–20.

93. Ibid.; Sitkoff, "Racial Militancy," *JAH*, p. 662.

94. Louis Ruchames, *Race, Jobs, and Politics: The Story of the FEPC* (New York: Columbia University Press, 1953), pp. 22–23, 156–64.

95. James A. Nuechterlein, "The Politics of Civil Rights: The FEPC, 1941–46," *Prologue* 10 (Fall 1978): 171, 174, 189; Polenberg, *War and Society*, pp. 102–5.

96. Wynn, *Afro-American*, pp. 39–58, 129–30; James S. Olson, "Organized Black Leadership and Industrial Unionism: The Racial Response, 1936–1945," *Labor History* 10 (Summer 1969): 475–77; A. Russell Buchanan, *Black Americans in World War II* (Santa Barbara: ABC-Clio Press, 1977), p. 39; John Hope II, "The Employment of Negroes in the United States by Major Occupation and Industry," *Journal of Negro Education* 22 (Summer 1953): 309–14; Norval D. Glenn, "Changes in the American

Occupational Structure and Occupational Gains of Negroes during the 1940's," *Social Forces* 41 (December 1962): 188-91.

97. Polenberg, *War and Society*, pp. 126-28; Warren Schaich, "A Relationship between Collective Racial Violence and War," *Journal of Black Studies* 5 (June 1975): 385-87; Sitkoff, "Racial Militancy," *JAH*, pp. 671-75.

98. Ibid., pp. 668-69.

99. John Hope Franklin, *From Slavery to Freedom: A History of American Negroes*, 5th ed. (New York: Knopf, 1980), p. 376; Polenberg, *War and Society*, pp. 123-24.

100. Franklin, *Slavery to Freedom*, pp. 576-77.

101. Foner, *Blacks and Military*, pp. 156-58, 163, 168-74; Wynn, *Afro-Americans*, pp. 21-24, 30, 35-38; Morris J. MacGregor, Jr., *Integration of the Armed Forces, 1940-1945* (Washington: Center of Military History, 1981), pp. 17-151. See also Alan M. Osur, *Blacks in the Army Air Forces during World War II: The Problems of Race Relations* (Washington: Office of Air Force History, 1977), Alan L. Gropman, *The Air Force Integrates, 1945-1964* (Washington: Office of Air Force History, 1978), and Richard M. Dalfiume, *Desegregation of the US Armed Forces, 1939-1953* (Columbia: University of Missouri Press, 1969).

102. Neil A. Wynn, "The Impact of the Second World War on the American Negro," *Journal of Contemporary History* 6 (1971): 51-52.

103. Buchanan, *Black Americans*, pp. 131-34; Wynn, *Afro-Americans*, pp. 100-2, 109, 115, 121; McCoy and Ruetten, "Civil Rights," *Midwest*, pp. 16-17.

104. Lois W. Banner, *Women in Modern America: A Brief History* (New York: Harcourt Brace Jovanovich, 1974), p. 171; William H. Chafe, *The American Women: Her Changing Social, Economic, and Political Roles, 1920-1970* (New York: Oxford University Press, 1972), p. 135.

105. Ibid., pp. 140-41, 148; Chester W. Gregory, *Women in Defense Work during World War II: An Analysis of the Labor Problem and Women's Rights* (New York: Exposition Press, 1974), pp. 40, 68, 79-81, 94, 114, 131; Karen Anderson, *Wartime Women: Sex Roles, Family Relations, and the Status of Women during World War II* (Westport: Greenwood Press, 1981), p. 4.

106. WMC director quoted in Gregory, *Women in Defense Work*, p. 16; Chafe, *American Woman*, pp. 155-58; US, Census, *Historical Statistics*, series D830-844, 1:172.

107. Chafe, *American Woman*, pp. 141-46; US, Census, *Historical Statistics*, series D49-62, 1:133.

108. Chafe, *American Women*, pp. 180-82; Anderson, *Wartime Women*, pp. 27-28, 164.

109. Arthur M. Schlesinger, Jr., *The Imperial Presidency* (Boston: Houghton Mifflin, 1973), pp. 124-30; Richard E. Darilek, *A Loyal Opposition in Time of War: The Republican Party and the Politics of Foreign Policy from Pearl Harbor to Yalta* (Westport: Greenwood Press, 1976), pp. 4-5.

110. Young, *Congressional Politics*, pp. 29–31, 219; Nathan D. Grundstein, *Presidential Delegation of Authority in Wartime* (Pittsburgh: University of Pittsburgh Press, 1961), p. 28; Schlesinger, *Imperial Presidency*, pp. 107–22.

111. Roosevelt quoted in Swisher, *Constitutional Development*, p. 1010; Schlesinger, *Imperial Presidency*, pp. 107–22.

112. Young, *Congressional Politics*, pp. 4–8, 90–95, 101, 234; Swisher, *Constitutional Development*, pp. 1010–11.

113. Donald H. Riddle, *The Truman Committee: A Study in Congressional Responsibility* (New Brunswick: Rutgers University Press, 1964), pp. 8–11, 154–56, 165; Louis Smith, *American Democracy and Military Power: A Study of Civil Control of the Military Power in the United States* (Chicago: University of Chicago Press, 1951), pp. 213–25.

114. Osmond K. Fraenkel, "War, Civil Liberties and the Supreme Court, 1941 to 1946," *Yale Law Journal* 55 (June 1946): 733–34; William F. Swindler, *Court and Constitution in the Twentieth Century: The New Legality, 1932–1968* (Indianapolis: Bobbs-Merrill, 1970), pp. 145–46; Clinton L. Rossiter, *The Supreme Court and the Commander in Chief* (Ithaca: Cornell University Press, 1951), pp. 60–64.

115. Jack R. Pole, *The Pursuit of Equality in American History* (Berkeley: University of California Press, 1978), p. 292; Robert G. McCloskey, *The American Supreme Court* (Chicago: University of Chicago Press, 1960), pp. 178–81.

116. Otis L. Graham, Jr., "The Democratic Party, 1932-1945," in *History of U.S. Political Parties*, ed. Arthur M. Schlesinger, Jr., 4 vols. (New York: Chelsea House, 1973), 3:1946–47; Young, *Congressional Politics*, pp. 220–25.

117. Taft quoted in Polenberg, *America at War*, p. 62; Donald R. McCoy, "Republican Opposition during Wartime, 1941–1945," *Mid-America* 49 (July 1967): 174–84, 186, 188–89.

118. Ibid., p. 180; John R. Moore, "The Conservative Coalition in the United States Senate, 1942–1945," *Journal of Southern History* 33 (August 1967): 368–76; James T. Patterson, "A Conservative Coalition Forms in Congress, 1933–1939," *Journal of American History* 52 (March 1966): 757–67.

119. Polenberg, *War and Society*, pp. 188–89, 203–13.

120. Brooks, *Great Leap*, describes the transformation of America between 1940 and 1965.

Notes. War and Society: A Few Answers

1. Arthur M. Schlesinger, Jr., *The Bitter Heritage: Vietnam and American Democracy, 1941–1968* (Boston: Houghton Mifflin, 1967), p. 80.

GLOSSARY OF ACRONYMS

AFL	American Federation of Labor
CCC	Civilian Conservation Corps
CIO	Congress of Industrial Organizations
CMP	Controlled Materials Plan
FEPC	Fair Employment Practice Committee
FSA	Farm Security Administration
GMPR	General Maximum Price Regulation
GNP	Gross National Product
IMP	Industrial Mobilization Plan
IWW	International Workers of the World
MOWM	March on Washington Movement
NDAC	National Defense Advisory Commission
NDMB	National Defense Mediation Board
NRPB	National Resources Planning Board
NWLB	National War Labor Board
NYA	National Youth Administration
ODT	Office of Defense Transportation
OEM	Office of Emergency Management
OES	Office of Economic Stabilization
OPA	Office of Price Administration
OPAC	Office of Price Stabilization & Civilian Supply
OPM	Office of Production Management
OSRD	Office of Scientific Research & Development
OWI	Office of War Information

GLOSSARY

OWM	Office of War Mobilization
PRP	Production Requirements Plan
REA	Rural Electrification Administration
ROTC	Reserve Officers Training Corps
SPAB	Supply Priorities & Allocations Board
WFA	War Food Administration
WIB	War Industries Board
WMC	War Manpower Commission
WPA	Works Progress Administration
WPB	War Production Board
WRA	War Resources Administration
WRB	War Resources Board

INDEX

Adams, Abigail, 9–10
Adams, Samuel, 1
Afro-Americans. *See* Black Americans
Agricultural colleges, 46, 67
Agriculture, 173
   American Revolution experience, 22–23
   Civil War experience, 44–46, 52–53, 67
   food supply control, 102–103, 138–139
   World War I developments, 91–93, 110, 127
   World War II advances, 137–139, 151–152, 157
Agriculture Department, 46, 67, 150
Alien and Sedition Acts of 1798, 121
Alien Registration (Smith) Act of 1940, 158
America First Committee, 158
American Civil Liberties Union, 129, 159
American College of Surgeons, 151
American Council on Education, 160
American Federation of Labor (AFL), 97, 98
American Medical Association, 151
American Protective League, 121
American Revolution
   black Americans' experience, 8–10
   central government strengthening, 34–40
   civil liberties curtailment, 17–19
   cost of, 6–8
   economic effects, 22–27
   educational improvements during, 11–12
   effects of, summary, 5–6, 40–41

ethnic groups' experiences, 12–14
financing of, 27–31, 173
Indians' experience, 19–20
inflation during, 6, 25, 29–31
mobilization of resources, 26–27, 35–36
number of soldiers, 6, 21
Old Northwest settlement during, 19–20
religious discrimination, 13–15, 17
social changes, 20–22
state government structures, 31–34
weakening of churches' influence, 15–16
women's experience, 10–11
American Society of International Law, 115
American Union Against Militarism, 116
Anderson, Marian, 160–161
Anthony, Susan B., 72
Arms and munitions industries, 24, 48, 49, 55, 90, 102

Banking system, 28, 38, 44, 69
Bank of North America, 26
Barton, Clara, 73
Baruch, Bernard, 148
Black Americans, 175
   abolition of slavery, 10, 72, 78, 79, 83
   American Revolution experience, 8–10, 20
   Civil War experience, 70–71, 77–79
   World War I experience, 96–97, 124–125
   World War II advances, 160–164
Blockade running, 53, 55
Board of Economic Warfare, 146

Board of War Communications, 146
Bourne, Randolph S., 87, 129
Brock, Peter, 81
Brooks, John, 169
Brown, Joseph E., 56, 57
Buchanan, James, 71
Bureau of Colored Troops, 70–71
Bureau of Investigation, 121
Business changes, 26, 49–51, 126–127, 150
Butler, Ben, 79
Byrnes, James F., 148

Capital Issues Committee, 108
Carnegie Endowment for International Peace, 115
Carroll, Charles, 15
Catt, Carrie Chapman, 119
Chandler, Alfred, 150
Chase, Salmon P., 44, 65, 67, 69
Child labor, 155, 156
Churches. *See* Religious institutions
Church Peace Union, 116, 118
Civilian Conservation Corps (CCC), 155, 156
Civil liberties curtailment
  during American Revolution, 17–19
  during Civil War, 60, 63–64
  wartime stimulation, 175
  during World War I, 121–123
  during world War II, 156–159
Civil Rights Act of 1866, 79
Civil rights movement, 161–162. *See also* Black Americans
Civil War, 43, 84–85
  abolition of slavery, 78, 79, 83
  antebellum nativism, 73–77
  black Americans' experience, 70–71, 77–79
  church disunity, 82
  civil liberties curtailment, 60, 63–64
  Confederate political system, 60–61
  cost of, 85
  executive power, 63–66
  financing of, 58–59, 67–69, 173
  Indians' experience, 79–80
  inflation during, 59, 67
  Northern economic growth, 44–51
  peace movement, 80–81
  political party competition, 61–63
  Southern economic collapse, 52–56
  Southern mobilization, 56–59
  Union mobilization, 67–71
  western settlement during, 80
  women's experience, 71–73
Clark, George Rogers, 19
Clark, Victor S., 55
Clayton Antitrust Act, 98
Coal industry, 48, 51, 103–104, 145, 149
Cobb, Frank, 123
Cochran, Thomas, C., 25, 26
Commerce
  American Revolution disruption, 6, 8, 22, 24–25
  Civil War experience, 46–47
  World War I exports growth, 88–89
  World War II control, 146–147
Committee on Public Information, 120
Committee on the Conduct of the War, 65, 127
Communication industries, 105, 146
Congress of Industrial Organizations (CIO), 153, 168
Conscientious objectors, 16–17, 80–81, 115, 120, 158–159
Controlled Materials Plan (CMP), 136, 137
Conzen, Kathleen N., 75
Cooke, Jay, 68
Copperheads (peace Democrats), 63–64
Corbin, Margaret, 11
Cornish, Dudley, 78
Council of National Defense, 102, 104
Creel, George, 120

Daughters of Liberty, 10
Daughters of the American Revolution, 160
Davis, Jefferson, 60, 61, 79
Davis, Rebecca Harding, 85
Debs, Eugene V., 122
Defense Transportation, Office of (ODT), 146

de Kalb, Baron, 14, 27
Department of. *See* specific department names
Dix, Dorothea, 73
Donald, David, 61
Douglas, Stephen A., 64
Douglass, Frederick, 77
Dred Scott decision, 66, 78
DuBois, W. E. B., 124
Dunmore, Lord (John Murray), 9
Dwight, Timothy, 15–16

Economic Bill of Rights, 159–160
Economic change
  American Revolution effects, 21–26
  Confederacy collapse, 52–56
  Union growth, 44–51
  wartime stimulation, 172–173
  World War I effects, 88–93, 126–127
  World War II effects, 148–155
Economic Stabilization, Office of (OES), 148
Economic Stabilization Act of 1942, 142, 144
Education, 8, 11–12, 46, 67, 160
Einstein, Albert, 151
Elkins, Stanley M., 39
Emergency Fleet Corporation, 105, 147
Emergency Management, Office of (OEM), 133, 147
Emergency Price Control Act of 1942, 141
Employment Service, US, 107
Engineering profession, 12
Espionage Act of 1917, 121
Ethnic tension
  American Revolution experience, 12–14
  antebellum nativism, 73–77
  divided response to World War I, 113–114, 116–117
  pre-World War I nativism, 114–115
  World War I experience, 121–125
  World War II experience, 156–157
Executive power. *See* Federal government strengthening

Export industry. *See* Commerce

Fair Employment Practice Committee (FEPC), 161
Farming. *See* Agriculture
Farm Security Administration (FSA), 155, 156
Federal Bureau of Investigation (FBI), 157
Federal Council of Churches, 118
Federal government strengthening
  American Revolution experience, 34–40
  Civil War experience, 63–71, 83–84
  Confederate developments, 60–61
  Roosevelt power, 165–167
  state executive power, 31–34
  wartime stimulation, 173–174
  World War I developments, 87–88, 129
  World War II acceleration, 131–133
Federal Reserve System, 99, 101, 108, 140–141
Fellowship of Reconciliation, 118
Finance Department, 37
Financing of war, 173
  American Revolution, 27–31
  Civil War, 58–59, 67–69
  World War I, 107–108
  World War II, 139–141
Flexnor, Eleanor, 72
Food Administration, 102–103
Food and Fuel Control Act of 1917, 102–103
Food supply control, 102–103, 138–139
Foreign Affairs Department, 37
Fourteenth Amendment, 79
Fox, Dixon, 12
Franklin, Benjamin, 27
Friedman, Leon, 62
Friends of Irish Freedom, 117
Fuel Administration, 103–104
Fuel supply control, 103–104
Funding Act of 1864, 59

General Maximum Price Regulation (GMPR), 141–142

German-Americans, 12–14, 74–75, 113, 114, 116–117, 121–122, 157
German pietists, 13, 16–17
GI Bill, 160
Gompers, Samuel, 97, 98
Grain Corporation, US, 103
Grand Army of the Republic, 62

Hatch Act, 158
Heilbroner, Robert L., 24
Herkimer, Nicolaus, 14
Hesseltine, William, 71
Higham, John, 76–77
Hillman, Sidney, 135, 155
Holmes, Oliver Wendell, Jr., 43
Homestead Act, 46, 80
Hoover, Herbert, 103
Houston, David, 112
Hudson, Winthrop, 16, 125

Immigration, 73–74, 77, 97, 114. *See also* Ethnic tension
Indentured servants, 26
Indians, 19–20, 79–80
Industrial Mobilization Plan (IMP), 133
Industry, heavy, 48–51, 91, 148–149
Industry, manufacturing. *See* Manufacturing industries
Inflation, 173. *See also* specific wars
International Workers of the World (IWW) (Wobblies), 97, 122
Inter-Parliamentary Union, 115
Interstate Commerce Commission, 104, 145
Irish-Americans, 14, 74–76, 113, 117
Iron and steel industry, 48–51, 91, 148–149
Italian-Americans, 74, 157

Japanese-Americans, 156–157, 167
Jay, John, 37
Jehovah's Witnesses, 159
Jewish-Americans, 12, 15, 74, 114, 117, 157
Johnson, Andrew, 62
Johnson, Joseph E., 59

Kerber, Linda, 11
Knights of the Golden Circle, 63

Know-Nothing movement, 75
Knudsen, William, 135
Ku Klux Klan, 126, 157

Labor Administrator, 106
Labor Division, WPB, 155
Labor force
   1939–1945, 132–133, 148, 162, 164
   unemployment, 88, 148
   World War I changes in, 93–97
Labor movement
   American Revolution experience, 25–26
   wartime advances, 175
   World War I gains, 97–99, 106–107, 119, 127
   World War II developments, 143–145, 152–155
LaFollette, Robert, 128
League to Enforce Peace, 117
Lend-Lease, 146–147
Leyburn, James G., 14
Lincoln, Abraham, 61–67, 71, 78, 81, 83, 121, 174, 175
Lincoln, Benjamin, 37
Lippmann, Walter, 118
Livingston, Robert, 37

McAdoo, William G., 104, 107–108
McKinley, William, 66
McKitrick, Eric L., 39, 61
Madison, James, 34
Manufacturing industries
   American Revolution experience, 23–24
   Civil War experience, 48, 55–56
   wartime stimulation, 172–173
   World War I developments, 89–91, 102
   World War II activities, 134–137, 148–150, 168–169
March on Washington Movement (MOWM), 161
Maritime Commission, 147
Massey, Mary E., 73
Medical profession, 12, 151
Meigs, Montgomery C., 49
Memminger, Christopher, 58, 59

Index

Mennonites, 13, 115, 159
Merchant marine, 46, 105, 147
Merryman, John, 66
Mexican-Americans, 157
Military service
   American Revolution, 6, 21
   black Americans, 8–10, 70–71, 77–79, 124, 163–164
   central government control, 57, 70–71, 120, 142–143, 173
   national service concept, 145
   women, 10–11, 119
Military technology, 12, 24, 36, 49, 93, 110–111, 132
Miller, John C., 13, 27, 38
Milligan, Lambdin P., 66
Mobilization of resources, 173–174
   American Revolution, 26–31, 35–36
   Civil War, 56–59, 67–71
   World War I, 101–112, 141
   World war II, 133–139, 142–148
Morrill Act, 46
Morris, Richard B., 21
Morris, Robert, 37
Morton, O. O., 61–62
Muhlenberg, Peter, 14
Murray, John (Earl of Dunmore), 9

Nash, Gary, 10
National Academy of Sciences, 151
National Banking Act of 1863, 69
National Civil Liberties Bureau, 129
National Defense Advisory Commission (NDAC), 102, 134, 151, 155
National Defense Mediation Board (NDMB), 143
National Resources Planning Board (NRPB), 155
National War Labor Board (NWLB), 106–107, 143, 144, 148
National Women's Loyal League, 72
National Youth Administration (NYA), 155, 156
Nativism. *See* Ethnic tension
Nelson, Donald, 134
Nevins, Allan, 49
New Deal, 155–156

New York Times, 112
Nineteenth Amendment, 119

Office of. *See* specific office names
Olson, James S., 12
Order of American Knights, 63
Overman Act, 127

Pacific Railway Act, 48, 67, 80
Pacifists, 16–17, 80–81, 115, 120, 158–159
Parish, Peter, 77
Paxson, Frederick L., 130
Peace Democrats, 63–64, 175
Peace movements, 80–81, 115–118, 158–159
People's Council of America for Democracy and Peace, 118
Pershing, John J., 124, 132
Petroleum Administration for War, 147
Pickering, Timothy, 27
Political Action Committee, CIO, 168
Political change
   American Revolution effects, 21
   World War I effects, 127–129
   World War II impact, 165–168
   See also Federal government strengthening
Political parties, 33–34
   Civil War experience, 61–64
   wartime competitiveness, 174
   World War I politics, 127–128
   World War II competition, 167–168
Prager, Robert, 122
Preparedness movement, 116
Price Administration, Office of (OPA), 141, 142, 144, 147, 148, 155
Price Administration and Civilian Supply, Office of (OPACS), 141
Price controls, 141–142, 167, 102–103
Price-Fixing Committee, 141
Price Stabilization Division, NDAC, 141
Privateering, 25
Prize Cases, 66
Production Management, Office of (OPM), 134–135, 147, 155
Production Requirements Plan (PRP), 136, 137

Progressivism, 118–119, 128
Prohibition amendment, 118–119
Prohibitory Act of 1775, 24
Propaganda agency, 120, 158
Protestantism, 15–16, 82, 117–118, 125–126

Quakers, 16–17, 115, 159

Racism. *See* Black Americans; Ethnic tension
Railroad Administration, 104–105
Railroads
  Civil War experience, 44–45, 47–48, 51, 53, 67
  World War I developments, 88, 91, 104–105
  World War II experience, 146
Randall, James G., 64
Randolph, A. Philip, 161–162
Rasmussen, Wayne, 23
Rationing, 142
Reform movement, 118–119, 128–129, 155–156, 159–160, 165
Religion, civil, 16, 81, 82
Religious discrimination, 13–15, 17
Religious exemption, 81, 120, 159
Religious institutions
  American Revolution experience, 15–16
  Civil War disunity, 80–82
  World War I stance, 114, 117–118
Reorganization Act of 1939, 133
Revolutionary War. *See* American Revolution
Roman Catholics, 14–15, 74, 75, 82, 114, 117, 125–126
Roosevelt, Eleanor, 160–161
Roosevelt, Franklin D., 133–136, 138, 141–148, 156, 158–161, 166, 174
Rose, Willie Lee, 9
Rossiter, Clinton L., 66
Rural Electrification Administration (REA), 155, 156
Rush, Benjamin, 5

Sampson, Deborah, 11
Sanitary Commission, US, 72, 73
Scandinavian-Americans, 74, 113
Schlesinger, Arthur M., Jr., 165, 171
Schurz, Carl, 75
Scientific research, 150–151
Scientific Research and Development, Office of (OSRD), 151
Scotch-Irish Americans, 12, 14
Sedition Act, 121
Selective Training and Service Act of 1940, 142–143. *See also* Military service
Servicemen's benefits, 62, 119, 160
Servicemen's Readjustment Act (GI Bill), 160
Seward, William H., 65
Shannon, William V., 76
Shipbuilding industry, 90, 147
Shipping Act of 1916, 105
Shipping Board, 105, 147
Shipping industry, 105, 147
Shy, John W., 6, 21
Sigel, Franz, 75
Sixteenth Amendment, 107
Slavery, abolition of, 10, 72, 78, 79, 83
Smaller War Plants Corporation, 149
Smaller War Plants Division, WPB, 149
Smith, Bessie, 161
Smith, Louis, 65
Smith and Wesson Arms Company, 107
Social change, 20–22, 123–126, 174–175. *See also* Black Americans; Ethnic tension; Women
Socialists, 97, 122
Sons of Liberty, 63
Stalin, Joseph, 131
Stanton, Edwin M., 65, 70
Stanton, Elizabeth Cady, 72
Stettinius, Edward R., Jr., 133
Sunday, Billy, 118
Supply Priorities and Allocation Board (SPAB), 147
Supreme Court, 66, 167, 174

Taft, Robert A., 167–168
Taney, Roger B., 66
Taxation
  Civil War experience, 47, 58, 67–69

Continental Congress absence of authority, 28
income tax, 68, 69, 107, 140
World War I developments, 107–108
World War II measures, 140
Thirteenth Amendment, 72, 79
Thomas, Emory M., 60
Trade. *See* Commerce
Trading-With-the-Enemy Act of 1917, 146
Transportation, 44–45, 47, 145–147. *See also* Railroads
Transportation Division, NDAC, 145
Tredegar Ironworks, 55, 79
Trumbull, Benjamin, 16
Truman, Harry S., 166

Union party, 62
United Mine Workers, 153

Vallandigham, Clement L., 66
Vance, Zebulon B., 57
von Steuben, Baron, 14
Voting right, 11, 15, 20, 119, 125

Wade-Davis bill, 64, 65
Wages
  controls, 142, 144
  See also Labor movement
Wallace, Henry A., 147
War
  effects of, overview, 1–3, 171–176
  See also specific wars
War Department, 37, 70, 78
War Finance Corporation, 108
War Food Administration (WFA), 138, 141, 147
War for Independence. *See* American Revolution
War Industries Board (WIB), 102, 141
War Information, Office of (OWI), 158
War Labor Disputes Act, 145
War Manpower Commission (WMP), 143–145, 155
War Mobilization, Office of (OWM), 148, 168
War Production Board (WPB), 135–138, 147–148, 155

War Resources Administration (WRA), 133, 147
War Resources Board (WRB), 133
War Shipping Administration, 147
Washington, Booker T., 161
Washington, George, 9, 11, 14, 27
Western settlement, 19–20, 80
Western Union, 107
Wiley, Bell I., 73
Wilson, Woodrow, 102, 104, 106, 112–113, 116–117, 119–124, 127–128, 174
Women
  American Revolution experience, 10–11
  Civil War experience, 71–73
  voting right, 11, 119, 125
  wartime advances, 175
  World War I employment, 95–96, 119, 125
  World War II employment, 164–165
Women's Land Army, 119
Women's Peace Party, 116
Work force. *See* Labor force
Works Progress Administration (WPA), 155, 156
World Peace Foundation, 115
World War I
  civil liberties curtailment, 121–123
  divided public response to, 112–116
  economic changes, 88–93, 126–127
  effects of, overview, 87–88, 129–130
  financing of, 107–108, 173
  inflation during, 99–101, 108–110
  labor force changes, 93–97
  labor movement gains, 97–99, 106–107, 119, 127
  mobilization of resources, 101–107, 110–112, 141
  molding of public support for, 116–120
  moral changes, 125–126
  number of soldiers, 120
  political changes, 127–129
  postwar antiradical nativism, 123–125
World War II
  civil liberties curtailment, 156–159

cost of, 139
economic consequences, 148–155
effects of, summary, 168–169
Federal government strengthening, 131–133
financing of, 139–141, 173

mobilization of resources, 133–139, 142–148
political changes, 165–168
price controls and rationing, 141–142
social reforms, 155–156, 159–165

www.ingramcontent.com/pod-product-compliance
Lightning Source LLC
Chambersburg PA
CBHW032022230426
43671CB00005B/168